RUNNING WITH DILLINGER

RUNNING WITH DILLINGER

THE STORY OF **RED HAMILTON** AND OTHER FORGOTTEN CANADIAN OUTLAWS | **EDWARD BUTTS**

DUNDURN PRESS

TORONTO

Copy-editor: Marja Appleford
Design: Jennifer Scott
Printer: Transcontinental

Library and Archives Canada Cataloguing in Publication

Butts, Edward, 1951-
  Running with Dillinger : the story of Red Hamilton and other forgotten Canadian outlaws / Edward Butts.

Includes bibliographical references.
ISBN 978-1-55002-683-2

    1. Outlaws--Canada--Biography. 2. Criminals--Canada-- Biography. 3. Crime--Canada--History. I. Title.

HV6805.B88 2008   364.1092'271   C2007-907080-9

1   2   3   4   5   12   11   10   09   08

We acknowledge the support of the **Canada Council for the Arts** and the **Ontario Arts Council** for our publishing program. We also acknowledge the financial support of the **Government of Canada** through the **Book Publishing Industry Development Program** and **The Association for the Export of Canadian Books**, and the **Government of Ontario** through the **Ontario Book Publishers Tax Credit program**, and the **Ontario Media Development Corporation**.

Care has been taken to trace the ownership of copyright material used in this book. The author and the publisher welcome any information enabling them to rectify any references or credits in subsequent editions.

J. Kirk Howard, President

Printed and bound in Canada.
Printed on recycled paper.

www.dundurn.com

Dundurn Press	Gazelle Book Services Limited	Dundurn Press
3 Church Street, Suite 500	White Cross Mills	2250 Military Road
Toronto, Ontario, Canada	High Town, Lancaster, England	Tonawanda, NY
M5E 1M2	LA1 4XS	U.S.A. 14150

For Mum:
Patricia Margery Butts
1925–2007

CONTENTS

ACKNOWLEDGEMENTS

I would like to thank the many people and institutions who were of assistance to me in one way or another while I was researching and writing this book: Tony Hawke, Michael Carroll, Marja Appleford, and Jennifer Scott of Dundurn Press; Dillinger biographers Tony Stewart, Ellen Poulsen, Jefferey S. King, Bill Helmer, and Rick Mattix; Bob Bates, for his excellent article on Blackie Audett; Dave St. Onge of the Kingston Penitentiary Museum; Norina Dagostini of the Metropolitan Toronto Police Museum; Irene Novaczek, Jim Hornby, and the P.E.I. Institute of Island Studies; Bruce Woodruff, and Brian Beerman; Library and Archives Canada; Veterans Affairs Canada; the Rooms Archives of Newfoundland; the provincial archives of Ontario, Manitoba, and Alberta; the Galt Museum and Archives of Lethbridge, Alberta; the Vermont State Archives; the *Toronto Star*; the Metropolitan Toronto Reference Library; the Sault Ste. Marie Public Library; and of course my ever-helpful friends at the Guelph Public Library. A special note of thanks to Bruce Hamilton of Shiprock, New Mexico.

INTRODUCTION

While I was researching *The Desperate Ones: Forgotten Canadian Outlaws*, I came across a Toronto newspaper article from May 1934 about the American bank robber John Dillinger. The story, under a banner headline, said the FBI believed Dillinger might be aboard a Canadian ship heading for Britain. I also found a terrific editorial cartoon that depicted Jack Canuck offering Uncle Sam the services of one Mountie to catch Dillinger. I thought this little-known "Canadian connection" to the Dillinger saga would make a good closing chapter for the book, so I started searching for information on Dillinger's life. Among other sources, I found two websites, dillingertimes and gangsterologists (both Yahoo groups). These groups are operated by and for people with a serious interest in the "gangster era" of the United States, particularly the 1920s and 1930s. It was through these groups that I met (online) Tony Stewart, author of *Dillinger: the Hidden Truth*; Ellen Poulsen, author of *Don't Call Us Molls: Women of the John Dillinger Gang*; Jefferey S. King, author of *The Rise and Fall of the Dillinger Gang*; William J. Helmer, co-author (with G. Russell Girardin) of *Dillinger: the Untold Story*; Rick Mattix, a historian who helped prepare the expanded edition of the Helmer/Girardin book; and gangster-era expert Bob Bates.

These people, individually and collectively, undoubtedly know more about America's gangster era than anyone else in the world. After the publication of *The Desperate Ones*, I learned from them that there was much more of a Canadian connection to the Dillinger story than I had realized. John "Red" Hamilton, a core member of the Dillinger Gang from its beginning to its bloody end, was Canadian! Moreover, there is a quite believable story that Red Hamilton was not killed in 1934 as the FBI claimed, but escaped to Canada and lived until the 1970s. This story has been supported by John Hamilton's great-nephew, Bruce Hamilton of Shiprock, New Mexico, as well as other members of the Hamilton family.

The story of how this Ontario-born desperado fell into a life of crime and became a gunman with one of the most legendary bandit gangs in American history is told here. It is every bit as intriguing as the story of Alvin "Creepy" Karpis, the Canadian-born member of the Barker Gang whose autobiography, *Public Enemy # 1*, was published in 1971. So is the story of how Hamilton allegedly survived a near-fatal bullet wound, evaded capture, and ended his days as a free man in Canada.

Not all of the historical characters the reader will meet in this book were bank robbers. Some preferred to rob trains, such as the gang that hit a mail car at Toronto's Union Station for one of the biggest holdups in Canadian history. Others were counterfeiters, smugglers, and kidnappers. A convicted bandit named Sam Behan won public admiration, not for his lawlessness, but for his courageous attempt to bring to the nation's attention the inhumane conditions in the Kingston Penitentiary. Albert Dorland, a failed bank robber, gained the public eye when overzealous members of the Toronto Police Department framed him for a bank robbery.

As I stated in my introduction to *The Desperate Ones*, my intention is not to glorify criminals or to excuse or condone the things they do. Certainly there are often extenuating circumstances involved in an individual's descent into a criminal lifestyle. Sometimes, as we shall see in these pages, the very system that was supposed to correct the wayward actually pushed them back into outlawry. But many people mired in bad circumstances have had the courage to make better choices. Most of the individuals whose stories are presented here did not, in the final analysis, have that kind of courage, though nearly all would have considered themselves "tough guys."

THE POWER GANG OF
NEWFOUNDLAND

"UNTIL YOU ARE DEAD, DEAD, DEAD!"

Outlawry was nothing new to mid-eighteenth-century Newfoundland. In the previous century the island had been home base to
the arch-pirates Peter Easton and Henry Mainwarring. Newfoundland waters had once been the hunting grounds of rogues like Eric
Cobham and Bartholomew Roberts, better known in the annals of
piracy as Black Bart. The Newfoundland interior was the domain
of the Masterless Men. These were Royal Navy deserters and in-
dentured servants who had fled the harsh conditions of the fishing
plantations to live a rough but free life in the woods. The very fact
that they had run away from their "rightful" lords and masters made
them outlaws. The Masterless Men further angered the authorities
in St. John's by raiding outports to steal food, guns, ammunition,
fishing nets, and other equipment. However, banditry of a different
sort was to strike St. John's in 1754. The crime would have serious
social repercussions for the colony of Newfoundland.

William Keen, formerly of Boston, Massachusetts, was one of the
wealthiest men in St. John's. He first arrived in the Newfoundland
capital in 1704 as the young agent for a New England firm involved
in the cod trade. By 1713 he was an independent trader, dealing
principally in salmon. He founded his own import-export business,
with connections in the West Indies. Keen also had fishing and
trading premises in at least two Newfoundland outports and owned
a considerable amount of real estate in St. John's.

Keen was a strong advocate for an improved legal system in
Newfoundland. He was among those who stressed the need for
appointed officials in St. John's during the winter months when the
"fishing admirals" were absent. In 1729 Keen became one of the first
justices of the peace appointed in Newfoundland. In 1736 he was
appointed magistrate and commissary of the vice-admiralty court. In

View of St. John's, Newfoundland, not long after the time of the Power Gang. (The Rooms Archives, St. John's, Newfoundland, C1-192)

1742 he was commissioned a naval officer, and in 1744 a prize officer. That meant he had the authority to preside over the distribution of proceeds from "prizes," enemy ships captured by Newfoundland privateers in times of war. In 1750 Keen was appointed the first commissioner of oyer and terminer. In the presence of a naval governor, he could hear all court cases except treason. He was not only one of the wealthiest men in the colony but also one of the most prominent. However, his wealth would make Keen the target of thieves, and his high social rank would not protect him from a vicious assault. Most of what is known of the events leading up to the crime comes from the testimony of one of the perpetrators.

Sometime around the end of August 1754, six people took a skiff from the little port of Freshwater Bay to St. John's. They were Eleanor Power and her husband, Robert, Matthew Halleran, Paul McDonald, Nicholas Tobin, and Lawrence Lamley. The males in the boat were all fishermen, and Eleanor Power had been employed in William Keen's house in St. John's as a washerwoman and maid. On this night, however, their purpose was robbery. Eleanor had told the men she knew where Magistrate Keen kept his money, and that if they helped her steal it, they would have enough money to last them the rest of their lives.

The skiff landed at the King's Wharf, where the band of would-be robbers was joined by Dennis Hawkins, a soldier from the local garrison. Two more soldiers fell in with them on their way to Keen's house at Quidi Vidi. Their names were Edmund McGuire and John Mulhall. McGuire had joined the gang for another reason besides robbery. He had appeared before Magistrate Keen once and believed he had been dealt with unjustly. McGuire wanted revenge as much as he wanted a share of the loot.

Before the gang proceeded, Eleanor Power took out a prayer book. She made each of her henchmen kiss it and swear an oath "to be true to each other." Then they continued on to the perimeter of Keen's property.

It was now about midnight. While the others remained hidden, McGuire, Halleran, and Lamley went on ahead to scout the house. They returned a short while later and reported that people were in the stages near the house splitting fish. (Stages were the places where fish were processed. It was not unusual for workers to be kept at their labours until the small hours of the morning.) With all those people around, it did not look like a good night for a robbery. After making plans to try again in a fortnight, the soldiers returned to their lodgings and the rest of the Power Gang went back to Freshwater Bay.

On the night of September 9, the Power Gang again gathered for a raid on Keen's home. It seems that Matthew Halleran had been keeping a watch on the place. One other robbery attempt had been called off when he told the others that "young Mr. Keen" (Keen's son William) was in the house and they could not do anything that night. This time Halleran had sent Tobin to Robert and Eleanor Power's house to inform them "it was a good time that night to rob Keen's house."

As midnight approached, the gang once more crept up to the perimeter of Keen's property. Another soldier, John Moody, had come with McGuire, Hawkins, and Munhall. The robbers had amongst them two muskets and two bayonets. Matthew Halleran carried a scythe with a broken handle. Eleanor Power was dressed in men's clothing.

Eleanor placed Tobin, armed with a musket, at the corner of one of Keen's storehouses. He had orders to fire on anyone who came along and asked questions. Robert Power, who also had a musket, and Dennis Hawkins kept watch on the house of Edward Whelan, Keen's neighbour. If Whelan heard anything and came to investigate, they would stop him. Paul McDonald was to guard the door to Keen's house after the rest of the robbers gained entry.

Halleran broke the door open with a hatchet, and then he, Eleanor, McGuire, Lamley, Moody, and Mulhall went inside. When they came out McGuire was carrying a large case that Eleanor had identified as Keen's moneybox. Lamley and Halleran had also pilfered several silver spoons. Eleanor called in her sentinels, and the gang withdrew to the shadows beyond Keen's property to divide the loot. Edmund McGuire broke open the case. It contained bottles of liquor!

Now the gang became divided over what to do next. Under British law, hanging was still the punishment for most crimes, although a merciful court might sentence a convicted thief to be transported. Only four years earlier a man named William Gilmore had been hanged in St. John's for stealing a cow. Eleanor Power and some of the men were more than disappointed at their failure to find Keen's hoard of money. They were afraid they had risked their necks for a few silver spoons and a case of liquor. Eleanor and Lamley withdrew from the group and disappeared into the night.

Then Nick Tobin and Dennis Hawkins said that they, too, wanted out. Edmund McGuire levelled a musket at them and threatened to shoot anyone else who tried to leave. He said he was "sorry he had not shot the woman." McGuire was determined to have his revenge on Magistrate Keen. He told the others they were going back to Keen's house, and if the old man wouldn't tell them where the money was, they would "punish him" until he talked. Mulhall told Tobin to fortify himself with a dram of Keen's liquor.

The men returned to Keen's house. Hawkins and Tobin kept watch on Edward Whelan's door. Robert Power guarded the main path to Keen's house. Paul McDonald posted himself at Keen's kitchen door. McGuire, Halleran, Moody, and Mulhall crept into the house once again. Halleran and McGuire started up the stairs to Keen's bedroom while the others watched the door to the servants' quarters. Halleran still had his scythe and McGuire had a musket.

The two robbers entered the bedroom and found Keen asleep in bed. While McGuire held a candle, Halleran started to pull a box out from under the bed. Suddenly the old man sat up, wide awake. McGuire pulled a quilt over Keen's head as the magistrate cried, "Murder! Murder!"

Keen's arms flailed and he snuffed out the candle in McGuire's hand. With his other hand Keen grabbed Halleran by the leg. Halleran slashed down with the scythe and buried the blade in Keen's body, striking him just above the stomach. Then McGuire slammed the butt of his musket into Keen's breast. The old man fell back, unconscious.

The robbers did not find any money. The swag consisted of nothing but a belt buckle and a pair of knee buckles. When McGuire and Halleran rejoined the others their hands and clothes were covered with Magistrate Keen's blood. The bandits left the house and vanished into the darkness, each man no doubt trusting that the others would keep the oath of loyalty they had sworn on Eleanor Power's prayer book.

Keen's body was discovered the next morning and news of the brutal murder of one of Newfoundland's most prominent men swept through St. John's. Nick Tobin heard it and decided he was not about to rely on an oath for his own safety. He knew that every member of the gang would be held accountable, no matter who had struck the actual blows. Tobin went straight to the British authorities. In return for immunity, he gave them the names of all the others. Soon every member of the Power Gang was rounded up and locked in the guardhouse of the St. John's garrison.

On October 8 Robert and Eleanor Power, Edmund McGuire, Dennis Hawkins, John Munhall, John Moody, Paul McDonald, Matthew Halleran, and Lawrence Lamley went on trial before Justice Michael Gill. McGuire and Halleran pleaded guilty. The others denied they were guilty of murder.

Nicholas Tobin took the stand and in his testimony he described everything that had happened leading up to the murder — or at least his version of it. He said Halleran and McGuire had told the others what had happened in Keen's bedroom. Halleran had nothing to say in his own defence. McGuire, while he admitted that he and Halleran were the only ones to go into Keen's bedroom, said Robert

Power had said from the start they should murder Keen, and that he (McGuire) had been against any killing.

Robert and Eleanor Power, Lawrence Lamley, and Paul McDonald had little to say in their defence but that they were not guilty of murder. John Moody testified that on the evening of the robbery and murder, he had been on guard duty at the garrison's magazine, when Edmund McGuire approached him, telling him he had an eye on a way to get some money if Moody could keep a secret. Moody swore on a prayer book that he would keep quiet, and then went with McGuire. Moody told the court he did not know the gang intended to commit a robbery when he joined them. He begged the court not to hang him but to transport him.

John Munhall also blamed McGuire for persuading him to join the robber gang. He testified that Robert Power wanted Keen killed, but McGuire would not agree. Then Power changed his mind and decided that killing Keen wasn't such a good idea after all. Munhall, too, pleaded that the court "would not take away his life but would transport him."

Dennis Hawkins testified that Eleanor Power was the chief instigator for the robbery. She had promised the men £1,000 each (a small fortune at that time). He also blamed McGuire for drawing him into the plot. After Hawkins begged the court for transportation, the jury retired.

The jury took only half an hour to find all nine accused guilty of robbery and murder. The prisoners threw themselves on the mercy of the court. But a magistrate presiding over a trial for the murder of a fellow magistrate was not likely to be lenient. Justice Gill's sentence was a foregone conclusion:

> That you Edmund McGuire, Matthew Halleran, Robert Power, Eleanor Power, Lawrence Lamley, Paul McDonald, John Moody, John Mulhall and Dennis Hawkins be sent back to the place from whence you came and from thence to the place of execution and there be hanged by the neck until you are Dead, Dead, Dead, and the Lord have mercy upon your souls.
>
> And that you Edmond McGuire and Matthew Halleran after being Dead and taken down are to be

hanged in chains in some Publick Place when and where the Governor shall be pleased to appoint.

In those days there was no drawn-out process of appeal. On October 10 Matthew Halleran and Edmund McGuire were hanged from a gallows erected on William Keen's wharf. Then their bodies were bound in chains and gibbeted in a public place as a warning to other would-be criminals.

On October 11 Robert and Eleanor Power were hanged back to back on the same gallows, and their bodies were buried nearby. Eleanor Power had the distinction of being the first woman hanged in Newfoundland. Lamley, McDonald, Moody, Mulhall, and Hawkins were granted a last-minute reprieve. They were transported, quite likely to the British penal colony in what is now the American state of Georgia. Given the conditions under which transported convicts lived, they might well have wished they'd been hanged. Meanwhile, Governor Richard Dorrill recommended that permanent gallows be erected in St. John's and other districts as a deterrent against crime.

With the exception of Nick Tobin, who had escaped punishment by informing on his comrades, every member of the Power Gang was dead or labouring in a penal colony. But the trouble was not over. Every one of the robber band had been Irish and Roman Catholic. At that time, even though the political power and economy of Newfoundland were in the hands of a small, English Protestant elite, a large percentage of the population was Catholic Irish. The Irish had traditionally supported England's Catholic enemies, France and Spain. Less than a decade earlier the Irish had sympathized with Catholic Bonnie Prince Charlie in the Jacobite Rising of 1745.

Now France and England were at war again, and the English in Newfoundland did not trust their Irish neighbours. Most of the Irish settlers simply wanted to make a living and be left alone. But with Keen's murder the English had visions of Irish renegades slaughtering them in their sleep so they could turn Newfoundland over to the papist French.

Governor Dorrill forbade the saying of the Catholic mass. Priests had to go into hiding. Any Irish settler found guilty of allowing mass to be said in his home or fishing rooms was fined and had his property destroyed. He was then banished from Newfoundland. Hugh Palliser, who became governor in 1764, further ordered that no Irishman could own a tavern and no two Irishmen could live under the same roof. Not until 1784, under Governor John Campbell, did this official persecution on the part of the colonial government in Newfoundland come to an end.

THE SMUGGLERS OF
LAKE CHAMPLAIN

THE *BLACK SNAKE* AND THE *PHOENIX II*

At the end of the Revolutionary War, when British negotiators sat down with their American counterparts to draw the border between British North America and the new United States, Benjamin Franklin proved — in most instances — to be much sharper at the game than the representatives of King George III. He convinced the British to sign over to the Americans such real estate as Isle Royale in Lake Superior, which the British thought worthless but which Franklin guessed (correctly) would contain valuable mineral deposits. A lot of border country that is American today would be Canadian were it not for the astute Mr. Franklin. On one point, however, the British held firm. They wanted to keep a bit of Lake Champlain shoreline. Thus, though the lake is almost entirely in the United States, between the states of Vermont and New York, the northern tip is in Quebec. Franklin might have bargained a little harder had he known this little bulge in the pencil line on the map would create a smuggling hot spot that lawless men on both sides of the border would exploit for many years. Canadian and American smugglers would make the little port of Saint-Jean-sur-Richelieu, just to the north of Lake Champlain, a "duty-free" capital. Canadians, for the most part, benefited from the illicit trade. But for honest customs collectors, the situation could be a nightmare.

In the early nineteenth century, Britain was locked in a deadly struggle with Napoleon. The British government passed its orders-in-council forbidding all nations, including the United States, to trade with France. This policy was enforced by the Royal Navy and was devastating to the American economy. Britain added insult to injury by stopping American ships on the high seas and taking off sailors they claimed were Royal Navy deserters.

President Thomas Jefferson responded with the Embargo Act of 1807, which forbade Americans to engage in commerce with Britain or with British colonies. Of course, the Act applied to Canada. People living around Lake Champlain were horrified. Their economy depended largely on trade with Canada. They ridiculed the new law by calling it *dambargo*. They turned the word backwards into *o-grab-me*. They said the federal government had no right to interfere with their business. From leading merchants like Gideon King, who held mortgages on just about every American boat on Lake Champlain, down to common farmers, people of the district ignored the embargo and continued to trade with the Canadians. Over the border and on to Montreal went timber, cattle and pigs, farm produce, and leather goods. Down the lake from Saint-Jean went rum, cloth, salt, tobacco, and manufactured items. One of the most important commodities smuggled over the line into Canada was potash. This was the packed-down ash left over from the wood fires of hearths throughout the region. British industry used tons of it in the manufacture of soap and glass. Before the embargo British merchants had bought potash at Boston for $165 a ton. Now they were willing to pay smugglers even more for it. Potash became a major cash crop in Vermont. Soon people in other parts of New England were sending their potash through the Lake Champlain corridor.

Much of the trade was done overland because it was almost impossible for customs officers to patrol a border that was all hills and forest. The smugglers had some ingenious ways of getting their goods across the line. An American would pile his merchandise on the ground just a few yards from the international line and leave it there for some Canadian to "happen by" and pick up. This method worked best if someone moved the border marker a few feet.

A Vermont newspaper reported that some smugglers carried goods to a hill right on the border. "On the top a slight building is erected, in which barrels, pipes, and other articles are deposited. The construction of the house is such, that on removal of a stone or a piece of wood, the whole edifice and its contents immediately falls on the British territory, by which means though accidental, the laws are evaded." One Vermonter, using the pen name "Ethan Allen," and with tongue firmly in cheek, wrote the following to the *Vermont Centinel*:

This fag end of the Embargo goes to prohibit the farmers of Vermont and New Hampshire from driving their swine into Canada for sale. Now, suppose a man should drive a herd of hogs close up to the line of the United States, *but not over*, and a Canadian should accidentally make his appearance just within the boundary of that British colony, with a basket of corn in his hand and should cry *Pig-pig-pig* and the whole drove should run over the line into Canada and *voluntarily* place themselves under the government of the tyrant of the ocean, who should be punished; the farmer who drove his hogs so near despotism, the swine, who regardless of the blessings of a free country, thus ran over the line, or the Canadian who tempted them to this anti-republican act?

Of course, the most obvious smuggling route was by water. Lake Champlain is 125 miles long. It is fourteen miles across at its widest point. It has many islands, bays, and river mouths. An international border crosses its northern extremity. It was still a pretty wild area in 1808, with a largely rural population on both sides of the border supporting the smugglers — the "Robin Hoods" who were saving them from an unjust law. That combination of factors made for a smugglers' paradise.

Some smugglers took advantage of a little accident of political geography. The northern head of the lake and Missiquoi Bay, both in Canadian territory, are separated by a small American-owned point of land that juts down from the Quebec border. Canadian boats travelling between the lakehead and the bay had to pass through American waters to round that point, and inspectors generally left them alone. Smugglers would rendezvous with these boats and load them up with potash and other goods. Another ploy the smugglers used was to build a wharf right on the border. Smugglers would legally unload their goods on one country's side of the dock, and someone would then legally pack the merchandise into boats on the other side.

Many smugglers, however, simply brazened it out on the lake, loading their sailing vessels and rafts with contraband cargo and heading for the other side of the line. Some travelled by night, playing hide-and-go-seek with the revenue patrols, darting from island to hidden creek mouth. Others went with heavily armed crews of ruffians who openly dared anyone to try to stop them. When ships or rafts did get caught by federal officers, they were often subsequently "liberated" by gangs of armed thugs.

One clever New Yorker, John Banker, actually obtained letters of marque (the licence under which privateers sailed) from some uncertain source, commissioning his little sailboat the *Lark* as a privateer. Armed with a few muskets, the *Lark*'s crew would "capture" a raft or boat loaded with American goods. Cargoes taken by armed privateers came under international law and were beyond the authority of the American revenue officers. Banker would take his "prize" to Canada, sell the merchandise, and then return to the American side, where he would turn the cash over to the original owner of the goods, after taking a percentage for himself.

The Canadians were enjoying all this immensely. Business in little Saint-Jean was booming. Because of the potash and other goods pouring into Montreal via Lake Champlain, Canada's exports to Britain that year were double the total of the previous five years. One Saint-Jean resident wrote to a friend in Vermont, "God grant that your Embargo Law may continue forever."

Dr. Jabez Penniman, the American collector of customs for the Lake Champlain district, had the unenviable job of enforcing the unpopular law. He had at his disposal a twelve-oared revenue cutter called the *Fly*. This little boat was on constant patrol but could hardly stem the flow of contraband up and down the lake. The crew of the *Fly* often received death threats from the smugglers. Penniman asked for military help, and throughout the spring and summer of 1808 various detachments of Vermont militia were sent to Lake Champlain. They generally proved to be unreliable. Some of them were in cahoots with the smugglers. Many refused to fire upon or arrest people who were their neighbours or relatives. Sometimes they just allowed smugglers to sail on by, saying they "could not command the wind and the waves and consequently could not prevent the passage of rafts and potash into Canada." A few took what they called "leg bail" and deserted, rather than perform the disagreeable duty.

The most notorious smuggling vessel was the forty foot-long *Black Snake*. She was powered by oars and sail, and had a hull com-

George Ramsay, the Earl of Dalhousie and governor general of Canada, grew weary of the stream of letters from Bartholomew Tierney, an honest customs officer whose life was made miserable by smugglers. (Metropolitan Library of Toronto T-31639)

pletely covered in tar, making her practically invisible at night. The *Black Snake* could carry one hundred barrels of potash, making every illegal visit to Canadian waters very profitable indeed.

The *Black Snake* had a crew of a dozen men, all of them reputed to be tough and dangerous. They were armed with muskets and clubs, and had long pikes for repelling boarders. Their most fearsome piece of armament was a eight-foot-long wall gun, a type of blunderbuss, which fired a load of sixteen one-ounce lead balls, similar to the canister shot used by the military of the time. The *Black Snake* had the look and the notoriety of a pirate ship. The owner might have been her captain, Truman Mudgett of Vermont. But there were rumours that Gideon King, the unofficial "Admiral of the Lake" had an investment in the *Black Snake*'s lawless exploits.

Originally a ferry boat, with the passing of the Embargo Act, the *Black Snake* was converted to a smuggler. For months she slid up and down Lake Champlain like a phantom, always giving the government men the slip. Jabez Penniman would not learn until much later that Samuel Mott, one of the men he had enlisted to track down smugglers, was a member of the *Black Snake*'s crew. He had been using his position to obtain arms for the vessel and to harass rival smugglers.

By mid-summer President Jefferson was getting reports that Vermont was in a state of insurrection, with gun battles on Lake Champlain and casualties among the smugglers and the revenue men. In his own letter to the president, Penniman dismissed the stories.

"You may consider three parts out of four of the reports in circulation as false … no man is killed … no man hurt … Gideon King has not drowned me yet." But the bloodless aspect of the smuggling war was about to come to a dramatic end.

On August 1, 1808, Penniman sent a trusted militia party of fourteen men commanded by Lieutenant Daniel Farrington to find and seize the *Black Snake*. These men were officially designated as revenue officers, with the full legal authority of the federal government. To fire upon them was tantamount to an act of treason. They set out on their mission in the *Fly*.

On August 2, going on either a tip or a very good hunch, Farrington was searching along a stretch of water called the North Hero Shore near the town of Burlington, Vermont. The *Black Snake* was in the area. Captain Mudgett had taken his ship up the Winooshi River (also called the Onion River) to pick up a cargo of potash. That night, before the cargo could be taken aboard, a friend warned Mudgett the *Fly* was nearby and would probably be coming up the river. A witness later testified: "[Joshua] Day [one of the smugglers] said that if they did come they would see their God before night. Others said they [the officers] would never get out of the river alive. The men loaded their guns with powder and leaden balls … and said that would make some others sup sorrow."

The same day a smuggler named Francis Ledyard had apparently been tipped by a militia informer that the *Fly* was looking for the *Black Snake* and went off to warn Mudgett. He rowed up the Winooshi River after nightfall and missed the *Black Snake* in the foggy darkness. He found it when he backtracked in the morning. Ledyard gave the smuggler captain the message and advised him to hide or sink the *Black Snake* because the revenue men would be on them by noon. Mudgett said he knew all about the approach of the *Fly* and was prepared to fight.

According to Ledyard's later description of the scene, the smugglers carried on like a gang of pirates. They swilled rum and boasted that the revenue men would never take the *Black Snake*. The owner of the potash Mudgett was picking up told the captain, "to kill every man belonging to the Revenue boat and not let one escape alive."

Eight smugglers were concealed in the bush when the *Fly* came into view. As the revenue boat pulled up alongside the *Black Snake*, Mudgett shouted out a warning. He said the first man to set foot in his boat would have his brains blown out. Lieutenant Farrington said he was taking the boat. He was not intimidated when one of the smugglers fired a shot into the air. Ledyard shouted a challenge to Sergeant David Johnson of Farrington's party, calling him a coward. Johnson placed his hand over his breast and told Ledyard that if he was going to shoot, there was a target for him. Ledyard said later that he did not shoot, "for we were both men of honour."

Ledyard claimed that he tried unsuccessfully to scare the revenue men off by telling them there would be "gallons of blood" if they tried to take the *Black Snake* down the river. The *Fly* pushed off to block the mouth of the river. The *Black Snake*, with a few smugglers aboard, followed the *Fly* out into the channel. Several more angry smugglers kept pace along the shore. Ledyard said he did not go with them and had no part in what happened next.

The smugglers were shouting that the revenue men would not get out of the river alive. Before the boats had gone very far, two smugglers opened fire. The *Fly*'s helmsman, Private Ellis Drake, was struck in the head and killed instantly. More gunfire erupted, but witnesses were never sure if the officers or the smugglers were shooting. Farrington told his men to steer for shore. As they were landing, the *Black Snake*'s big wall gun roared, and sixteen lead balls tore into the closely bunched revenue men. Five of the missiles ripped into the head and body of Jonathan Ormsby, a civilian who had volunteered to help the officers. Three hit Farrington in the arm, shoulder and head. Private Asa Marsh was also struck down. Farrington would survive his wounds, but the other men were dead. They would go down in history as the first United States revenue officers to be slain in the line of duty. They were buried with military honours.

Led by Sergeant Johnson, the remaining revenue men charged the smugglers and caught all but two of them. The two fugitives were soon apprehended. One of them, Samuel Mott, was arrested in Quebec. Others known to be associated with the smugglers, including Francis Ledyard, were soon in jail.

The local people may have been willing to look the other way when the crime was just a profitable bit of smuggling in defiance of a hated law, but the murder of three men doing their duty was shocking. The officers had not drawn their weapons before the smugglers opened fire. They were simply taking possession of a boat engaged in smuggling.

In the trials that followed, several smugglers were acquitted on technicalities. For whatever reason, the prosecution decided not to proceed against Captain Truman Mudgett. Perhaps he had connections. Samuel Mott and a man named David Sheffield were found guilty of manslaughter and sentenced to the pillory and fifty lashes, followed by ten years in prison. Francis Ledyard was also convicted of manslaughter and sentenced to ten years. Only one smuggler, twenty-seven-year-old Cyrus B. Dean, was found guilty of first-degree murder and sentenced to hang. He went to the gallows at Burlington on November 11, 1808. He did not go quietly.

Ten thousand people crowded into Burlington to see the first hanging in the state of Vermont. From the gallows, Dean protested his innocence and claimed that one of the witnesses at his trial had lied. He laughed, chewed tobacco,and spat into the waiting open coffin. When he prayed, no one in the crowd prayed with him. Finally, in the words of one spectator, "he was swung off."

No one claimed ownership of the *Black Snake*. She was sold at auction for $13. The Embargo Act, which had hurt the United States much more than it had Britain, was withdrawn in 1809. But Lake Champlain would remain a smuggler's haunt for many years to come.

More than a decade after the demise of the *Black Snake*, smuggling on Lake Champlain was still a thriving business. It was, in fact, one of the earliest documented instances of organized crime in Canada, with unscrupulous men on both sides of the border cooperating to cheat the customs agents. The tribulations of one customs agent who could not be bought shows that sometimes crime *did* pay, and a man who stood in its way could be ruined.

Bartholomew Tierney of England arrived in Quebec in 1820 with sterling letters of recommendation as to his character, his honesty, and his work ethic. He was hired as a junior customs inspector at the port of Saint Jean. The Customs House there had been the very first one established on the Canadian-U.S. border. Tierney had a wife and seven children to support on a very small salary, £40 a year. But he was told he could make an adequate income through the seizure of contraband goods. Seized goods were sold at auction, and the officer responsible for confiscating them received a percentage of the money. Tierney was also told that smuggling went on at Saint-Jean at an incredible rate. Tobacco, tea, whiskey, and silk were the most frequently smuggled commodities. His superiors told him an "active, vigilant officer was required." If he showed "energy and exertion" on the job, he would make a good living and earn promotion.

He was *not* told until much later — and even then he heard it from personal friends and not from his colleagues in the Customs House — that he also had the right to seize any vessel involved in smuggling, and was entitled to a share of whatever the boat fetched at auction. He was tipped that two ships, the *Congress* and the *Phoenix II*, belonging to the Lake Champlain Steamboat Company of Vermont, were heavily involved in smuggling. That wasn't surprising, since Gideon King, one of the most notorious smugglers on the lake, had shares in the company. The company's first ship, the *Phoenix*, for which the *Phoenix II* was a replacement, had sunk in 1819 under mysterious circumstances and with the loss of six men. Officially she sank because of an accidental fire. But there was circumstantial evidence of sabotage by a rival company. Competition on Lake Champlain was stiff, and smugglers were not above informing on each other and destroying each other's property.

In 1821 and 1822 Tierney made several seizures of contraband goods on the *Congress* and the *Phoenix II*. Then he learned of the law regarding the seizure of vessels. He warned the respective captains that the next time he caught one of them smuggling he was going to enforce the law and seize the ship. On August 21, 1821, acting on a tip from an informant, Tierney went aboard the *Phoenix II* in search of some bags of silk hidden in a secret compartment. The hiding place was just where the informant had said it would be, but the silk was gone. Following some wet footprints, Tierney saw the ship's pilot, a man named Wilson, dragging two large bags. Instead of going after Wilson, Tierney went to the skipper, Captain Sherman. (The account does not specify if this was Captain Jehaziel Sherman, a legendary Lake Champlain skipper or his son Captain Richard Sherman, who had been in command of the original *Phoenix* when she went down.)

Tierney told Sherman that Wilson was engaged in smuggling and was endangering the Company's property, namely the *Phoenix II*. He advised Sherman to dismiss Wilson, and warned him again that the ship would be seized if the smuggling continued. Captain Sherman swore he knew nothing about the silk or a secret hideaway. At that time, under British law, just the presence of a secret storage room on a ship was enough to have the vessel seized. There did not have to be any contraband in it. Tierney was giving Captain Sherman every chance to straighten out.

Four days later, acting on yet another tip, Tierney went aboard the *Phoenix II* looking for ten bales of silk. He had the district bailiff, Robert Davies, with him. The room in which the informant had said the silk was hidden was locked. Captain Sherman said he couldn't find the key. Tierney and Davies started to break the door down. The captain finally forced it open with a chisel. There lay the ten bags of contraband silk.

Tierney had the bags taken ashore and turned over to the chief customs collector, William Macrae. Macrae put the silk in his own residence. He said the crew of the *Phoenix II* might try to "rescue" the silk if he put it in the Customs House. Tierney then went back on board the ship and "branded the *Phoenix II* with the King's mark in due form." That meant the vessel was seized.

To Tierney's surprise, Macrae tried very hard to dissuade him from taking this action. Captain Sherman tried to bribe him into letting the ship go. Tierney's response to both of them was that the matter was now in the hands of the colonial government. Macrae then gave Tierney a letter for the commander of the local garrison, requesting two soldiers to guard the *Phoenix II*. Tierney complained later that Macrae could have asked for more soldiers, as he had the authority.

When the two soldiers had taken their stations, Macrae and Captain Sherman said they had to go into town to see to some details concerning the bonding of the ship. Tierney should have been asked to accompany them, since he was the officer who had made the seizure. Instead, Macrae sent him to the Customs House to do some routine paperwork. An impartial witness who had gone aboard the *Phoenix II* to see what all the fuss was about would later state in writing that he clearly heard Captain Sherman tell a crewmember to keep the engine's steam up.

About twenty minutes later Tierney's son hurried into the office to tell him the *Phoenix II* was getting under way. The landwaiter (another customs officer) came in right behind the boy and said it wasn't so. Then a third person arrived and confirmed what the younger Tierney had said. Tierney immediately sent for more soldiers, but they arrived too late. The crew of the *Phoenix II* had charged aboard the vessel, disarmed the two soldiers, and put them in the hold, and then steamed up the river to Lake Champlain and safety. (The soldiers were put ashore unharmed.) Then Bartholomew Tierney's nightmare began.

From the safety of the American side of the line, Captain Sherman wrote letters proclaiming his innocence and publicly denouncing Tierney. Bailiff Davies came to Tierney's defence, stating in writing that Captain Sherman frequently smuggled tea, tobacco, silk, and other contraband. He said the captain knew about the smuggled silk, and he knew about the smuggling activities of Wilson. Macrae threw Davies's deposition away, and said he didn't want to hear anything about Tierney.

Macrae was now determined to make life miserable for Tierney. He spoke to him abusively and spread lies about his character. He demanded to know the name of the informant who'd told him about the silk and said he would see to it that Tierney lost his position if he did not co-operate. Tierney would not betray his informant. Macrae angrily called Tierney "a damned impudent blackguard." That was pretty strong language in 1822; the sort that would compel a gentleman to demand satisfaction via pistols at twenty paces. Tierney wrote of the incident, "My first impulse was to fell him to the ground." But it seems Tierney was a man who was loath to resort to violence.

Fearful of losing his job, Tierney wrote to the governor-in-chief of Canada, who at that time was the Earl of Dalhousie. He was an autocratic Scot who really didn't like his social inferiors — which meant pretty well everyone else in Canada. Tierney explained that if he gave up his informant's name, he would be putting the man's life in danger. Dalhousie had already received a letter of complaint about Tierney from Macrae. Now His Excellency's secretary wrote to Tierney, telling him he was not obliged to name his informant. The secretary rather testily added that he hoped neither Macrae nor Tierney would have to bother his Lordship again.

Meanwhile, the Lake Champlain Steamboat Company had to straighten matters out, or the *Phoenix II* would be seized again the next time she docked at Saint-Jean. In September an influential Vermont merchant known as "General" Amos Barnum approached Mrs. Tierney with a letter. This document stated that the seizure of the *Phoenix II* had been a mistake, and that Captain Sherman was innocent of smuggling and of assaulting the two soldiers. Barnum said if Tierney would copy the letter in his own hand and send it to Lord Dalhousie, the steamboat company would pay him well for the favour.

An indignant Tierney would have nothing to do with the scheme. He sent Barnum a flat refusal, stating, in short, that he could not be bought. The paper war was about to heat up.

A week later Barnum showed up at Tierney's house at 10:00 p.m., a very late hour to come calling in those days. He had a letter that an agent for the Company had received from Lord Dalhousie. His Lordship said he was sure Captain Sherman was innocent of smuggling, but trade laws had been broken and the British flag dishonoured by the assault on two soldiers doing their lawful duty. He insisted that the *Phoenix II* be returned to Saint-Jean to await the decision of the law officers of the Crown, and an apology be made for the outrage to the two soldiers. Then, in a postscript, Dalhousie said the *Phoenix II* could resume trade if the Company was willing to post sufficient bond. Barnum had come to talk to Tierney about the bond. He said the company was willing to post a bond of £1,000, and that Macrae had agreed to that, on the condition that Tierney would also agree, and if Tierney would accept the £1,000 as his own full share and as the final acquaintance of the Company.

Tierney smelled something fishy. He didn't have the legal authority to make such a decision. He knew the *Phoenix II* was worth about £20,000. What if the government decided the ship had in fact been smuggling? Not only would he be on the spot for letting the ship go for a pittance, he would also forfeit his share from the auction. This was just another attempt to buy him off! Tierney told Barnum the bond should be set at £8,000. Barnum left in a rage. Tierney wrote another letter to Dalhousie, explaining what had happened. His Lordship's secretary replied that Tierney had done the right thing. Meanwhile, in an American port on Lake Champlain, the *Phoenix II* was placed under armed guard.

For several months nothing dramatic happened. Tierney was aware of rumours detrimental to his character being circulated. By now he realized that Macrae and others in the Customs House were part of the smuggling operation. He spoke with Macrae only when it was absolutely necessary. Things were so uncomfortable for Tierney, he requested a transfer to another job in Montreal. The governor turned down the request. Tierney in turn declined all invitations to communicate with Barnum. Then in March 1823 a captain from the steamboat company came to Tierney with a new offer. If he would relinquish his legal claim against the *Phoenix II*, the company would remunerate him privately, or, if he wished, make a gift of the money to his wife. Again, Tierney refused.

Now a flurry of letters fell upon his Lordship's desk. Some were from Tierney, explaining with a growing sense of desperation that he was only trying to do his job and claiming the reward that was his lawful due. Other letters were from Barnum, pleading the case for Captain Sherman and the owners of the *Phoenix II*, and presenting falsehoods and twisted facts.

Dalhousie, fed up with the whole affair, finally reached a decision. He accepted the company's apology for the assault on the two soldiers. He dismissed any charges against Captain Sherman. He dropped all legal claims against the *Phoenix II*, allowing the ship to once again enter Canadian waters. Dalhousie also said Customs Officer Tierney was entitled to a third of the proceeds from the confiscated silk. The last point left Tierney scratching his head; if the silk had been legally seized, how could the captain and his ship not be guilty of smuggling? His Lordship went on to say that Tierney was entitled to some small compensation from the steamboat company for his pains, which he should make arrangements for privately. The closing line of the letter bluntly informed Tierney that his Lordship wished to hear no more about the tiresome matter.

The letter was dated March 29, 1823, but Tierney did not receive it until April 18. Dalhousie's secretary had sent it to Tierney by way of Macrae. Tierney believed (probably correctly) that Macrae had deliberately withheld the letter, expecting that Tierney — being kept in the dark — would do something that would cause himself embarrassment.

Tierney's share from the confiscated silk should have been £122, but he did not get any of it, and he still had to pay his informant. He wrote to Barnum about the compensation he was supposed to receive from the company. He afterwards learned that Barnum read the letter aloud to a bunch of drunken louts in a tavern, to much laughter and "ribald appellations."

In May Tierney wrote to Dalhousie again, pointing out that he had done everything according to the law and had nothing to show for his efforts except abuse. His Excellency's reply was, "Case Closed!" Dalhousie did not want to hear another word about it.

Tierney's troubles weren't over. Word went out that he had profited from the seizure of the *Phoenix II*. Now people to whom he owed debts were demanding their money. One creditor sued Tierney and had most of his personal property seized.

Things got worse. In August 1823 Tierney caught Macrae, the landwaiter, and another man in a scheme to smuggle some printing equipment through customs. When he confronted them in the office, Macrae called him "a damned impudent scoundrel." At that Tierney lost his temper.

He replied, "*No man* should use such language *to me;* that I had a mind to and *would – if he repeated it –* pull his nose; adding that he was a *low minded coward,* sheltering under *his office* to insult a man *he feared to meet in the way a gentleman should.*"

The next thing Tierney knew, he had a letter from Dalhousie's office, informing him that he was dismissed from his position for the "gross and insulting language" he had used with Macrae, and for other misconducts. He was told he could go to Quebec City to plead his case, if he had any defence to make. Tierney was stunned. He was out of a job, and he had no money to travel to Quebec City. He wrote back, explaining what had happened and why he couldn't go to Quebec. He wanted to know just what charges of "misconduct" had been made against him. The response he received was unbelievable. His Lordship had visited Saint Jean — unbeknownst to Tierney — and was entertained by Macrae and Captain Sherman. Those two had nothing good to say about Tierney, and His Lordship did not bother to seek Tierney out and listen to his side of the story. "You yourself are to blame," Dalhousie's secretary wrote. At the end of the letter Tierney was advised, "Furthermore, His Excellency will not notice any future letters or applications from you."

In his lengthy statement on the events surrounding the seizure of the *Phoenix II*, published in Montreal in 1823, Tierney concluded that in his three years as an honest Customs House Officer he had been: "Condemned ... placed in an infinitely more disadvantageous situation than a publicly accused criminal ... despoiled of my character [and] deprived of my rights as a British subject." In the parlance of today, Tierney might say the smugglers had railroaded him.

EDWIN JOHNSON

MASTER COUNTERFEITER

The counterfeiting of currency has been around for as long as mankind has used money to conduct business. In ancient times, when gold and silver were poured into molds to make coins, counterfeiters made copies of the coins from base metals, covered them with a thin coating of precious metal, and then put them into circulation. Then as now, the profits from counterfeiting could be enormous. Of course, should the ancient counterfeiter be caught at it, he could lose his head, or find himself working as a slave in a mine that the gold or silver came from in the first place.

In England during medieval and Renaissance times, counterfeiting was considered an act of treason against the monarch. A convicted counterfeiter would be hung, drawn, and quartered. Nations at war have found counterfeiting to be a handy way to undermine the enemy's economy. During the Revolutionary War, the British government counterfeited the American Continental dollar in an attempt to sabotage the economy of the rebelling Thirteen Colonies. The Americans considered this a foul way indeed to fight a war, but eighty-seven years later the Lincoln administration used the same tactic to knock the cotton stuffing out of the Confederate dollar during the Civil War. During the Second World War, Nazi Germany had a grand scheme to hurt the British and Americans by printing millions of bogus notes in dollars and pounds but never actually managed to put the fake cash into circulation.

Most counterfeiting, however, is done by criminals. Today any high school student understands why fake money is harmful to a nation's economy. Modern technology has made paper money harder and harder for the counterfeiter to reproduce. It is also increasingly easier for police, banks, and business people to spot phony bills.

During the ninteenth century, though, counterfeiters had a heyday. In North America, governments, banks, and even companies issued their own paper money. Most of it was relatively easy to counterfeit. If you could engrave a copper plate with all of the features on a bill, and forge the signature of a treasurer, bank manager, or company president, you had a money-making machine. It certainly helped the counterfeiter that many people were illiterate or had so little exposure to handling actual cash that they wouldn't know a bad bill from a good one. A phony bill could be in circulation for a long time before it was finally spotted. For obvious reasons, counterfeiters were considered as dangerous to the community as bank robbers and burglars.

One of Canada's earliest counterfeiters was a man named Morrall Magoon. He lived in Lower Canada (Quebec), and between 1821 and 1834 he was charged and convicted three times for counterfeiting. Magoon's trick was to alter a banknote of a low denomination so that it looked like a larger note. For example, he changed a £10 note to a £1,000 note. Magoon wasn't the brightest of criminals, and he kept getting caught. He was fined, jailed, pilloried, and finally dragged onto a prison ship and sent away to hard labour in Bermuda.

In Canada and the United States, counterfeiters were called "koniackers" or "cooney men." Counterfeit money was called "boodle" or "the queer." Circulating fake money was "passing the boodle" or "pushing the queer."

Browse the pages of ninteenth-century newspapers, and it is clear to the reader that cooney men were a major problem. Issue after issue carried warnings about counterfeit money. The papers would give the vicinity in which the bad bills had appeared, the name of the institution whose currency had been forged, the denominations, and the flaws to watch out for. If you found yourself in possession of a bad bill, you had to take the loss. You were required by law to give it to the police. If you were caught trying to pass it on, you could be arrested.

Canada had fallen well behind the United States in fighting counterfeiting. The quality of paper used for American banknotes was much better than that used in Canada. The Americans also wove coloured silk threads into their paper money, which the Canadians did not. This did not make the American bills 100 percent counterfeit-proof, but it did discourage the lowly rank-and-file koniackers. Duplicating the tough American bills was a crime usually pulled off by the elite of the counterfeiting profession.

At the top of the boodle-making hierarchy was the engraver. He was the man who made the copper plates used to print the "queer." The engraver had to make three plates: one for the front of the bill, one for the back, and one for something called the wedge. (It seems the meaning of the term "wedge," as far as paper currency is concerned, has been lost. According to a curator at the Bank of Canada's Currency Museum, "wedge" might refer to elements of the printing plate that were left blank where the issuer's name and place of issue were to be added. It might also refer to extra plates required to print notes in multiple colours.) To make a good set of plates took a lot of time and required considerable skill. In the criminal world a master engraver was regarded with the kind of respect and admiration legitimate society reserved for a great artist. A fine set of plates was valued in the tens of thousands of dollars, which in today's terms could be beyond the million-dollar mark. It was said that banks would pay rewards of several thousand dollars for counterfeiting plates, just to get them out of operation. Publicly, the banks denied this, saying they would pay a nominal reward of forty or fifty dollars.

The engraver would rarely pass the boodle himself. That was beneath his station. Besides, he wanted the fake money to go into circulation as far as possible from the vicinity where he lived and worked. The engraver would sell bundles of his bad money to a wholesaler for a percentage of the face value of the bills; perhaps 30¢ for each $1 bill, $2 for each $5 bill, and so on. The boodle would then pass through the hands of other middlemen until it reached the "shovers" who put it into circulation on the street. This system ensured that the phony bills were spread far and wide, making it difficult for the police to trace them to the source.

In the United States, tracking down counterfeiters was a job for the Secret Service. In Ontario the task fell to John Wilson Murray, the man who has gone down in history as Canada's "Great Detective." Born in Scotland in 1840, Murray immigrated to the United States as a boy and during the Civil War served on the Great Lakes gunboat USS *Michigan*. After the war he was a policeman in Erie, Pennsylvania, and then a rail-road detective. In 1873 he became a detective for the Canada South-

John Wilson Murray, Canada's "Great Detective," finally tracked master counterfeiter Edwin Johnson to a house in Toronto. (Library and Archives Canada, Amicus 2373268)

ern Railway. Within two years he was working for the Ontario government as the province's only full-time detective, with the full authority of a constable in every city, town, and county in the province. Murray would be Ontario's principal criminal investigator right up until his death in 1906. Over the years he ran to ground many thieves, murderers and other fugitives from the law. In 1904 a book about some of his cases was published. Murray tended to embroider the stories of his exploits, but when checked out against other sources, the basics of most of his accounts of criminal cases are relatively accurate. One of Murray's most challenging assignments was the hunt for a particularly skilled and elusive counterfeiter. The Great Detective admitted to a Toronto newspaper reporter that tracking this man down took him about two years.

Sometime in 1875 American authorities became aware that bogus $5 bills were in circulation. These bills were so good, even bank managers couldn't tell them from the real thing. It was only because one of the bills looked *too* good that a Treasury Department official checked on the serial number and learned it was counterfeit. Secret Service agents began the hunt. They rounded up the usual suspects, looked in every nook and cranny, and came up empty-handed. When no leads materialized in American cities, the Secret Service men suspected the bad money was coming over the border from Canada. Two agents went north to do some sleuthing, and again came up with nothing.

Then in 1878 Canada experienced a flood of counterfeit bills. Once again, the fakes were almost impossible to tell from the real thing. The Canadian "queer" included: Bank of Ontario $10 bills, Canadian Bank of Commerce $5 bills, Dominion Bank $4 bills, and Dominion Bank of Canada $1 and $2 bills. Today one might wonder why counterfeiters would bother to fake $1 and $2 bills, but back then a dollar still had a lot of buying power, and people were much less likely to look closely at bills of such low denomination. Something in the order of a million dollars' worth of this boodle was in circulation. A large number of the phony bills found their way into northwestern Ontario. They were still in use in the fur trade there long after the counterfeiter had been caught and his plates destroyed.

The Americans were sure the U.S. $5 bill and the Canadian boodle were all coming from the same source. They sent Isaac N. Plotts, a member of the U.S. Treasury Department and a famed "Counterfeiter Detector," to Toronto. Plotts had compiled a "Blue Book" in which he had detailed every scrap of information the United States government had on known counterfeiters. John Wilson Murray was not a man who liked to share the glory when he solved a tough case, and his account makes no mention of Mr. Plotts's Blue Book. But in all likelihood he had access to it when he was assigned to find the counterfeiter, and most importantly "get the plates." It would be a daunting task. Murray wrote later, "I started out, and I knew at the outset that I was tackling one of the hardest cases of my life."

Though the Americans were sure the bad money was coming from Canada, Murray began his investigation in the United States. He went to New York City, Philadelphia, and Washington, D.C. He showed the fake American and Canadian bills to officials, and looked up former "cooney men" in those cities, trying to find a lead. The government men weren't much help. But the ex-counterfeiters were. These men knew their business well, and they could often recognize a colleague's work.

Murray initially thought his quarry was a notorious counterfeiter known as Prussian Mark. This man's name was actually Charles F. Ulrich. He was born in Prussia but had gone to England where he joined the army. According to one story he was with the legendary six hundred in the Charge of the Light Brigade at Balaklava in 1854. Ulrich eventually went to the United States where he found work as an engraver. Soon he was engraving copper plates for counterfeiters. Criminals hailed him as one of the best. But Ulrich did some time in jail, and by the time of Murray's investigation he had given up counterfeiting, though his name was in Plotts's Blue Book.

A retired counterfeiter in Troy, New York, looked at Murray's fake bills. He said they were about the prettiest he'd ever seen, but they were not the work of the Prussian. He thought the American $5 note looked like the work of a notorious engraver named John Hill. He said Hill was the best in the business, next to a fellow named Ed Johnson.

Hill might have made the $5 plates and then sold them. Murray's contact in Troy believed he was currently in jail. As for the Canadian bills, they were so good, the man said only a master like Ed Johnson could have made the plates.

In Murray's own account he said he knew Johnson by reputation — though his information could have come from the Blue Book. Edwin Johnson, in his seventies by this time, was born in England and had gone to the United States with his family as a boy. He moved to Canada shortly after the 1837 Rebellion. At some point he learned the craft of engraving. By the time of the Civil War he was back in the Unites States, living in Indianapolis. He was involved in counterfeiting American $20, $50, and $100 bills and served five years in prison. All Murray could learn of his activities since that time was that he was suspected of working on both sides of the Canada-U.S. border.

Murray went to Indianapolis, where he learned that six years earlier Johnson and his family — his wife, two daughters, and five sons — had lived there in high style. They'd had a big house, carriages, and servants. The family spent money like water. Then Johnson had been accused of counterfeiting. A high-priced lawyer got him off the hook, but the family was no longer welcome in the city's best social circles. Murray was told they had moved to Cincinnati.

Murray went to Cincinnati and found that the Johnsons had continued their opulent lifestyle there, occupying a home in one of the city's upscale neighbourhoods. But then they had moved again, this time to Hartford, Connecticut. In Hartford Murray saw the house the Johnsons had lived in but had long since vacated. He also found there had been a change in the daily lives of the Johnson family. Gone was the flashy show of wealth they'd displayed in Indianapolis and Cincinnati. In Hartford they'd been reclusive, rarely showing themselves on the street. Then they'd moved on again, this time to Fall River, Massachusetts. Murray went there and found the big old house they had lived in. He was told they had been gone not quite a year. And that was where the trail ended. No one knew where the mysterious, wandering Johnsons had gone. Murray "worked like a beaver," as he put it, to find a trace but came up with nothing.

Murray went back to New York and conferred again with one of the cooney men he knew there. The man said he knew Ed Johnson but hadn't seen him in years. He examined Murray's counterfeit bills and had no doubt that the Canadian bills were Johnson's work. He also told Murray that Mrs. Johnson was a fussy type. She would always make sure the family had money "for a rainy day." The man had one other bit of information about Ed Johnson. "He used to get on drunks, and his family had a desperate time watching him."

Murray's informant had no idea where the Johnsons were. He thought they might have gone to England. At Murray's request he made inquiries through the underworld grapevine. He came up with nothing except the rumour that Ed Johnson had left the country.

Johnson had a history of border hopping, so Murray travelled to two of the busiest border cities, Buffalo and Detroit, in search of new leads. No one he spoke to had seen Ed Johnson in years. It was now 1880, and Murray was no closer to making an arrest than he'd been when he started out.

Sitting in his Detroit hotel room, Murray went over all the information he had on Ed Johnson and the circulation of the counterfeit money. He decided that the Johnsons had either left North America, or were somewhere nearby, and were passing the boodle themselves. If they were not in the United States, they had to be in Canada. The most obvious place to start looking was Toronto (which might indeed have been suggested by the American Secret Service men a couple of years earlier).

According to his own account, Murray was not back in Toronto for long when by sheer chance he saw Edwin Johnson's son Johnnie having a drink in a saloon. When Johnnie left the saloon, Murray followed him. Then he lost him when the young man hailed a cab.

Murray spent the next three nights hanging around saloons in that part of Toronto, hoping Johnnie would make another appearance. On the third night he saw him in a saloon on King Street. When young Johnson left, Murray followed him again. This time, when Johnnie hailed a cab, Murray had a hack waiting nearby so he could stay on the young man's tail.

Murray followed the cab to a fine-looking brick house on Hazelton Avenue, near present-day Queen's Park. He watched Johnnie unlock the door and let himself in. Murray was sure now, that after two years on the trail, he had finally found Edwin Johnson. But he still needed proof that Johnson was the source of $1 million in counterfeit money that had been in circulation all over Ontario.

With the co-operation of neighbours, Murray kept the Johnson house under surveillance for five days. In all that time no one left the house. Deliverymen — the butcher, the baker, and the milkman — came and went. Murray stopped them out of sight of the house and asked them about the people who lived there. The men said the house was occupied by elderly parents, two very attractive daughters, and a couple of sons. They knew nothing else, except that the girls liked to play the piano and sing.

From all appearances the Johnsons were a law-abiding (if reclusive) family. Murray had no solid evidence that the father was a counterfeiter, and he doubted the plates were in the house. But Murray had tenacity. He listened to the sounds of music and singing coming from the house, and he waited.

Finally he got his break. On the morning of Friday, June 11, old Edwin himself stepped out of the house, dressed like a dapper gentleman. He headed downtown, stopping in at almost every saloon along the way. Murray was close behind him. At each groggery where Johnson had gone in for a snort, Murray asked the bartender to show him the money with which the old man had paid. It was all good Canadian currency.

Johnson went to the train station and bought a ticket to Stouffville, a small community north of Toronto. Murray was in the same coach, just a few seats behind him. When the train stopped in Stouffville, Johnson got off and went to the nearest saloon for a drink. He paid for it with a $1 bill and pocketed the change. No sooner did he leave the tavern than Murray went in and gave the proprietor a dollar's worth of silver for the bill. He looked it over carefully and then knew, "I had my man at last." Murray had the proprietor initial the counterfeit bill. Then he continued to follow Johnson.

The old man bought a few more drinks and a cigar, paying each time with a counterfeit note. Murray went into each establishment and bought the phony bills. When Johnson finally got the train back to Toronto, Murray was again in the same coach. As Johnson stepped off the train back in the city, Murray came up behind him, tapped him on the shoulder and said, "How do you do, Mr. Johnson?"

Johnson told Murray he was mistaken, that his name was Anderson. Even after Murray told him how he had followed his trail from Indiana to Massachusetts to Ontario, Johnson insisted his name was Anderson. Murray told Johnson he had the bad bills he had passed in Stouffville, and that he was under arrest for counterfeiting. Johnson had been drinking all day, but now he seemed to sober up quite suddenly. "Is there no way of arranging this?" he asked. "It seems a serious matter."

Murray hailed a cab and took Johnson to the York County jail. Johnson tried once more to bribe the detective. "Can we not arrange this matter?" he asked. "Give me your terms. I have money. I mean, good money."

Johnson was wasting his breath, because Murray most certainly was not a crooked cop. He searched Johnson and found more bad bills on him. He gave Johnson a few cigars, told the jailer to make the old man comfortable, then told Johnson he would be back to see him on Monday. He said Johnson needed some time to dry out and think things over. He added that he wanted the plates.

The next day, Saturday, a sober and somewhat anxious Johnson sent for Murray. Once again he offered the detective money, saying he had friends who could raise a considerable sum.

"Nothing for me except the plates," replied Murray.

"Foolish fellow," Johnson said. Then he warned Murray against the evils of strong drink. "If I had not been drunk, this would not have happened," he said.

On Monday Johnson reluctantly agreed to turn the plates over to Murray. But they were hidden, and he would have to take Murray to the hiding place. Murray sent for Toronto Police Detective John Hodgins to assist him. Then the two policemen and the seventy-five-year-old counterfeiter got into a cab.

Johnson directed the cab driver north through Yorkville, then along the Davenport Road, past a tollgate, to a place called Wells Hill. The men got out of the cab and walked into the woods. Johnson pointed to the foot of a large elm and said, "There's where they are."

Murray and Hodgins had not brought shovels. They took off their coats and began digging with sticks. The ground at that spot did not seem to have ever been disturbed, and after toiling awhile in the June heat, Murray suspected that Johnson might be trying to pull a fast one. He told the old man this was no time for practical jokes. Johnson looked around the area again, pointed at the base of another tree and told Murray to dig there.

Murray sent Hodgins back to town to buy a spade. While he waited, he warned Johnson he had not time for any tricks. Old Johnson said, "They are here, Murray. I vow they are here."

Detective Hodgins returned with the spade and started to dig. In no time he struck what was pay dirt for Murray. "Careful, man, careful!" Johnson cried. "They took years to make and are worth over forty thousand dollars."

The plates were in a package about the size of two bricks. They were sealed with beeswax and wrapped in oilcloth. There were twenty-one of them, three for each of the seven notes Johnson had been counterfeiting. The old man looked at them lovingly and told Murray he was only part-owner. A man in the United States also owned an interest in them, he said.

Murray's find was, up to that date, the biggest seizure of counterfeit plates that had ever been made in North America. Johnson said the American $5 plate had in fact been made by John Hill, but he had made the Canadian plates himself. He proudly credited his daughters, Jessie and Annie, with forging the signatures on them. He said he'd spent years training the girls in the fine art of forging handwriting. He was also teaching his sons to be engravers, so they could follow in his footsteps.

Johnson said they printed large quantities of bills once a year. Then they buried the plates and destroyed all the other counterfeiting equipment. The old counterfeiter regretted that every so often he got drunk and stooped to the low level of a shover. "When I drink, I indulge in it, and because I drank and indulged in it, you got me."

Johnson could have been sent to the Kingston Penitentiary. But because of his age and his co-operation in handing over the plates, a judge gave him a suspended sentence. However, the Canadians were obliged to turn Johnson over to the Americans to face charges of counterfeiting in the United States. The old master died before he could be brought to trial. Murray said crime had lost a genius. Murray said that he, personally, had been "well used" by the banks for finding and destroying the plates, meaning he was handsomely rewarded.

Soon after Edwin Johnson's death, three of his sons, Johnnie, Sam, and Charlie, were in Canadian or American prisons for "pushing the queer." The plates Johnson had made, the masterpieces of his forty-year career as a counterfeiter, were scored so they could never be used again. John Wilson Murray kept them in his library as trophies. Some of Ed Johnson's actual counterfeit bills can be seen on display in the Bank of Canada's Currency Museum in Ottawa.

JACK KRAFCHENKO

THE SAGA OF BLOODY JACK

The man who would come to be known in Canadian criminal lore as Bloody Jack remains something of an enigma to this day. The facts about his life are often distorted by legend. Stories about him that were reported in the newspapers during his lifetime would now be very difficult to verify. Journalist James H. Gray wrote a chapter titled "On the Trail of Jack Krafchenko" in his autobiography, *The Boy From Winnipeg*. While discussing the fascination young boys in Manitoba had for the outlaw, Gray stated that there are two or three versions for most stories that surround Krafchenko. Had Krafchenko been an American desperado, there would quite likely be at least one Hollywood film based on his criminal exploits.

John Larry Krafchenko was born in Romania to Ukrainian parents in 1881. His family immigrated to Canada in 1888 and settled in the village of Plum Coulee, an agricultural centre at the western edge of the Red River Valley, not far from Winnipeg. There Jack's father worked as a blacksmith. Jack's mother died while he was still quite young, and his father married a German woman. Jack's stepmother, Catherine, loved the boy as though he were her own son, and stuck by him through all his troubles.

As a youth Jack Krafchenko had a lot going for him. He was handsome, and though somewhat under average size at five foot six, he was fit and muscular. He spoke Russian, Ukrainian, German, and English fluently. At school he was said to be a very bright student. But Jack didn't like school and rarely attended.

Indeed, Jack Krafchenko had a serious problem with any sort of discipline or authority. He would not be told what to do. Added to this were a hair-trigger temper and a violent streak that made him a bad man to cross in any way. Ordinarily a friendly and easygoing young man, Krafchenko could suddenly explode in a fit of volcanic

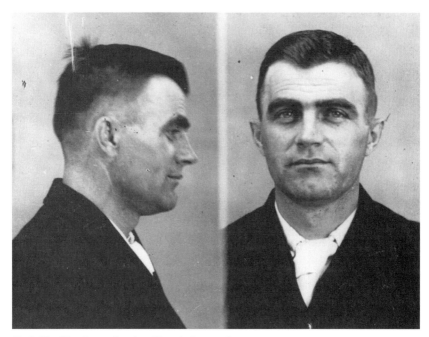

Jack Krafchenko — bank robber, killer, and escape artist.
(The Lab Works, Archives of Manitoba)

rage. As an adult, Jack allegedly expressed admiration for the train robber, Bill Miner.

Jack first got into trouble with the law in November 1892, when at the age of eleven he was charged with stealing five watches from a store. The judge let him off with a warning. A few years later at the age of fifteen Jack wasn't so lucky. He was arrested for stealing a bicycle and apparently was sent to jail, though documentary evidence is unclear. It would not be surprising if he did do jail time for bicycle theft because in those days stealing a bike was almost as bad as stealing a horse. Whether or not he spent a few months behind bars, as Jack approached twenty he seems to have decided to get out of Manitoba for a while.

Legend says that Krafchenko went to Australia. If so, he might have wanted to get in on the gold rush there. In Australia Krafchenko became a professional wrestler (in some versions, a boxer). He went to the United States and fought under the names Australian Tommy Ryan and Pearl Smith. The stories say he was successful, and even married a relative of "Gentleman" Jim Corbett, the heavyweight boxing champion who had defeated the great John L. Sullivan. Such tales of Krafchenko's career as a pugilist are rather suspect. The face of the man who was photographed by Winnipeg police in later years bore none of the marks that would be found on a man who made his living in the brutal rings of the late nineteenth and early twentieth centuries.

By 1902 Krafchenko was back in southern Manitoba, passing himself off as a temperance lecturer. As he travelled from town to town he was passing bad cheques. The police caught up to him in Regina, Saskatchewan. Krafchenko was sentenced to eighteen months in the Prince Albert Penitentiary. Krafchenko is said to have attempted to escape from the train taking him to prison by climbing out an open window. The train was moving, and Krafchenko was wearing handcuffs. His bid for freedom was short-lived. The guard escorting him to prison also climbed out a window and recaptured him.

If Krafchenko really did try to escape from the train, the prison authorities failed to read the signs about what sort of man he was. They put Krafchenko to work painting the *outside* of the prison walls. Jack seized the opportunity. He slugged a guard over the head with a bucket of paint, and he and three other convicts made a run for it. The other three escapees were quickly apprehended, but Krafchenko eluded all pursuers.

Here the Krafchenko legend begins to grow, and just how much truth is at the root of it is difficult to determine. Krafchenko allegedly returned to Manitoba, where he held up a money shipment between Plum Coulee and Winkler at gunpoint and got away with $2,500. Then he crossed the border into the United States and headed for New York City. After robbing several New York banks, he boarded a freighter for England.

In Europe Krafchenko was supposedly a one-man crime wave. He is said to have robbed banks in England, Germany, and Italy. During a bank robbery in Milan, Jack allegedly locked the manager in the vault, and then slipped outside and joined the crowd that had gathered to see what all the excitement was about. The *Winnipeg Free Press* would write of him: "He has a genius for robberies requiring desperate action."

These stories about Krafchenko circulated, picking up more and more colourful "facts" as they passed from one teller to the next. As with Billy the Kid and Jesse James in the United States, the stories presented Krafchenko as a larger-than-life figure. It was said of Jack that he was "… one of the most cultured men imaginable. He knows more about police work than most of the force." There was even a story that back in the old country, Jack's natural mother had been a notorious horse thief who disguised herself as a man when she went on raids.

In 1905 Krafchenko went to Russia. There he married a woman named Fanica — a fact that challenges the story of the marriage to Gentleman Jim Corbett's relative. In 1906 Krafchenko returned to Canada with his new wife, with whom he soon had a son. They settled near Plum Coulee, where Jack went to work as a blacksmith.

Krafchenko wasn't home long before he had his eye on a bank. The victim was the Bank of Hamilton, which was a short distance outside Plum Coulee on the road to Winkler. Krafchenko looted it of an undisclosed amount of money. However, he was recognized and once again had to hightail it to the United States.

On November 21, 1908, a young man named Eccles Lennox was shot dead during a drunken dispute in a Pullman car in the Winnipeg rail yards. Police found the body with a revolver beside it, and at first thought the man had committed suicide. But the autopsy revealed that it would have been impossible for the gunshot wounds to be self-inflicted. Police traced the suspected murder weapon to a man named Thomas Henry Hicks, a friend of Jack Krafchenko. Hicks was arrested and charged with murder. Winnipeg police hoped that with Hicks's arrest they might be able to clear up a few unsolved robbery cases, as well as the murders of two Chinese labourers.

Meanwhile, Krafchenko had returned to Manitoba, only to be caught by surprise and arrested at his aunt's house in Winnipeg. He was armed with two revolvers, but the police pounced on him so quickly, he didn't have a chance to use them. Jack said he was tired of being hounded for a crime he hadn't committed.

When Hicks went on trial for murder that December, Krafchenko appeared as a witness for the defence. He testified that the gun found next to Lennox's body was his, not Hicks's. Krafchenko could not be charged with the murder because he was in custody when the crime happened. But his claim of ownership of the gun placed enough doubt on Hicks's connection to it that the charge was dismissed. Even though Hicks walked out of the courtroom a free man, Krafchenko did not. He was tried for the 1906 bank robbery and sentenced to Manitoba's Stony Mountain Penitentiary for three years.

When Jack was released from prison, he and Fanica moved to the little community of Graham in the middle of the northern Ontario wilderness, about seventy-five miles northwest of Port Arthur (now Thunder Bay). Jack was employed there as a boilermaker for the Transcontinental Railway shops. For a while he stayed out of trouble, and by the summer of 1913 he had risen to the position of foreman. Ironically, he even did some service for the local police as an interpreter. But Krafchenko's vile temper was his undoing. That summer, because of his unpredictable and violent outbursts, Krafchenko was demoted. He found the experience so humiliating and infuriating, he quit his job and returned to Manitoba.

Krafchenko went to Winnipeg, where he caroused around, drinking and gambling with some of his old hoodlum pals. The Winnipeg Chief of Police Donald MacPherson thought that a man who was out of work and had underworld connections might be interested in earning a few dollars from the police. He paid Krafchenko a small sum of money to find the names of people responsible for a rash of burglaries. Jack took the police chief's money but never did squeal on any of his criminal associates.

On November 2 Jack was arrested as a suspect in a robbery in nearby Kildonan. He was carrying two revolvers when the police picked him up. But there was no evidence connecting him to the robbery, so he was released. Krafchenko believed the police were just getting even with him for stiffing the chief.

Jack made frequent trips between Winnipeg and Plum Coulee. Not long after the police had shaken him down for the Kildonan robbery, Jack decided to stick up the Bank of Montreal in Plum Coulee. This wasn't one of the more brilliantly planned bank robberies in Canadian crime history. Only about one hundred and fifty people lived in Plum Coulee, and they all knew Jack Krafchenko. In Manitoba in 1913 the roads — such as they were — became next to impassable in winter. Moreover, the cars of that time were extremely difficult to keep running in the cold weather. Most automobile owners took the wheels off and put the cars up on blocks until spring. Jack would have been better off using a horse, like an old-time desperado.

Krafchenko recruited two of his Winnipeg cronies to assist him in the heist. He had watched the bank carefully during his visits to Plum Coulee and noted that during the lunch hour only the manager, Henry Medly Arnold, was in the bank. That would be the perfect time for the outlaws to strike.

On November 18 Krafchenko bought two pistols in a Winnipeg gun shop: a 9mm Browning automatic and a 7.65mm Luger. Then, in the last week of November, he arranged for a taxi to take him and his two confederates to Plum Coulee. The bandits expected to hit the bank at lunchtime and then have their unsuspecting driver take them back to Winnipeg. But when they arrived at the village they found that manager Arnold had closed up early and gone home. Jack's two pals were disappointed, perhaps even disgusted. They returned to Winnipeg with their driver. Krafchenko, determined to rob the Plum Coulee bank, stayed behind.

Some historians have speculated that Jack Krafchenko was not an emotionally or mentally stable individual. The irrational hatred of authority figures and the violent outbursts of temper were certainly signs of personality problems. But for a man who had always been described as intellectually bright, the decision to go ahead with this bank job was unbelievably stupid.

On December 1 Krafchenko contacted a local man he had known for many years, a taxi driver named William Dyck, and arranged for Dyck to drive him out of the village after the bank robbery. Dyck later testified that Krafchenko forced him at gunpoint to agree to be the getaway driver. Dyck could easily have gone to the police. Why didn't he? Either he was in on the robbery, or he was too scared of the notorious Krafchenko to do anything but obey.

On Wednesday, December 3, 1913, at 12:30 p.m., while Henry Arnold was in the Bank of Montreal alone, Jack Krafchenko entered. He wore false whiskers, a heavy coat, and had a bandana wrapped around the lower part of his face. He pulled out the Browning 9mm and told Arnold to hand over the money. The startled banker shoved $4,200 through the wicket. The bandit fled out the back door to an alley where a car was waiting.

Arnold then did what every bank manager of the time was expected to do in the event of a robbery. He grabbed a pistol from his desk and went after the thief. Outside the bank's back door, about two feet from the building, Krafchenko had dropped some bundles of money and was half kneeling to scoop them up. Gun in hand, Arnold shouted at him to stop. Those were his last words on earth. The outlaw responded with a single shot. The bullet struck Arnold in the chest and went right through his body, severing his spinal cord. The bank manager was probably dead before he hit the ground. Krafchenko had now given Canadians good cause to call him Bloody Jack!

Krafchenko climbed into the car and told William Dyck to drive. At least three people witnessed the shooting. In spite of the disguise, one of them positively identified the killer as Krafchenko. The others gave police descriptions that matched his.

A few miles out of Plum Coulee, Krafchenko told Dyck to stop the car and let him out. He threatened to kill Dyck (or so Dyck told police) if he gave the police his name. He told Dyck to make up a good story about where he'd been. Then Krafchenko disappeared into the bush.

The Manitoba Provincial Police were soon in Plum Coulee, interrogating William Dyck. He told them two men had robbed the bank and then forced him to drive them about twenty-five miles to the southeast. Then, probably under tough questioning, Dyck gave in and told the truth. His fear of Krafchenko, he said, had compelled him to lie. A $1,000 reward was posted for Krafchenko's capture, and one of the biggest manhunts in Manitoba history was on.

Meanwhile, Krafchenko had made his way to Winnipeg, and under the cover of night he slipped into the city unseen. He had a room in a boarding house at 546 William Avenue, where he was posing as a visiting surgeon, Dr. Fairchild. The landlady's son seemed to become suspicious when Dr. Fairchild was unable to do much to help him with an aching tooth. Krafchenko stayed there just one night, and then moved on to a boarding house at 439 College Avenue, where he introduced himself as Mr. Andrews, a schoolteacher.

Krafchenko's problem was that even though Winnipeg was the biggest Canadian city between Ontario and the Pacific coast, it was no Toronto or Montreal. He could not effectively "lose himself" in the crowd. The police would be watching the roads out of town closely, as well as the trains. The longer he remained in Winnipeg, the greater the danger of being discovered. He had to get out of town quickly, but he would need help.

Over the next few days Krafchenko visited a few of his old pals, boldly (or foolishly) appearing on the streets, sometimes even on Main Street. He entrusted some of the robbery loot to friends, telling them to stash it away for him. He gave another friend $700 to take to his wife. He had an idea that he could sneak out of Winnipeg disguised as a woman, so he had a friend buy him a full set of female clothing.

One of the trusted acquaintances Krafchenko spoke to was a taxi driver named Benjamin Rolph. According to the rumour that swept through Winnipeg later, it was Rolph who went to former police chief J.C. McRae and informed him of Krafchenko's hideout. Rolph would deny this, possibly out of fear of retribution on the part of Krafchenko's friends. Rolph claimed the informer was an unsavoury underworld character named Bert Bell. One historian (author Bill Macdonald) has suggested that Krafchenko was actually spotted by a young deliveryman for the Great North West Telegraph Company named William Stephenson. This was the same William Stephenson who would become the master of espionage known as "Intrepid" during Second World War. Whoever the stool pigeon really was, the police kept the man's identity a secret.

Shortly before ten o'clock on the morning of December 10, Winnipeg policemen surrounded Krafchenko's College Avenue boarding house. Chief MacPherson, his deputy chief, his chief of detectives, and the chief of the Manitoba Provincial Police entered the house and went to the door of Krafchenko's room. One of them knocked. A sleepy-eyed Krafchenko opened the door. Evidently he had been expecting a visit from one of his criminal associates. He grew pale at the sight of four policemen with guns leveled at him. His own pistols were in the room but had he dared to go for them, he would not have made it.

Krafchenko was placed under arrest, manacled, and hauled off to jail. He was initially held on weapons violations until the police could gather enough evidence to formally charge him with the murder of Henry M. Arnold. The police did not find any of the bank money in Krafchenko's room, but they did uncover $2,800 concealed in the yard behind the house. Police acting on a tip eventually found more money hidden in another part of the city.

Krafchenko was officially a prisoner of the Manitoba Provincial Police because the crimes of armed robbery and murder had been committed in Plum Coulee. However, because of his record of prison escape, the police decided to keep him in the city jail rather than the provincial jail. The city jail was in the same building as the courtroom. The provincial jail was about one hundred yards away, which would have meant taking Krafchenko outside to get him to court and then back to his cell. By putting him in the city jail, the authorities kept him indoors at all times, considerably reducing his opportunities to make an escape attempt. Instead of putting Krafchenko in a regular cell, the police placed a cot in an old, unused kitchen down the hall from the cells and locked him in there. It seemed as secure a holding place as any in Winnipeg. But Jack Krafchenko wasn't about to give up yet. Not with an almost certain date with the hangman waiting for him.

Krafchenko's preliminary hearing began on January 5. The court-appointed defence counsel was Percy Hagel, son of a prominent Winnipeg family. Prosecuting for the Crown was W.H. Hastings. The hearing carried on over several days, and during that time Krafchenko regaled Hagel and his guards with stories of loot he had stashed away from other holdups. It was a real treasure, he told them: cash and jewellery. If he could just get out and lay his hands on it, he'd be only too willing to share.

One guard, Constable William Flower, was not impressed with Krafchenko's tall tales. But Constable Robert Reid was very interested indeed. So was lawyer Hagel.

On January 9 the hearing concluded, and Krafchenko was committed to stand trial for robbery and murder at the spring assizes. When the judge made the announcement, Jack said impatiently, "Oh, get through with this thing so that I can go rabbit shooting in the spring." Krafchenko was taken back to his lock-up in what was now known throughout Winnipeg as the Old Kitchen. The next morning he was gone!

According to the guards, Flower and Reid, Krafchenko spent most of the night pacing up and down, stopping only occasionally to ask the time. The two guards had cots at the entrance of the Old Kitchen. It would have been impossible for him to reach the door without passing them. In accordance with Canadian law, the guards were not armed, so as not to give the prisoner an opportunity to seize a gun. Both guards, however, were burly men. Reid was a former Toronto policeman. Either one could have easily overpowered the smaller Krafchenko.

The guards had books to read to help pass the monotonous hours, but keeping sharp watch for hours and days on end would eventually dull anyone's vigilance. The two constables were not paying much attention to Krafchenko when, sometime after two o'clock on the morning of January 10, a Saturday, Jack suddenly said, "I'm going out of here."

One of the guards looked up, and what he saw made him gasp, causing the other to look up, too. Bloody Jack had a Colt automatic in his hand and was pointing it at them. He waved it a little, so that both officers were covered. "Make a move and I'll shoot you both," Krafchenko warned. He told them to throw their keys on the floor, and then said, "Get into that closet."

Flower and Reid backed into a closet that had probably once been a pantry, and Krafchenko slammed the door. The inside handle had been removed, so they were effectively locked in. None of the guards' keys would fit the lock to the Old Kitchen door, but Jack easily opened it with a cheap skeleton key — the sort that could be bought in dime stores anywhere at that time. Then, with a coil of clothesline rope he had hidden in the room, Krafchenko made his way to a photography room that had an unbarred window overlooking Main Street. He opened the door with one of the guard's keys, and went to the window. It was a thirty-foot drop to the pavement, but Jack wasn't worried about that.

Krafchenko secured one end of the rope, slid the rest out the window, and began to climb down. But he was hardly out the window when the thin rope broke! Krafchenko fell almost the full thirty feet and hit the pavement hard. He sprained both his knees, one ankle and his back. In great pain, Krafchenko looked up and down the street. The bust-out had been planned for this late hour, when even Main Street would be deserted. But a car was supposed to be waiting for him. It wasn't there! (Or so Krafchenko claimed later.) Gritting his teeth against the pain and clutching his gun, Jack Krafchenko hobbled off into the night to seek shelter.

The news of Jack Krafchenko's escape stunned the nation. How could this accused killer, "the most dramatic and magnetic character in the history of all Manitoba crime," as the *Winnipeg Free Press* described him, have been allowed to get away with two strong policemen watching him every minute of the day and night? Where did he get the gun, the skeleton key (which was found in the photography room), and the rope? Without a doubt, the desperado had outside help. But from whom? Suspicion fell upon William Flower, Robert Reid, and Percy Hagel. While police officers combed Winnipeg, followed wild goose chases all over southern Manitoba, and watched the American border, a Royal Commission was called to investigate the escape.

Everyone associated with the Winnipeg jail was questioned. Flower, Reid, and Hagel all initially denied having anything to do with the escape. Hagel said he had given Krafchenko nothing but a package of cigarettes, and he had done that in plain view of others. While

the Commission was in session, reports of "Krafchenko sightings" were coming in from all over the Canadian West, as well as from northern Ontario and North Dakota, thanks in no small part to the $5,000 (soon raised to $7,000) reward being offered for information leading to his capture. (Offering rewards for a fugitive to be brought in "Dead or Alive" was illegal in Canada.) The *Winnipeg Free Press* rubbed salt into the wound by running an editorial cartoon that showed a smiling Krafchenko reading a wanted poster while

In this Winnipeg Free Press *cartoon, an artist picks up on Jack Krafchenko's statement that he wanted to get out of jail so he could shoot rabbits.*

rabbit hunting. Both unamused and undaunted, the Royal Commission continued to grill potential suspects. After five gruelling days, during which he was cross-examined for hours on end, Constable Robert Reid finally broke down and confessed.

Constable Flower, said Reid, had nothing to do with the escape. But Hagel did. Reid claimed that he and Hagel met several times in Hagel's office and at the Clarendon Hotel to discuss springing Krafchenko. Hagel brought two other men into the plot: John Westlake, a former employee in Hagel's law firm, and John Buxton, who had once been the custodian in the Builder's Exchange Building where Hagel's office was located.

Buxton's job was to get the rope and a gun. (Presumably Hagel or Reid had the foresight to realize the police would trace the rope to a local hardware or dry goods store, and did not want to be identified as the purchaser.) Buxton had two guns in a pawn shop, but did not want to use either of them in case the police traced the weapon to him. He had a friend steal a .32 calibre Colt automatic from a warehouse. Buxton gave the gun and rope to Reid, who smuggled them to Krafchenko, along with the skeleton key.

Westlake was to hide Krafchenko in his apartment in the Burris Building at the corner of Toronto Street and Ellice Avenue. The fugitive would stay there until a way could be found to spirit him out of the city. Then — the conspirators believed — Jack would reward them with shares from his ill-gotten gains.

The escape was originally planned for the night of January 8. Hagel was supposed to be waiting with a car to pick Jack up and drive him to Westlake's place. But the lawyer got drunk that night and the break-out had to be postponed.

It was on again for the early hours of January 10, and this time Jack made the break. How he got from the jail to Westlake's apartment remains a mystery. He denied being driven there by Hagel but might have been trying to protect the lawyer. In one story Jack said he got a lift from some young people out for a joyride. But in another version Krafchenko said a "Good Samaritan" — not realizing he had escaped from jail — stopped his car and gave him a ride.

It may well have been Buxton who first tipped the police off on Reid and Hagel's involvement. Whether he did or not, once Reid spilled the beans Buxton lost no time in confirming Reid's story and providing the police with any further information they required in order to apprehend Krafchenko. It was important the capture be made without bloodshed. Chief MacPherson did not want any dead cops. Nor did he want Krafchenko going down in a blaze of gunfire and looking like a martyr.

On January 18 the police surrounded the Burris Building. Once again Chief MacPherson and a "picked squad of detectives and constables" approached the door of Westlake's apartment. All had their guns drawn. MacPherson knocked on the door and said, "Are you in there, Jack?"

Krafchenko replied, "Is that you, Chief?"

MacPherson said, "Yes, it's me."

One of the detectives asked, "Are you still going to fight?"

Krafchenko answered, "I'm all right. Come on in."

The policemen entered and found Krafchenko lying on a bed, barely able to move because of his injuries. His gun was in a basket beside the bed but he made no attempt to reach for it. The outlaw was in such pain, the police didn't even bother to handcuff him for the trip back to jail. This time he was taken to the provincial jail and locked in a steel cage usually reserved for condemned prisoners.

Krafchenko told police he had planned on having himself shipped out of Winnipeg in a piano crate but could not go through with it because of his injuries. The police found the piano crate with food scraps inside that indicated Krafchenko and his would-be liberators had actually experimented with the plan.

Hagel, Reid, Westlake, and Buxton were all arrested and eventually tried. Because Buxton turned King's evidence against the others, he was released. To protect him from vengeance at the hands of Krafchenko's friends, the attorney general's office quietly helped Buxton relocate in Maryland, where he started up a business.

Westlake was sentenced to two years in Stoney Mountain Penitentiary. Hagel, claiming he'd been framed, got three years. When he was released he was dismissed from the Manitoba bar but was eventually invited back. Reid, the ex-Toronto policeman, got seven years. Though he was only in his thirties when he was incarcerated, Reid died in prison.

Jack Krafchenko made no further escape attempts. His trial for armed robbery and murder was held in Morden, Manitoba, and lasted from March 18 to April 9. Krafchenko admitted to setting out that fateful day to commit a robbery but said he had no intention of hurting anyone. He claimed to have been armed only with a "gas gun" (air gun). He said he had an accomplice who was carrying a real pistol. Krafchenko further claimed that the victim, Arnold, had been in on the robbery but had messed things up by running out with a gun. Jack said it was the accomplice, and not he, who had shot the banker. He refused to identify his fellow bandit.

The jury didn't buy the story. None of the witnesses had seen another man. The jurors found Krafchenko guilty of murder. Justice J.C. Mathers sentenced him to hang on July 9, 1914.

Krafchenko protested his innocence to the very end. The fact that between ten and twenty thousand people signed a petition for clemency shows that, while there was no doubt about his guilt, Krafchenko certainly had sympathizers. But the plea to the government fell on deaf ears.

The hanging was to be carried out in Winnipeg's Vaughan Street jail. On the night before the execution, Krafchenko was sitting with the chaplain, Mr. Bertal Heney, praying. Jack picked up a teaspoon, and to the amazement of the clergyman, picked the lock of his cell door with it and opened the door wide. This was not an attempt to escape. Krafchenko just wanted people to know that he could have made another break for it if he'd wanted to but had resigned himself to his fate.

At about 4:00 a.m., as his final hour approached, Krafchenko fainted and lay unconscious on his cot. At 6:45 a.m. he came around, just in time to be escorted to the gallows. Though he went, "like a man of iron nerve," according to one witness, he stopped halfway up the stairs of the scaffold and complained that he didn't feel well. Hangman Ellis dropped him at one minute before seven o'clock.

Outside the jail a crowd of some two thousand people watched in silence for the black flag that signaled the death of a condemned prisoner. An anonymous person sent white lilies into the jail. The body was turned over to Jack's long-suffering stepmother, Catherine Krafchenko. In a bizarre show of grief, she tried to revive Jack. She had brought along a man who claimed to be a warlock, another who called himself a soothsayer, two witches, and a practitioner of voodoo. When this assembly of charlatans failed to resurrect Jack, she tried to breathe life back into the body herself. Catherine finally had to allow the corpse to be buried in a grave that would remain unmarked.

Jack Krafchenko had captured the attention of the Canadian public in a manner matched by few other Canadian criminals. But within weeks of his death, Canada and most of the world were drawn into the crucible that would be known as the Great War. By the time that unprecedented bloodbath was over, the case of Bloody Jack Krafchenko was all but forgotten.

TOM BASSOFF

SHOOTOUT IN BELLEVUE

It was the afternoon of August 2, 1920, and the days of the Wild West were long past. But to the people in the passenger car of CPR train number 63, westbound from Lethbridge, Alberta, the scene in the coach must have looked like something straight out of one of the Hollywood westerns that were already popular on the silent movie screens. Three men suddenly rose from their seats, drew pistols and announced they were pulling a holdup. When Conductor Sam Jones reached for the emergency cord, a bandit fired a warning shot in his direction. One man — the leader — seemed to be a caricature of Pancho Villa, the notorious bandit-turned-revolutionary guerrilla who had been in the news recently. The train robber wore a Mexican sombrero, riding breeches, and cowboy boots. He had a thick black moustache, and one bad eye gave him the look of a genuine desperado. One of his companions also wore a sombrero, high boots, and a mauve bandana around his neck. The third man, somewhat more nondescript, wore what was described as "a cast-off khaki jacket."

Brandishing their guns, the three robbers went through the coach, relieving passengers of cash and valuables. They also took a large sum of money and a watch from the conductor. Evidently the robbers had been told the local bootlegging boss, Emilio "Emperor Pic" Picariello, would be aboard the train with a roll of about $10,000 on him. Legend has it that Picariello stuffed his wad of cash under a seat cushion and then quietly moved to another seat. Actually, the bootlegger wasn't even on the train.

The bandits jumped off the train at Sentinel, near the British Columbia border. They were believed to have fled in a car driven by a fourth accomplice. The victims described the robbers to police and said they had thick accents that were anything but Mexican. The bandits were soon identified as three men who were known by police in Calgary as small-time thugs: Tom Bassoff, age thirty-one; Ausby Aulcoff, age thirty; and George Arkoff, age uncertain. One police spokesman told the press these train robbers were amateurs. But not everyone was certain of that. Some journalists suspected (though it was never proven) that Tom Bassoff was in fact Dzachot Bekuzaroff, a bandit from Siberia who was wanted for bank robberies and a murder committed in New Hazelton, British Columbia, a few years earlier. Even if Bassoff was not actually Bekuzaroff, newspapers would soon describe him as being "as cold blooded a gunman as ever operated in the west."

The police didn't have much information on Bassoff and his henchmen except that they had worked in the mines in The Pass the previous winter. They were known to hang around saloons and pool halls and were said to have friends in the "foreign community." However, most of the immigrant workers seemed to be afraid of them. Unfortunately for the investigators, the immigrants were just as much afraid of police and other government officials as they were of the bandits and were reluctant to talk. Their fears stemmed only partially from bad experiences with officials in their countries of origin. Some Anglo-Canadian police officers had a tendency to be rather heavy-handed with "foreigners."

After the robbery the outlaws took to the hills. Police blocked every road to the U.S. border, making escape in that direction unlikely. On Friday, August 6, Bassoff, Aulcoff, and Arkoff appeared in the town of Coleman where they bought some groceries and tried to cash some stolen cheques at the bank. They failed to cash the cheques and managed only to draw attention to themselves. The following morning Arkoff and Bassoff were seen boarding a train for Bellevue. Someone called the Bellevue police station and tipped the officers there that the train robbery suspects were heading their way.

In Bellevue, Justice of the Peace Robert Morrison recognized the pair as they got off the train. He quickly informed the local constables. The police believed Bassoff and Arkoff were in town to rob the bank, but there was no proof of this.

Unaware they were being watched, Bassoff and Arkoff went into the Chinese-owned Bellevue Café, which was only a few feet from the police station. The booths within were curtained, which was not unusual in those days, so when the outlaws sat at a table, they drew the curtains closed. Three policemen — Corporal Ernest Usher of the Royal Canadian Mounted Police; and Constables Frederick Bailey and James Frewin of the Alberta Provincial Police — moved in on the Bellevue Café to trap and arrest the suspects. Usher and Frewin entered through the front door, while Bailey went around to the rear of the building to prevent an escape through the back door. What followed was described in the press as "a typical frontier-town battle."

When Usher and Frewin entered the café, they could see that only the second booth had drawn curtains. Fortunately, there were no other customers in the restaurant. The Chinese proprietor, Joe Mah Ki, seemed to have ducked out of sight. Each officer had his gun in his hand when Usher yanked the curtain open and ordered, "Hands up!"

Both outlaws were covered, and in the next instant they should have either surrendered or been shot. But a moment's hesitation can make a world of difference. This time it would prove fatal.

"Why for we put our hands up?" Bassoff asked. Even as he spoke, his hand dropped to his gun. Arkoff reached for his gun, too, and Frewin shot him. But for some reason that will never be known, Usher — who had Bassoff covered — did not shoot. Bassoff pulled his gun and fired several shots at the officers, ducking under the table for cover as he did so. Arkoff, who was wounded but not yet out of the fight, also returned fire. Frewin emptied his gun into Arkoff. Then he backed off to reload. Usher, who had still not fired a shot, retreated with him to the front door. Whether he had already been hit by one of the outlaws' bullets is not known.

Bailey heard the gunshots and burst in through the back door. By now the air in the café was thick with gunsmoke. Frewin stepped outside where he could see better to load his pistol. Bailey took his place beside Usher.

Suddenly Bassoff charged out of the booth firing two automatics. Usher and Bailey both went down in the hail of lead. Bullets struck twenty-six-year-old Usher in the neck, head, and shoulder. Bailey, age thirty, the father of two young children, was shot in the chest and neck. Bassoff stopped to take the guns from the hands of the dying officers. He fired three more bullets into each man and then ran out to the street. He hurtled past a surprised Frewin, who was shoving bullets into the chamber of his gun. Bassoff turned and backed up the street, holding his guns at the ready.

Arkoff, now mortally wounded but somehow still on his feet, staggered out of the booth. At the doorway he emptied his guns into the bodies of Usher and Bailey. Autopsies would later reveal eight bullets in Usher and fifteen in Bailey. Constable Bailey was the first Alberta provincial police officer to be slain in the line of duty.

Arkoff made it out to the street. He lurched along about seventy-five feet, trying to catch up to Bassoff. Then he collapsed and died, his guns still clenched in his fists. Bassoff, who so far had not a scratch on him, hesitated, as though considering going back for Arkoff. Meanwhile, Robert Morrison had armed himself when he heard the shooting. He took a shot at Bassoff from across the street and hit the outlaw in the leg, almost toppling him. But the Russian bandit was nothing if not tough. He limped out of town, and managed to lose himself in the vast jumble of rocks known as the Frank Slide (named for the town that had been partially demolished by the infamous landslide of 1903).

The area covered by the two-mile wide fan of rubble from the landslide was like the surface of an alien planet. Many of the limestone boulders were the size of four-storey buildings. Hunting an armed man amongst them could be futile and unnecessarily dangerous. The police put a cordon of two hundred officers and armed civilian volunteers around the expanse of fallen rock, knowing that sooner or later Bassoff would have to come out.

Then they received information that Bassoff had doubled back before all of the men in the posse were in place. He'd skirted the edge of town unseen. Then some Russian miners, out of loyalty to a countryman — or out of fear — had helped him to temporary refuge in a miner's shack.

Now the police had the difficult task of tracking a fugitive through the rugged country surrounding the Crowsnest Pass. Bassoff had friends among the Russian immigrants in settlements like Hillcrest, many of them Cossacks with a proud ancient tradition of looking out for their brethren. And those who felt no sense of loyalty to the criminal could be intimidated by his reputation — and his gun.

Throughout the night and the next day police raided and searched one isolated miner's cabin after another. They learned that two teenaged boys, camping on the mountainside above the Frank Slide, had an unpleasant visit from Bassoff and Arkoff the night before the shootout. The bandits had pointed guns at them and robbed them of $14. A miner told police Bassoff had entered his cabin at about 4:30 Sunday morning and made him brew a pot of coffee.

As the search continued, more Mounties and provincial police poured into Bellevue. So did newspapermen, who were already comparing the manhunt to the chase after Bloody Jack Krafchenko. Help came from the United States, too, with the arrival of two Seattle deputy sheriffs and their bloodhounds: Lightning, Dynamite, and Dan. These dogs were famous for the number of fugitives they had helped run to earth. While Usher and Bailey were given heroes' funerals and Arkoff's body was trucked in a rough wooden box to a pauper's grave, the hounds were put on Bassoff's scent.

The third member of Bassoff's gang, Ausby Aulcoff, had not been seen since the bandits made their appearance in Coleman. Police and the press speculated that he had joined Bassoff in the bush to give him assistance. Then on August 9 the police in Bellevue had a phone call from a Mrs. Holloway, who lived in a cottage less than a mile from Frank. She said Bassoff had come to her home and demanded a meal. He was limping and using a stick for a crutch, she said. And he was alone. The outlaw asked, "Do you know who I am?"

The woman replied, "No, I don't. But I want you to leave."

Funeral procession for Royal Canadian Mounted Police Corporal Ernest Usher, one of two policemen slain by Tom Bassoff and George Arkoff. (Galt Museum and Archives, Lethbridge, Alberta)

Mrs. Holloway made Bassoff something to eat. She had once worked as a nurse, so she examined his wounded leg. It was badly swollen, and she believed the bullet was still in it. When Bassoff finished his meal he warned Mrs. Holloway not to notify the police. Then he left without doing her any harm. She immediately phoned the police and reported what had happened. In ten minutes the police had the cottage surrounded, but Bassoff had disappeared into the bush.

As the officers continued to search cabins and question Russian immigrants, they could not help but notice a growing sense of sympathy for Bassoff. As the hours and days passed, people seemed to be more and more on the side of the lone fugitive, even if he was a suspected thief and a known killer, and less willing to assist the police. Rumours of his hiding place that proved to be groundless flew from one Crowsnest Pass community to another. These rumours may have been deliberately planted to throw the police off track.

Then tragedy struck again. Just after dark on August 9, police were searching a house in Hillcrest. One of the searchers was a civilian named Nick Kyslik, who had been sworn in as a special constable. For some unknown reason he suddenly jumped out a window and began to run. A policeman waiting outside saw the figure of a man running in the twilight and took it to be Bassoff. He shouted "Stop!" but the man kept running. The officer fired, and Nick Kyslick tumbled to the ground, dead with a bullet through his heart. No one had the slightest idea why he had acted the way he had. The officer who had mistakenly shot him was overcome with remorse and was exonerated of any blame by a coroner's jury.

Bassoff had not pulled the trigger on the unfortunate Kyslik, but as far as the public was concerned he was as much responsible for the death as if he had done the actual shooting. Had the manhunters not been out beating the bushes in search of Bassoff, Kyslik would still be alive. Nonetheless, the police came under some critical fire themselves. Why had the Russian desperado — with a wounded leg — been allowed to slip out of Bellevue in the first place? The press also complained that the various law enforcement agencies, the Mounties, the provincial police, and the CPR police, were working independently of each other, with no senior officer taking overall command. Police spokesmen replied that they were doing their best under difficult circumstances, that constables had been in the field for days with little sleep and barely time to eat. It didn't help matters, they said, that Bassoff was obviously getting help from "foreigners." They assured the public Bassoff would soon be taken, but they predicted the outlaw, once cornered, would put up a stiff fight.

The police still concentrated their search around the communities of Bellevue, Frank, and Hillcrest. The celebrated bloodhounds, Lightning, Dynamite, and Dan, had so far been of no help in leading the hunters to their quarry. Then a break came from a totally unexpected quarter.

On the night of August 11, CPR engineer Harry Hammond was making a run between Pincher Creek and Burmis, twenty-seven miles east of the area police were searching, when he caught a quick glimpse in the beam of his locomotive's light of a man walking along the tracks. As soon as the light hit him, the man dashed for the cover of the woods.

At Burmis, Hammond reported what he had seen. Four CPR railway policemen named Glover, Touler, Hollworth, and Sawyer had Hammond take them back down the line to the place where he had seen the man. It was truly a shot in the dark because the railways were always the haunts of tramps and hobos looking for free rides on the freight trains. Hammond's suspicious character might have been nothing more than an innocent transient.

When they reached the spot, the four railway police spread out to search. It was very dark, and the chances of finding anything were slim. Then Glover heard a noise. He crouched down and saw the silhouette of a man against the night sky. He cried, "Throw up your hands!"

The man stood still. Touler hurried to Glover's side. They saw the man reach into his coat. Once again Glover called to the man to raise his hands. He and Touler had their guns drawn and were quickly joined by Sawyer and Hollworth. One of them caught the suspect in the beam of a flashlight. At that moment Bassoff knew the game was up. Four guns were aimed at him. If he pulled the gun from inside his coat, he'd be dead. The outlaw raised his hands. As Glover handcuffed him, Bassoff said, "I am the man you are after." He had a fully loaded Colt automatic but no extra ammunition.

Bassoff was wearing a stolen cap and coat and had a lot of money in his pocket. He was hungry, dirty, and his wounded leg was in terrible condition. Official papers he had on him told police his name was indeed Thomas Bassoff, born in Alegar in the Caucasus in 1889. He was not the elusive Dzsachot Bekuzaroff after all. According to his documents, Bassoff had landed at Halifax in 1913. He'd then headed west to work in the mines and on sheep ranches. He denied involvement in the train robbery, but Conductor Jones identified him.

The police wanted to know where Ausby Aulcoff was. Bassoff said that as far as he knew, Aulcoff was hiding in Coleman. The police found no trace of him there, nor anywhere else.

Bassoff was charged with two counts of murder and one of train robbery. He was tried at Macleod on October 12. His defence counsel argued that Usher and Frewin had failed to identify themselves as police officers, and Frewin had fired first, making the Russians' actions self-defence. But the fact that Bassoff and Arkoff had both fired several bullets into the policemen after they were already down pretty well sealed Bassoff's fate. He was convicted and sentenced to death. On December 22, 1920, Tom Bassoff was hanged in the Lethbridge jail.

For a while it seemed that Aulcoff had made a clean getaway. Then in 1924 he pawned the conductor Sam Jones's watch in Portland, Oregon. This was a distinctively engraved CPR watch, and Canadian police had sent a description of it to law enforcement agencies throughout Canada and the United States. The Portland police were able to trace Aulcoff to Butte, Montana, where he was arrested. Aulcoff was extradited to Canada and tried for train robbery. He was sentenced to seven years in the Lethbridge jail but died there two years later. Ironically, Emilio Picariello, the bootlegger the Bassoff gang had wanted to rob in the first place, was himself convicted of murdering an Alberta Provincial Police constable. He and convicted accomplice Filumena Lassandro were hanged in 1923.

BLACKIE AUDETT

LIAR, LIAR

> I've tried to tell the story of my life in my own way,
> just like I lived it — which was in my own way, too.
> I hope you'll enjoy reading it, because I sure didn't
> enjoy living it.
> — James Henry Audett, from *Rap Sheet*

In 1953 journalist Gene Lowall, a special investigator for the district attorney of Denver, Colorado, sat down with James Henry "Blackie" Audett, (who also went by Theodore James) to record the career criminal's life story. The autobiography Lowall was helping Audett write was titled *Rap Sheet*, a slang expression for a criminal's police record. In his introduction to the book, Lowall expressed admiration for Audett's candour. Blackie was straightforward about his criminal exploits. He did not whine that he was "driven to it" or that he "never had a chance." Lowall even confessed that he had grown to like the hoodlum who had seen the insides of so many jails and prisons, including notorious Alcatraz.

Rap Sheet, published in 1954, is a two-hundred-and-fifty-page narrative in Blackie's own words — butchered grammar included. It is an amazing story, worthy of a Hollywood film. The speaker, in his early fifties when he spilled it all out for Lowall, had an incredible recall of names, dates, and details of events going back almost forty years. He remembered every heist, every shot fired, and every hour spent behind bars. Blackie's lawyer, Merlin Estep, called Audett's memory "phenomenal."

James Henry Audett was born in Pendleton, Oregon, in 1902 or 1903. While he was still a baby his family moved to a farm just outside Calgary, Alberta. There young Audett grew up in fear of an alcoholic father who beat him with a harness strap and who routinely battered the boy's mother. At the tender age of ten Audett ran away from home. He was big for his age and survived by doing menial work for the Canadian Pacific Railway. The railroad men nicknamed him Blackie because of his thick, jet black hair.

For a little over a year Blackie worked for the CPR, dreaming of one day becoming a railroad man himself. Then he got word that the Mounties were looking for him as an underage runaway. He bought a ticket for the next train to Spokane, Washington.

For two years Blackie was happy in Spokane. He had a job at a power plant and a crush on the teenaged daughter of the family he boarded with. Then, he recalled years later, World War I changed his life forever.

According to Blackie's account, on "New Year's 1916" (he isn't clear on whether it was New Year's Eve or New Year's Day) he fell in with a man named Joe who got him drunk. When Blackie awoke with a king-sized hangover he learned that "Joe" was a sergeant in the Canadian army. Blackie also learned that he had signed up as a volunteer for the Canadian Expeditionary Force, which was fighting in France. In spite of his protests, he was soon on a train for Alberta. He was only thirteen years old. But as Blackie had explained, he was big for his age.

After an adventurous training camp, *Rap Sheet* says, Blackie was sent to France. He spent some time in the stockade for shooting and wounding a Canadian soldier who had made an insulting remark about his girlfriend. Then he and a buddy named Eddie volunteered for the tank corps. The pair of them captured more than two hundred German soldiers all by themselves. For this action they were decorated and promoted to lieutenant. Not long after that Blackie was wounded in action and sent back to Canada, where surgeons put a steel plate in his skull. He recovered from his injuries in a Winnipeg hospital. There he met a fellow veteran whom he identifies only as Henry. Months later, when the war was over and Blackie was no longer in the army, he met Henry again, along with a few of Henry's friends. They were all unemployed and broke. But Henry and his pals knew how to get their hands on a lot of money fast. They had plans to rob the "Spokane Special," a train that ran out of Calgary and would be loaded with bank money. They wanted tough Blackie Audett in on the job.

James Henry "Blackie" Audett, formerly of Calgary, actually smiles for the camera as he becomes a resident of Alcatraz. (U.S. National Archives and Records Administration, Courtesy Bob Bates)

The gang of five armed men stopped the train outside Calgary by sidetracking it to a spur line and showing the stop signal. They looted the express car of $560,000 and made their getaway in Blackie's car. After dividing the money, the bandits split up. Blackie and Henry went to Lethbridge where they put up in a hotel. Unfortunately for Blackie, his car had been identified. An Alberta Provincial Police detective named Scotty Lawrence was hot on his trail. That officer caught up with Blackie and Henry in the little town of Granum. The pair were arrested and locked in jail in nearby McLeod.

The boys had stashed most of their share of the loot, and the idea of sitting in prison while all that money was out there waiting for them wasn't very appealing. Blackie thought up an escape plan. He and Henry made their break after Blackie struck the lone guard, Alberta Provincial Police Corporal William Watt, over the head with a brick, knocking him out cold. They stole a car, but a couple of days later as they made a dash for the American border they were captured again. Corporal Watt, his head wrapped in bandages, welcomed them back to the McLeod jail.

Blackie and Henry stood trial in McLeod. Representing them, Audett told Gene Lowall, was a lawyer named William Lyon Mackenzie King, the future prime minister of Canada. But in spite of that kind of legal talent, the two were found guilty and sentenced to ten years each in the prison at Prince Albert, Saskatchewan. Blackie was not even twenty years old.

Blackie and Henry had no intention of spending the next decade behind bars. Moreover, during their break from the McLeod jail they had not had an opportunity to pick up their hidden loot. They weren't in the Prince Albert prison for long when they made another attempt to escape. It failed, and the boys were soon on their way to the maximum-security prison at Stony Mountain, Manitoba.

Seven months later, during a blizzard, Blackie and Henry escaped from the penitentiary by hiding under the hood of a delivery truck. This time the breakout was successful. After dodging the police for a few days the escapees crossed the border into Minnesota. Blackie told Lowall that he never returned to his old haunts in Canada, although "business" took him to other parts of the country.

Blackie went back to the state of Washington, where he soon got into the smuggling trade. Sometimes he drove truckloads of illegal Chinese immigrants from British Columbia into Washington and Idaho. Prohibition was now in effect, so Blackie also got into the lucrative bootlegging racket, hauling Canadian whiskey over the border. He made a lot of money at it, but his real criminal calling lay elsewhere.

In 1925 Blackie met a bank robber named Danny Powers. "He taught me a lot of things," Audett told Lowall. With a third accomplice, Blackie and Powers held up a bank in Portland, Oregon, and got away with it. The boy who had run away from his Alberta home at the age of ten was well on his way to becoming one of America's most prolific bandits.

With Lowall listening in awe and asking only occasional questions, Audett took him through the heady years of the Roaring Twenties and the Depression-blighted Dirty Thirties. Lowall heard tales of daring holdups, arrests, trials, imprisonment, and spectacular jailbreaks. There was even a sensational escape from a train taking Audett to the dreaded penitentiary at Leavenworth, Kansas. Then there was Alcatraz — the Rock — where Blackie was incarcerated with America's toughest, most desperate criminals. (Years after *Rap Sheet* was published, Audett — who just couldn't stay out of jail — would claim to be the last prisoner taken off the island when the prison was closed in 1963.)

Audett claimed to have robbed over 120 banks. As he told his story to Lowall he rolled off names that made up a who's who of American criminals. Blackie had worked for Al "Scarface" Capone in Chicago, before the Big Man finally went down for income tax evasion. He once ran afoul of Capone when he pulled a job in Chicago without Scarface's permission. Blackie had to hightail it to Europe for awhile until Big Al cooled down.

As a bank robber, Blackie kept illustrious company. He told of pulling jobs with the Fleagle Boys, Baby Face Nelson, Pretty Boy Floyd, Homer Van Meter, and the Barker Gang. He met Bonnie and Clyde and robbed a bank with Buck Barrow, Clyde's brother. Blackie was in tight with Kansas City crime boss Tom Pendergast, Louisiana's corrupt governor, Huey "The Kingfish" Long, and Chicago's crooked mayor, Big Bill Thompson. Blackie shared a prison cell with gangster Frank "Jelly" Nash. Blackie was a witness on June 17, 1933, when Nash and several policemen were slain by machine-gun bullets at Kansas City's Union Station in an ambush that has since been known as the Kansas City Massacre.

What Blackie was most proud of was his association with Public Enemy Number One, John Dillinger.

"I've heard a lot of people say that Dillinger had shifty, beady eyes," Audett recalls in *Rap Sheet*. "I've even read that in the papers. That just plain wasn't true. He was a man completely without fear and he could look you square in the eye as long as you could stand it."

Blackie told Lowall that he and "Johnnie" were pals, that he'd been one of the few people Dillinger trusted. In fact, Blackie learned of the deal Dillinger's lady friend Anna Sage (the legendary Woman in Red) had made with the FBI to betray the bandit. Blackie hurried to Chicago's Biograph Theater that July 22, 1934, to warn his friend. He was too late. He arrived just in time to see FBI agents gun Dillinger down without giving him a chance to surrender.

All this and more Blackie Audett recounted for Gene Lowall. The journalist got it all on tape and then wrote the book. *Rap Sheet* was a rare insight into a storied era of American (and Canadian) crime, provided by a man who had seen it all. Poor Lowall did not realize that 90 percent of what Blackie had told him was false.

In criminal circles, Blackie Audett had long had a reputation as a compulsive liar. He was most certainly a criminal; he had a lengthy record to prove it. But he had not had the amazing career he described in *Rap Sheet*.

This author investigated Audett's claim that he had served with the Canadian Expeditionary Force in France. The Department of Veteran's Affairs in Ottawa could find no record of a James Henry Audett or a Theodore James Audett — or any of the aliases Blackie was known to have used — enlisted in the Canadian army (let alone being decorated in France and promoted to lieutenant). A correspondent in that office said that while some Americans did cross the border to join the Canadian army, Canadian military personnel did not go to the United States to shanghai young Americans into Canadian uniforms. Moreover, though some boys of sixteen and seventeen did lie about their age in order to enlist, for a thirteen-year-old to have gotten away with it, no matter how "big for his age" he was, would have been highly improbable. As for the head wound Blackie claimed to have received in action, American doctors could find no evidence of it. Nor could they detect a steel plate in his skull.

A thorough search of the archives of the *Globe* and the *Toronto Daily Star* covering the period just after the war turned up no story about a half-million-dollar train robbery in Alberta. Train holdups that occurred in other parts of the country at roughly the same time, but which netted the bandits substantially smaller sums, were front page news. Nor could the Alberta Provincial Archives find any reference to the train robbery Blackie had described in such detail.

The records of the Alberta Provincial Police, a force that existed from 1918 to 1931, show no officer named Scotty Lawrence. There was a Corporal William Watt, the officer Blackie supposedly slugged with a brick in his escape from the McLeod jail, and whom Blackie said he later saw with his head bandaged up "like a turban." But Corporal Watt's record indicates that he was never injured in the line of duty.

Audett's Canadian record shows that he was indeed jailed in McLeod in 1921 for theft of liquor and escaping custody. Whoever Blackie's lawyer was, he could not have been William Lyon Mackenzie King. The future prime minister never practiced law in Alberta. Blackie evidently escaped custody at some time, because in 1922 he was given a two-year sentence in Lethbridge for breaking out of prison. His name does not appear in the records for Stony Mountain Penitentiary. Audett quite likely did get involved in bootlegging during Prohibition. What crook didn't? He may well have run Canadian booze into the state of Washington. But for all the wild stories given in such detail in *Rap Sheet*, Blackie Audett's criminal activities in Canada were never more than those of a small-time hood. His claim that an escaped convict from a Canadian prison was legally free if his sentence expired while he was still at large is absolute nonsense.

Blackie Audett's blatant lies about his military and criminal careers in Canada quite naturally cast doubts on his stories about hobnobbing with America's criminal elite. He certainly could have met some of those notorious people — besides as acquaintances made in prison, that is. Criminal organizations run by the likes of Capone and Pendergast employed hundreds of thugs, gunmen, bagmen — all of the anonymous two-bit punks necessary to do the daily legwork and dirty jobs of keeping a criminal empire functioning.

The infamous "automobile bandits" of the early thirties, men like Baby Face Nelson, Pretty Boy Floyd, and John Dillinger, also mixed with a lot of rank-and-file underworld riff-raff during their short careers as public enemies. Blackie *could* have met some of them. But there is no evidence that he ever robbed banks with any of them. Furthermore, Blackie could not have witnessed the Kansas City Massacre, because his real rap sheet shows he was in jail at the time that atrocity occurred. Blackie claimed to have pulled jobs with Al Sutton, brother of the infamous Willie Sutton. Willie did not have a brother named Al.

Blackie's claim to have escaped from a train taking him to a maximum-security prison was only partially true. He did escape from a train. But he was being transported to a mental institution. It seems that Blackie had been telling his wild stories to the police long before he ever met Gene Lowall, and the authorities decided that he was crazy. They described him as "a man without conscience … low, mean, vile and despicable." Psychiatric testing placed his mental age at fourteen and his IQ at ninety.

According to American crime historian Bob Bates, between 1927 and 1934 Audett was incarcerated at McNeil Island, Washington, three times for auto theft. During his third stint he escaped but was re-captured and sent to Leavenworth, then to Alcatraz. In December 1940 Audett was caught trying to burglarize a bank and was again sent to Alcatraz. Ten years later another act of larceny landed him in the Oregon State Penitentiary. In 1956, after the publication of *Rap Sheet*, Audett was nailed on another bank burglary charge and returned to his old home in Alcatraz to do a twenty-year stretch. He was eventually paroled, but in 1974 he tried to rob a bank in Seattle and wound up back on McNeil Island.

In 1979, with his health failing, Audett was paroled to the custody of a well-known American crime historian and writer. This author had written a book based on his theory that John Dillinger was not the man the FBI killed in front of the Biograph Theater. Dillinger staged his own death, the book claims, and lived out his life in quiet anonymity in a western state. The author wanted to interview Dillinger's "good friend" Blackie Audett about Dillinger's "true" story. Of course, Blackie was happy to oblige. He was never short of stories. Not long after taping a series of interviews in which he discussed his close relationship with the legendary bandit, Blackie Audett died in Chicago.

Audett was in Alcatraz at the same time notorious criminals like Alvin Karpis were there. Quite likely he spoke to them — at least, the ones who *would* speak to him (he was reputed to be an informer) — and so got the names and stories he eventually used in *Rap Sheet*. Generally, men like Karpis held Audett in pretty low regard. The word they usually used to describe him was *rat*. Blackie's main claim to notoriety was the fact that he was the only criminal to be sentenced to Alcatraz three times.

Crime historians who have studied Audett's book and found little in it that can be substantiated have speculated that had Blackie stuck to the truth, he probably could have produced a compelling factual narrative. He was involved in the criminal worlds of both Canada and the United States in the heady years of the 1920s and 1930s, and even though he was not the major player he pretended to be, he could have provided an insight into the underworld that would be useful to historians today. In the opinion of crime historian Bob Bates, Blackie Audett's biggest crime was writing *Rap Sheet*.

MATTHEW KOLIDEE

"ME FOOL ... ME GET 'FRAID"

Matthew "Danny" Kolidee of Hamilton, Ontario, did not want to turn to crime. In the thirteen years since he and his wife, Annie, had left their native Ukraine, he had been a hard-working, honest man. But now the thirty-three-year-old, who still spoke only broken English, had his back against the wall.

The year 1925 had not been good to Kolidee. Bad luck and even worse decisions had changed a man whom neighbours described as a good husband and father — they'd never heard him even raise his voice to his wife — into a desperate character. Early in the year he'd lost his job. For months he'd been able to get only an occasional shift as a labourer in a quarry. That wasn't enough to support a wife and three children.

The Ontario Temperance Act was in effect, making the province officially "dry." Like so many other men, Kolidee had done a little bootlegging, selling illegal booze from his home. But he'd been caught at it twice and fined. Annie had been afraid of the strange men who came to the house while he was in that business and begged him to give it up. He had done so.

Then Kolidee thought of another way to reverse his fortunes. He and Annie had a nest egg of $2,000 stashed away in the bank: their life savings, scraped together over the years. Kolidee withdrew some of it and went to the Hamilton racetrack. He bet heavily and lost! Hoping to recoup his losses, he withdrew more money and went back to the track. This went on until only a few dollars remained in the account. Annie knew nothing about this.

Now Danny Kolidee decided to risk everything on one big gamble. On Monday, July 13, he told Annie he was going away to find work. They might even have to move to another city. When he found a job, he said, he would send for her and the children. When

Kolidee left the house he had in his pockets a .38 calibre revolver with the barrel cut short and the serial number filed off, some extra cartridges, a flashlight, and a pair of kid gloves. He already had a bank picked out.

William "Ross" Rodger had been the manager of the Imperial Bank of Canada in the village of St. David's, near Niagara Falls, for two-and-a-half years. He and his wife Lillian and their two small daughters lived in an apartment on the second floor of the bank building. Like all bank managers of the time, Rodger was expected to try to protect the bank's money in the event of a holdup, even at the risk of his own life. So, like every other bank manager, he kept a gun on the premises, a .38 revolver. To give the weapon extra stopping power, in case he ever had to use it, Rodger had cut nicks into the tips of the soft lead bullets. That would cause the bullet to spread open when it struck a target, having the same terrible effect on flesh as a dumdum bullet. In the daytime Rodger kept the gun in a drawer in his office. At night he put it on a ledge on the second floor, side verandah where he and Lillian slept on warm summer nights. As an added precaution against bank burglars, every night Rodger put the family's pet collie, Rover, in the basement.

On the evening of July 14, Ross and Lillian went to bed early, as usual. Before retiring, Rodger put their kitten, Betty, outside. At eleven o'clock they were awakened by the furious barking of Rover coming from the basement. Rodger went downstairs to investigate. There he found that someone had forced open a basement window but had evidently been frightened off by the dog. Rodger took a look around outside the building but saw no one. He did not think it worthwhile to call the police at that hour, so he went back to bed.

The dog had given Danny Kolidee a terrible scare. A few days earlier he had "cased" the St. David's bank by going in to cash a small cheque. It had not occurred to him that there might be a watchdog. Now he would have to try something else.

A few doors away from the bank was the home and office of Dr. C.E. Duggan. Kolidee silently broke into the doctor's office and ransacked it. Perhaps he was looking for chloroform he could use to put Rodger's wife and children out in case they posed a problem. Whatever he was searching for, all he took was a case of Dr. Duggan's cigars. Then he slipped back into the darkness and

The bank Matthew Kolidee attempted to rob in St. David's, Ontario, is on the right. The balcony in which the fight took place had not yet been added when this picture was taken in 1910. (Bruce Woodruff)

waited until he could be sure the banker and his family would be asleep again.

At about 4:30 in the morning, Lillian Rodger awoke when Betty the kitten jumped on the bed. But Ross had put the animal outside! How did it get back in? She woke her husband. Again Ross got out of bed to investigate. He did not take his gun, which lay on a ledge next to the bed.

Rodger passed through the dining room and kitchen on his way to the back door, which opened onto a small balcony at the top of a stairway. Even in the darkness he could see that someone had cut the screen on the door to reach in and undo the latch. That person had inadvertently let the cat in. Alarmed now that someone was in the house, Rodger turned and headed back to the verandah to get his gun. He was partway through the dining room, when someone who had been crouched on the other side of the table suddenly stood up and pointed a gun at him. The stranger commanded, "Hands up!"

Rodger raised his hands, but the gun in the hand of the nervous Kolidee went off. The bullet only creased one of Rodger's fingers, but now the manager was certain his life and the lives of his family were in danger. He threw himself at Kolidee and tried to seize the gun.

The two men grappled in a savage wrestling match. Rodger twisted Kolidee's arm behind his back, trying to force him to drop the gun. Kolidee broke Rodger's grip and struck him on the head two or three times with the gun. His head and face now bloody, Rodger threw a punch that caught Kolidee square in the face and dropped him to the floor. The gun fell from his hand and Rodger dove for it. But Kolidee recovered quickly and beat him to it. Once again Rodger seized his opponent's arm before the man could aim the weapon.

The fight carried the men from the dining room into the kitchen, then through the back door onto the balcony. Kolidee repeatedly pistol-whipped Rodger, but the banker wouldn't go down. The whole time Kolidee roared and snarled like an animal.

Kolidee lifted Rodger right off his feet and tried to throw him from the balcony to the ground, twenty-five feet below. Fortunately for Rodger, the railing was too high. Nonetheless, the banker was getting the worst of the fight and didn't think he could last much longer.

Then a voice called from a second-floor window in the house next door, "Will I shoot, Mr. Rodger?"

It was his neighbour, Mrs. Woodruff, wife of Archie Woodruff, local merchant and the town reeve. Mrs. Woodruff was a sporting woman, and she was pointing her pump-action shotgun out the window. She called to Rodger to step aside so she could shoot his assailant.

"No!" Rodger cried, fearful that a shotgun blast would hit them both. "I've got him! Send Archie over!"

From the dining-room doorway Lillian looked across the kitchen and saw the men struggling on the balcony. She could easily tell them apart because her husband was wearing white pajamas and the intruder was dressed in dark clothes. She watched in horror as the man struck Rodger on the head with the gun again and again. Certain the stranger was trying to kill her husband, Lillian hurried back to the verandah and grabbed Rodger's gun.

When Lillian returned to the kitchen she saw that the attacker's back was to the screen door. He had Rodger down and was still hitting him with the gun. Lillian called, "Will I give it to him?"

"Yes!" Rodger cried. "Go ahead!"

Lillian had never fired a gun in her life. Now she pointed it at the man's back and squeezed the trigger. The gun roared. The bullet pierced the screen and struck Kolidee in the back just below the shoulder blade. The nick in the soft lead bullet caused it to widen as it smashed through muscle and then tore into the victim's lung. Kolidee slumped down and a groggy Rodger got to his feet and picked up his opponent's gun. About three minutes had passed since Kolidee said, "Hands up!"

Archie Woodruff and a man who was visiting him came bounding up the stairs. Archie had his wife's shotgun. He was unaware the stranger sitting on the balcony with his back against the wall had been shot. He saw the man put his hands in his pockets. Thinking he was going for a gun, Archie pointed the shotgun at him and said, "Don't you move or I will blow your brains out."

"Me fool," the wounded man said. "The damned dog did it." He asked for a cigarette and Archie gave him one.

Lillian put down the gun and hurried into the bedroom where her two daughters, age two and four, huddled on their bed in mute terror. Ross, his head and face a mass of blood, angrily said to the strange man, "You shot at me!"

The man replied, "Yes. Me fool ... me disgusted."

Someone went down the road to fetch Dr. Duggan, whose cigars were still in Kolidee's pocket. When the doctor opened his office door to get his black bag, he was shocked to see the room in a shambles. He hurried over to the Rodgers' place and went right to work on Ross's head. Kolidee moaned that he had been shot and needed the doctor's help right away. Wounded bank managers, however, had priority over wounded bank robbers.

Meanwhile, the police had been notified. Provincial Police Sergeant G.E. Kedward arrived with the town constable and began to question the wounded man while they awaited an ambulance. Kolidee gave the officers his name and address. When he said he had a wife and three children, Kedward responded, "Then you have no business being here."

The ambulance took Kolidee to the hospital in St. Catherines, where he was treated by Dr. Duggan. At first it was thought that his wound was not very serious. But four hours after he'd been shot, Danny Kolidee died. His last words were, "Me fool ... me got 'fraid."

Lillian Rodger was extremely distraught when she was told Kolidee was dead. "I hated to do such a thing," she said. "Yet, he would have killed Ross if it had gone much farther."

Annie Kolidee was overwhelmed when she heard the awful news. The shock of her husband's death was made doubly hard by the shameful circumstances. Shot down as a common criminal!

"Nobody in this country will think Danny was a good man," Annie said bitterly to a reporter. "Nobody knows how much he cared for me and the children, and how he tried to make us happy. He did his best for me and the little ones."

Annie had another unpleasant surprise when she went to the bank to take out money to pay for her husband's funeral and coffin. Almost nothing was left of her $2,000! The bank manager told her Danny had withdrawn the money. Police would eventually learn of his spree at the racetrack.

Meanwhile, the undertaker was about to remove Danny's body from the coffin Annie had chosen, and put it in a cheaper one. Friends and neighbours quickly took up a collection to cover the undertaker's bill. They would spare Annie at least that humiliation.

The newspapers heaped praise on Ross Rodger for the manner in which he had protected the bank's money. "Few if any exploits on the part of bank managers to defend their banks can equal the struggle that Rodger went through," gushed the *Toronto Daily Star*. But the real focus of the press coverage was Lillian, whom Ross gave full credit for saving his life. The fact that a *woman* had shot a bank robber was sensational. Lillian slipped away to a cottage to escape all the attention, but the newspapermen still wrote glowing reports of her courage and heroism. The Rodgers' pictures were all over the papers. Mrs. Woodruff posed for a photo, holding the shotgun she hadn't fired. One editor even devoted a few words to Betty the kitten.

The police believed Kolidee intended to force Rodger to go downstairs and open the vault for him — which the banker would not have been able to do because it was on a time lock. The fact that he had filed the serial number off his gun and wore kid gloves to avoid leaving fingerprints indicated that he had planned the whole thing out. But he hadn't taken into account the dog nor a banker's wife with a gun.

At the coroner's inquest into Kolidee's death, not only was Lillian found guiltless of any wrongdoing, she was also commended.

"We also appreciate the heroism shown by Mrs. Rodger and recommend that recognition be shown her for her quick action in saving the life of her husband and the property of the bank," said the coroner's jury.

For Annie Kolidee the future was very uncertain. "I do not know where to go now. I have no relatives here. Only two sisters in the Ukraine. But I won't go back there. My husband has relatives here, but I can't say yet what I am going to do for my children. They must grow up to be good, honest men."

TORONTO'S GREAT TRAIN ROBBERY

"LIKE HAWKS AT MIDNIGHT"

James Hutcheon, an Ontario provincial government employee, thought there was something peculiar about the dark blue, 1928 Buick sedan parked on the north side of Front Street, west of York Street. Hutcheon was driving along Front when he spotted the other car. He passed it slowly and so had a good look. Four men sat in the car and two more stood beside it. That wasn't what caught Hutcheon's attention, even though it was about ten minutes before midnight and there didn't appear to be any reason for the men to be on the otherwise deserted street.

The licence plate was what caught Hutcheon's eye. It was *wrong*! The entire car was dirty, as though it had just been down a country road. But the licence plate was clean! Moreover, it was not a current 1928 plate but one from 1920 with some of the numbers altered with paint. Hutcheon thought that suspicious enough to go in search of a policeman. By the time he found an officer and brought him back, the Buick was gone. It was now a few minutes past midnight on June 20, 1928. Hutcheon didn't realize he had just seen the six men who were about to pull what was to date the biggest armed robbery in Ontario history.

In the railyard of Toronto's Union Station the engineer of train number nine, westbound for Windsor and Detroit, sat at the controls of his locomotive. As he awaited the signal to proceed, he talked to the conductor, who was on the platform. The mail car, three cars back, had just been loaded with dozens of bags of mail and six bags stuffed with half a million dollars in bank money. The cash was destined for banks in Hamilton, London, Detroit, and Chicago.

Just after midnight a blue Buick sedan (which had been stolen in Hamilton two weeks earlier) crept down York Street and turned right onto Station Street. It stopped and backed up to the big loading door of the old Canadian National Railway Express building. The barn-like structure had that very day been vacated in favour of new premises. It was empty, and its doors unlocked. The Buick backed into the building, where it stopped so the occupants could remove the back seat. Then the car backed out through the loading door on the railyard side.

Continuing in reverse, the sedan rolled over three sets of tracks, stopping once so a man could get out and push a handcar out of the way. Because of darkness and the positions of idle cars on the tracks, and of train number nine itself, no one saw a thing. The Buick stopped at the open door of number nine's mail car. Five men armed with shotguns and automatic pistols got out. The driver stayed at the wheel and kept the engine running.

Inside the mail car J.M. Farrow, a forty-five-year veteran of the postal service, and his assistants E.N. Allen and J.D. Robertson were busy sorting the mail sacks. They were taken completely by surprise when two gunmen jumped into the car. One robber jammed a shotgun in Farrow's stomach and growled, "Are you the registry clerk?"

Farrow, who perhaps had more nerve than sense, did not answer immediately. He thought if he played for time, help would come. But the bandits meant business. The one who seemed to be the leader twisted the shotgun barrel in Farrow's stomach and commanded, "Hand over the mail bag. The small bag! That's what we want. And make it quick! The moneybags, damn it! Dig 'em up. Dig 'em up quick, or we'll fill you full of lead."

Farrow gave them a bag of money, then tried to pass off a bag of ordinary mail as a moneybag. The bandit knew what he was up to. "If you don't hand over those bags, I'll shoot you where you stand. I have a good mind to shoot you anyway, and take the money after. It would be easier. I'll give you three to come across. Then, damn you, I'll bump you off. One … two …"

Before the outlaw could say three, Farrow kicked at a moneybag. The other bandit tossed it out to the platform. "Come on, the rest!" the gunman barked. Five more bags went out the door.

Out on the platform two bandits held three or four railway men at gunpoint while another threw the bags into the Buick. An assistant CNR night agent named William Venton stumbled upon the scene. He was startled when two men pointed guns at him and told him to stay back. One told him, "Lie down on the platform and stay down."

"I won't," Venton protested. "What are you fellows trying to do anyway?"

In response, one of the gunmen pushed him off the platform. Venton fully expected he was about to be shot. He rolled under a railway car for cover. Then he rolled out the other side and ran up the track, shouting to the conductor and engineer that the mail car was being robbed. They thought he was joking.

When Venton disappeared under the railway car, one bandit shouted, "Hell, boys, there goes the transfer clerk!" Another one yelled, "Beat it!" The stickup men jumped from the mail car. They all piled into the waiting sedan.

The whole operation had taken less than three minutes. Where the sedan's back seat had been there were seven mailbags. Two were full of money. Four more contained valuable registered mail and bonds. The last one was stuffed with nothing but empty sacks. Farrow's tactics had been at least partly successful. Bags containing $200,000 were still in the mail car. Nonetheless, the raid had netted the bandits $300,000 in cash and bonds. No armed robbers in Ontario history had ever made such a haul.

The Buick that had sneaked into the railyard like a phantom now roared across the tracks, through the old express building, and into the dark streets of Toronto. Witnesses who caught a glimpse of it said it was "rocketing along as if propelled by thunderbolts." One person said it took the Bay Street bridge on two wheels.

By the time William Venton convinced the engineer and the conductor he was serious and police were notified, the robbers had all the head start they needed. The Toronto Police Department had recently purchased a fast Cadillac. This was their "speed car," intended to give them an advantage over highly mobile "automobile bandits" whose powerful (stolen) cars always left the cops behind. A call went out to the Cadillac's driver, James Hamilton. He made it to Union Station in record time, but the robbers were out of sight.

The country was shocked that a mail car loaded with money should be such easy pickings for a gang of thieves. The robbers swooped down "Like Hawks At Midnight," as the headline declared in the *Toronto Daily Star*. Clearly, the press said, it was an inside job. How else could the crooks have known about the money shipment, not to mention the conveniently empty CNR building? And why, the papers wanted to know, were the mail clerks not armed so they could protect His Majesty's Mails and the property of the banks? The answer to that was simple. Mail clerks were not policemen or security guards. Not a shot had been fired during the robbery. If the robbers had thought the clerks had guns, the city might well be burying three innocent men.

The robbers had not been masked, and the clerks and witnesses on the platform were able to give the police good descriptions. They were all young men, except for the driver of the getaway car, who seemed middle-aged. All were well dressed. Farrow said the one who did most of the talking seemed well acquainted with postal terminology.

In the hours following the holdup every available Toronto police officer was called in, and the news was sent to communities across the province and to American border towns. Police swept through Toronto, rousting out every possible suspect. They watched all roads out of town. No one knew for sure if the bandits had made a run for it or if they were hiding in the city. Police in Detroit speculated that the robbery was the work of a well-known American gangster named Paul Jaworski, whose notorious Flathead Gang had recently pulled a spectacular daylight robbery of the *Detroit News* payroll. Meanwhile, a vaudeville producer offered money to the mail clerks and the railroad men who had been on the platform if they would go on stage and tell of their thrilling experience. It does not seem that anyone accepted the offer.

Toronto's chief of police, D.C. Draper, was new to the job. He knew the future of his professional career rested on how he handled this sensational crime. He announced that the Toronto Police Department would follow Detroit's example and put radios in their patrol cars. All constables were to report for pistol practice. He would also look into the purchase of armoured cars for dealing with armed robbers. Meanwhile, he was taking personal charge of the investigation into the train robbery, with Chief Inspector George Guthrie as his right-hand man.

Two nights after the robbery, the blue Buick was found parked on a quiet street not far from the intersection of Yonge and St. Clair. In it was a mailbag containing $120,000 in bonds that the bandits evidently thought they'd be unable to fence. In addition the police found the remains of some sandwiches, some Toronto newspapers opened to stories about the robbery, and hundreds of rounds of ammunition.

Over the next few days there was considerable speculation as to the whereabouts of the bandits. Many believed they were still holed up in Toronto. Some Essex County residents reported seeing well-dressed strangers camped on the shore of Lake Erie. In the morning they were gone. Could they have been the bandits now escaped by boat to Ohio? Almost everyone was certain the mail car robbers were Americans. Everyone, that is, except the Toronto police.

On July 12 the newspapers suddenly announced that the Toronto police had five suspects — none of them American — in custody. They had actually made the first arrests on July 8. At their request the papers withheld the news so as not to jeopardize further investigation. In jail were Findley McLeod, age forty-eight; his son Findley Jr., age twenty-four; Findley Sr.'s brother Alex, age forty-two; Everett McKibben, age thirty-three, and John Sullivan (alias Brown), age twenty-eight.

Findley McLeod Sr., a Toronto street cleaner, had done five years in the Kingston Penitentiary for stealing $130,000 in bonds and securities while employed as a truck driver for the post office. He had been out of prison for a little more than a year. Alex McLeod, a Toronto cab driver, and Findley Jr. had no previous criminal records.

Everett McKibben had done eight years in Kingston for receiving $18,000 from a Windsor holdup. He had occupied the cell next to McLeod's. After being paroled McKibben found he could not get a job in Canada because of his prison record. With the permission of his parole officer, he went to Detroit where he was employed in a barbershop.

John Sullivan had served seven years in Kingston for burglary. He was the younger brother of Arthur "Curly" Sullivan, a member of the notorious Red Ryan gang. Curly had broken out of Kingston with the noted desperado in 1923 and shortly after was shot dead by police in Minneapolis. Since his own release from prison, John Sullivan had been working in a Toronto cigar store.

Because of his previous mail theft, police had suspected the elder Findley McLeod from the start. They put him under surveillance the day after the robbery. They even intercepted and read his mail before it was delivered to his home, a squalid apartment above a fruit store on Royce Avenue. One letter was from McKibben in Detroit, demanding money. He was coming to Toronto to get it.

The police knew that Findley Jr. had already made a trip to Detroit to give McKibben $1,000.

McKibben and his wife took the train to Toronto on July 7, unaware that two Pinkerton men were following them. The next morning the McKibbens were on the sidewalk in front of the Royce Avenue fruit store. McLeod came down to see them. The three began walking along the street, not knowing detectives had staked out the area.

Suddenly McLeod sensed something wrong. He began to walk very quickly away from the others. The detectives moved in and arrested all three. McLeod's son and brother were picked up later that day. Further investigation led the police to Sullivan, who was arrested in the cigar store on July 10.

Mrs. McKibben was charged with receiving stolen money. McLeod Sr.'s wife was in possession of 121 $2 bills that were identified as holdup money. But she was pregnant and due to deliver any day and so was sent to a hospital. Mrs. Harriet McPhee, Alex McLeod's elderly landlady, was held as a material witness.

Findley Jr. and Alex McLeod were also charged with receiving stolen money. Young Findley later told police that the day after the robbery he asked his father, "Are you in this mess?" The elder McLeod said yes. "I asked him why he had done it," young McLeod continued. "He said to me they had taken some years off his life and he was getting back at them."

In the McLeods' apartment police found money hidden in a compartment under a stairway. They also found two automatic pistols in a barrel of oatmeal. A search of the yard of Mrs. McPhee's house on Laing Street, where Alex boarded, turned up two hoards of buried money. A small amount of money was stashed in the barbershop where McKibben worked. In all the police recovered $37,400 of the stolen cash.

Young Findley McLeod, the only one of the arrested men not suspected of being part of the actual robber gang, was released on $3,000 bail. For the McLeod brothers, McKibben, and Sullivan, bail was set at $100,000 each. They could not raise that kind of money and so remained in the Don Jail.

The police did not believe any of the men they had captured was the gang's leader. They suspected he was an American and a hardened professional criminal. They were also sure he had double-crossed his Canadian partners and taken the lion's share of the swag and then fled to the United States. "There's no man's face I'd rather see than that chap's," Chief Draper told reporters. "He's a smart and dangerous customer. That's why I want him. He's somewhere between Detroit and Chicago, and the net is closing in on him."

Draper was working closely with American authorities. He sent two detectives to Detroit. From there the officers went to Chicago to work with that city's "secret service." That was a branch of the crime-ridden Windy City's police department that was so cloaked in mystery and secrecy, only its commanding officer, Deputy Commissioner William E. O'Connor, knew the names of all its agents. If anyone could track down the mastermind behind the Toronto robbery, the papers said, it was O'Connor's phantom force. But the next big news of the case did not come from Chicago.

Assisted by Detroit police, detectives of the Windsor Police Department had been looking into the backgrounds of two Windsor men, Ray Boven, age twenty-four, and his older brother Bill. The two, especially Bill, had been involved in bootlegging, and investigators had evidence that they were in Toronto the night of the robbery. Bill Boven had not been seen in Windsor or Detroit for several weeks. Ray, however, had been "living the high life" since the middle of June.

At 2:45 a.m. on July 24, Windsor police burst into a house and found Ray Boven sleeping off a drunk. Also in the house were Bill Boven's estranged wife Frances, her eleven-year-old-daughter and Frances's aged father. Pinned to the inside of a curtain was $900 that was identified as robbery loot.

Frances Boven said she had not lived with her husband for two years. She had split with him because of his "roaming all over the continent." She claimed to know nothing of the robbery. Frances explained that she kept the house in Windsor so she could look after her father and her daughter. Ray had a room there; that was all. Police believed, however, that Ray and Frances were romantically involved.

Ray Boven insisted he was in Windsor the night of the robbery. He said Bill had given him some money he'd made from bootlegging. He had pinned it inside the curtain, he said, because there had been so many robberies in the area. Ray swore he hadn't seen Bill in weeks and had no idea where he was.

While American police launched a manhunt for Bill Boven (who was almost certainly in the United States), Ray Boven and his sister-in-law were sent to Toronto. Police were now certain they had enough evidence to prove Bill Boven and John Sullivan were the gunmen in the mail car. William Venton picked Ray Boven out of a police lineup and identified him as the bandit who had told him to lie down on the platform. He also identified McKibben as one of the other gunmen on the platform. Police had little doubt Findley McLeod Sr. had been the driver.

In the preliminary hearings there was no evidence that Alex McLeod had been involved in the robbery. Mrs. McPhee testified that Alex had in fact been angry when he learned that his brother had buried stolen money in her yard, and told Findley Sr. to "Get it the hell out of there." Alex was released, and Findley Jr. was placed on probation for receiving stolen money. Frances Boven, Mrs. McLeod, and Mrs. McKibben were also released.

The court decided the four remaining suspects should be tried separately. Findley McLeod was the first to be put in the dock, in a trial that began October 30. Against his attorney's advice, McLeod insisted on taking the stand and telling the whole story, or at least his version of it.

McLeod told how he had met McKibben and Sullivan in prison. He said they and other convicts "pestered" him for information on how the postal system worked, especially the transport of money. McLeod said he wanted no part of any more robberies, but the others kept at him.

A couple of months before the robbery, McLeod continued, McKibben and Bill Boven approached him in Toronto. They wanted him to show them the layout of the railyard at Union Station. He said he told them the robbery could not be pulled off, but Boven said he'd already robbed some banks in the United States and knew how it could be done.

McLeod took McKibben and Boven down to the railyard for a look. After that Boven didn't want him going near Union Station anymore because employees there might recognize him and get suspicious. McLeod said he finally agreed to go along with the heist when Boven promised him 5 percent of the haul. He added that Ray Boven was not brought in on the scheme until late in the game, along with a man called Bucky Harris. He said the gang planned the robbery at John Sullivan's house. Bill Boven was unquestionably the leader.

McLeod's story accounted for all six bandits who had participated in the robbery: the two Boven brothers, Sullivan, McKibben, the previously-unheard-of Bucky Harris, and McLeod himself as a reluctant participant. When the time came to split up the loot, McLeod said, Bill Boven kept most of it and threatened to kill anyone who interfered with him. McLeod claimed Boven wanted to kill him because he was afraid he would talk to the police. He said he didn't get the full 5 percent he'd been promised.

Everett McKibben, John Sullivan, and Ray Boven had their turns in the dock, and they bitterly denied McLeod's whole story. They said he was a liar who was trying to get a light sentence. All denied participating in the holdup.

McKibben testified that McLeod had written to him in Detroit, asking if he knew any men who were interested in making some "easy money." He'd put McLeod in touch with Bill Boven. McKibben admitted to knowing about plans for a robbery but had witnesses who swore he was in Detroit when it happened. He said he'd been paid a $1,000 as "hush" money and then had lost most of it at the racetrack.

John Sullivan said he had seen McLeod in prison but didn't know his name and never talked to him about postal procedures. He knew nothing about the robbery, he said, until he read about it in the newspapers. The mail clerks who identified him as one of the bandits were either mistaken or liars. Sullivan produced witnesses who swore he was at the cigar store until late in the evening and then went home.

Ray Boven did not deny that his brother Bill could have been in on the robbery but said he himself had nothing to do with it. He testified he had never met any of the other accused men until he was arrested and taken to jail in Toronto. Findley McLeod, he insisted, was framing him to save his own skin. Boven's lawyer said that William Venton, who had identified Ray, must have mistaken him for Bill. Of course, this conflicted with testimony that Bill Boven was in the mail car, jamming a shotgun into clerk Farrow's stomach, not on the platform threatening Venton. Accusations would arise later that the Toronto police and the Crown withheld evidence that might have thrown doubt on Boven and Sullivan's presence at the crime scene.

The witnesses who were supposed to provide alibis for McKibben and Sullivan did not do very well on the stand. Under cross-examination they were tripped up and they contradicted each other. In the end, the jury chose to believe the mail clerks and railroad men who had looked the bandits in the eyes over gun muzzles. They found all four men guilty.

If Findley McLeod thought he would get off easy by turning stool pigeon, he was wrong. He was sentenced to fifteen years in prison, the same as John Sullivan and Everett McKibben. Ray Boven got ten years, perhaps because he was a last-minute addition to the gang and had not participated in the planning of the crime. Sullivan, Boven, and McKibben were packed off to the Kingston Pen. However, the judge thought McLeod might not live long in the same prison as the other three, so he sent him to Stony Mountain Penitentiary in Manitoba.

If a man known as Bucky Harris was indeed involved in the holdup, police never found him. But they kept up the search for Bill Boven, and from time to time got news of his activities. "Bad Billy," as the papers now called him, was said to be running with a gang of American bank robbers. Acting on tips, Canadian detectives travelled as far as Texas in search of the outlaw. But each time they thought they were closing in, Boven gave them the slip. In March 1929 a group of American crooks in Pittsburgh, including one Harry Meyers, alias "Dopey Davis," were caught with $80,000 worth of bonds from the Toronto mail robbery. Bad Billy had evidently unloaded some of the booty.

On the night of June 3, 1932, a burglar broke into a gas station in the town of Peru, Indiana. He was in the process of cracking the safe when someone saw him and called the police. Three patrolmen and a railroad detective responded. They called on the burglar to come out with his hands up. The robber answered with gunfire. The officers shot back, and the man died with a bullet in the head and four more in the body.

The dead man had a .25 calibre pistol in his hand and $400 in his pockets. In a nearby car the police found a .37 calibre pistol and a teargas gun. A passport identified the body as that of William R. Miller, of Columbus, Ohio, but the document was either forged or stolen. Police in Indianapolis matched the fingerprints with those on a circular they had received from the Toronto Police Department. An

Indianapolis police superintendent sent a telegram to Chief Draper. Bill Boven was lying dead in the Indianapolis morgue.

In October of that same year, prisoners in the Kingston Pen demonstrated over brutal and unsanitary conditions. One of the many men charged in the aftermath of the trouble was Ray Boven. When Boven was brought to trial for his part in the disturbance, a court official asked him about the big robbery that had landed him in prison. He responded with the three words that were part of every hoodlum's jargon. "I was framed."

JOHN BUROWSKI

"WHY SHOULD I SHOOT MY FRIEND?"

While the four Union Station mail car bandits were sitting in the Don Jail awaiting trial, and Toronto detectives were trying to track down Bill Boven, in the wild country overlooking Georgian Bay yet another train was hit by robbers. This crime did not involve as great a sum of money as the Toronto holdup did. But it had bloodier and far more tragic consequences.

Shortly after midnight on the morning of August 18, 1928, train number four from Vancouver to Toronto made a quick stop at Romford Junction just outside Sudbury to transfer mail. It was the only stop the train would make between Sudbury and Parry Sound, about one hundred miles to the southeast. Unseen by anyone, two men climbed onto the roof of the mail car. As the train pulled out of the junction, they went over the edge and swung through the open door into the car. The three clerks, M.J. Doyle, Harry Macdonald, and Charles Clarke, suddenly found themselves looking down the barrels of a pair of automatic pistols. The intruders had black cloth masks around the lower parts of their faces and wore caps pulled down low over their eyes. They had linesmen's leather belts strapped around their waists, which had probably enabled then to loiter around the junction without arousing suspicion while they awaited the train. "Where is the registered mail?" one bandit demanded. "We want it! Hand it over!"

Having no doubt read about the close call J.M. Farrow had brought upon himself in the Toronto robbery, the clerks attempted no foolhardy heroics. They told the outlaws where to find what they wanted. Speaking in thickly accented English, the bandits ordered the clerks to face the wall. Then they went to work, slashing open mailbags and rummaging for cash and bonds. They had plenty of time. Parry Sound was at least three hours away.

As the train rumbled through the night and the robbers tore into the mail, Doyle, Macdonald, and Clarke made furtive looks over their shoulders. One bandit allowed his mask to slip down, and the clerks saw his face. He was so intent on pillage that he didn't notice.

Sometime after 3:00 a.m. the train slowed down as it approached Parry Sound. About six hundred feet from the station, the bandits jumped from the car. They had taken about $20,000 in cash and bonds. By the time the three excited clerks could tell anyone about the holdup, the crooks were racing away from Parry Sound in a stolen car. And they were being pursued.

Police later suspected — though they were never entirely certain — that a third man was part of the robbery plan. While people at the train station were hearing the first news of the stickup, a car was stolen from the yard of a family named Laird. It was never determined whether the two train robbers had taken it themselves or if an accomplice stole the vehicle and picked them up. From this point, witnesses could not agree if there had been two bandits or a gang of three.

Walter Laird, age twenty-two, and his brother Haughton, age eighteen, were in bed asleep when they were awakened by noises from outside. They got dressed and went to investigate. The car belonging to their brother-in-law, who was visiting from Ohio, was gone. They awakened a neighbour, Harold Rolland. The three got into Rolland's automobile and went after the car thieves. They knew nothing of the train robbery and were not armed.

A rainstorm had swept through the evening before, and though the roads had largely dried up by now, there were still enough puddles that the stolen car left a trail of wet tire marks. The tire marks themselves were distinctive because the tires were of an American manufacture, unlike others in the Parry Sound area. The Laird brothers and Rolland followed them like Native scouts following a moccasin trail.

Outside of town the tracks turned onto a dirt road that led to the village of Waubamick, eight miles from Parry Sound. This road went all the way to North Bay, which might have been the bandits' destination. The prints from the American-made tires stood out from others in the dirt road.

A delivery truck came bouncing down the road. The Laird brothers asked the driver, whom they knew, if he had seen their brother-in-

An artist's sketch of John Burowski, who was charged with Thomas Jackson's murder. (Toronto Daily Star)

law's car. He had indeed, just a little way back, with three strangers in it. The Laird posse continued the chase.

Unaware that they were being chased as car thieves, the train robbers ran their vehicle into a ditch, right in front of the farm owned by a family named Jackson. No doubt they thought they had no need to hurry because the local police would not yet have a clue which way the robbers went. They decided their best bet was to have the car pulled out of the ditch and then continue on their way.

Sixty-two-year-old Thomas Jackson had been working the same farm for forty years and was well liked in the region. Like most farmers, he was used to city slickers who came knocking on his door, asking for help when their automobiles got stuck in the mud of the quagmires that passed for roads in rural Ontario. A farmer could make a couple of bucks just by hitching his team of horses to the bumper of a car and making them heave for a few seconds. And of course, it was always good to be neighbourly to strangers. Jackson's son Claude later told reporters what happened.

"We heard someone knocking at the door at about four o'clock in the morning. My father went to the door. There was a foreigner there. He said that his car was stuck in the ditch down on the highway and asked my father if he would pull him out. He offered him a lot of money, but did not say how much.

"My father agreed to do it and called me. We went out and hitched up the horses and went down to where the car was. It was stuck fast in the ditch."

Claude saw no other strangers except the man who had knocked on the door. Anyone else who had been in the stuck car must have been hiding nearby. As the Jacksons hitched the team to the car, the man got behind the wheel and started the engine.

Then another car roared past and stopped a short distance down the road. The Lairds spotted their brother-in-law's car. They turned around and went back. Just in case of trouble, they armed themselves as best they could. Rolland had a piece of a car jack, Walter a leaf spring from a car, and Haughton a wrench. Haughton later gave the press his eyewitness account.

"As we approached the car we saw that the lights were on and heard the engine running. We could see a man and a horse silhouetted in the light from the car. Another man with a lantern stood close beside him and a third man was at the wheel.

"Rolland went up to the car, stood on the running board and asked the driver if he wanted any help. The man replied in a gruff voice that he was all right. He spoke with a strong foreign accent.

"Rolland's reply was to step up to the car and say, 'You are the man we want. You stole this car.' He turned to me and said, 'Put the gun on him, Haughton.'

"I held a wrench in my hand and as I walked toward the car with it I held it close to my side and pretended it was a gun. The man at the wheel held up his hands and squealed, 'Don't shoot!' I ordered him to get out and he opened the door on the left-hand side. I was on the running board on the right side of the car and started around to the back of it to meet him … Then I saw a revolver in the man's hand spit flame and heard three shots. I ducked down beside the running board."

Walter Laird took up the story from there. "I just got around in time to see him make for the back of the car, grab his gun and shoot three times. I knew we had to stop him and made for him. Just as I was coming at him he wheeled and fired at me point blank. I saw the flash and felt the bullet strike me on the chest and then I closed with him.

"I got him down on the ground and got on top of him. He was squirming and kicking and struggling and he was so much bigger and heavier than I was.

"It was dark and I could not see a thing. I was afraid he had shot the others. We were there in the ditch covered with slime and mud and I was bleeding a lot. Funny I never thought about my wound or how badly I was hit. I just hung on. I was holding the wrist of the hand that held the gun and he was trying desperately to loosen my grip. I knew he meant business."

Walter called to Haughton for help. The younger brother struck the big man several times on the legs and head with his wrench. Finally the man stopped struggling and let go of the gun. Haughton picked up the weapon and pointed it at the now bloodied man. The stranger weakly said, "Don't shoot!"

A bullet had struck Walter Laird directly on the breastbone. Though the injury was serious, it was not life-threatening. Haughton found that a bullet had creased his hand. One other person had been struck by flying lead, and he was not as fortunate as the Lairds. In the first volley of three shots the gunman fired, a bullet tore through Thomas Jackson's throat. The old man put his hands to his face, staggered a few steps to his front gate and collapsed. After the gunman had been subdued, Claude Jackson found his father on the ground, dead. He and his brother Allen carried the body back to the house, where their mother sat in shock.

While the struggle had been going on by the car, someone had fired up to a dozen shots from the cover of nearby woods. Several bullets were embedded in the farm gate. Whoever had fired those shots fled into the bush. However, there was no doubt among the people on the scene that the gunman now on the ground had fired the shot that killed Thomas Jackson.

At the first sound of gunshots, someone in the house had phoned the police. The Lairds and Rolland tied their prisoner with rope until officers could arrive. The man said he had $1,800 in his pocket that they could have if they would just let him go. One of the young men told him to shut up.

When the police arrived the gunman gave his name as John Burowski. He said he had been hitchhiking and two men had picked him up. He could not satisfactorily explain the gun or the fat roll of money in his pocket. He also had several empty "cocaine decks," paper packets in which the narcotic was sold.

Burowski said he knew nothing about a mail car robbery. He

said he did not mean to shoot Walter Laird. He thought he was being attacked, so he fired a few shots to scare the other men off. He denied shooting Thomas Jackson. He insisted that the bullet that killed Jackson had to have been fired from the woods.

In the Parry Sound Police Station, detectives put Burowski through what the papers called "a modern third degree." They questioned him for hours on end but could get little out of him. He wouldn't budge from his "hitchhiking" story. There was no logic to this, unless Burowski thought his silence would help his friend(s) escape and he might be sprung from jail later.

A check on Burowski's fingerprints revealed that he had escaped from the Western Penitentiary in Pennsylvania in 1926. He'd been doing five to seven years for attempting to kill a man with a gun. He had also served time in New York's Auburn Prison for receiving stolen goods. The police would eventually learn that Burowski had left his native Poland in 1913 and landed at Halifax. He'd drifted around Canada and the United States using several aliases. After his break from the Pennsylvania prison he had crossed the border at Niagara Falls in the trunk of a car. He had a sister in France, a father and brother in Russia, but no family in North America.

The mail clerks Doyle, Macdonald, and Clarke identified Burowski as the bandit whose mask had slipped off. Still he denied any involvement in the robbery. But from his cell he wrote letters in Polish to someone in Winnipeg, asking for assistance in a jailbreak. It did not seem to occur to Burowski that the police would read his letters with the help of an interpreter. As a security measure they moved him from the Parry Sound jail to the fortress-like Don Jail in Toronto.

Meanwhile the hunt was on for whomever had been in the stolen car with Burowski. For some reason — perhaps something the prisoner had let slip during interrogation — the police did not seem sure if they were hunting one fugitive or two. All they were certain of was that two men had robbed the mail car, and *someone* had fired shots from the woods while the fight was happening in front of the Jackson home.

At the edge of the woods near the scene of that struggle, police found crushed foliage that indicated a man had lain there, perhaps to take a good firing position. They also found bundles that contained stolen bonds of an undisclosed value. Someone in a hurry to get away had dropped them.

The police launched a huge manhunt that involved dozens of Ontario Provincial Police officers and railroad detectives. The Toronto Police Department sent reinforcements. Over a hundred farmers joined the search as volunteers. Claude and Allen Jackson were with them. "They killed my father," Claude told a reporter. "But we will catch them."

The ground the posses had to cover was rough and heavily forested, which worked both for and against their quarry. In the bush the searchers could pass within arm's length of a fugitive and not see him. But it was also a land not friendly to anyone who did not know how to live on it. It was covered with streams, lakes, and swamps. If one did not encounter bears, wolves, or rattlesnakes, one most certainly endured swarms of mosquitoes. The woods provided berries for a man on the run but not much else.

The police were sure the man or men they were after would have to go to a farmhouse for food. They thought they had a break when seventeen-year-old Edward Welsh told them strangers had visited his family's farm not quite three miles from Parry Sound. Edward's father, a constable, was not home when two men came to the house and asked for food. The men left a canvas bag that looked like a mail sack by the gate before going up to the house. Edward was sure one of the men had a gun stuck in the waist of his pants, under his shirt. The boy and his mother were too scared of the men to refuse them food. The strangers bolted down their meal and then left as suddenly as they had appeared. The police went out to the farm, but the unwanted guests had left no trail.

The manhunt was, as one Toronto reporter put it, "a bad time for hoboes." This was the time of year when thousands of itinerant agricultural workers from eastern Canada headed west in search of jobs harvesting the prairie wheatfields. The few men who could afford it bought train tickets. The rest went the hobo way, hopping freight trains and riding in, on or under boxcars. Police and other searchers turned up scores of them as they swept through small-town railyards and beat the bushes along the railway in their rural dragnet.

At one railstop the constables saw a figure scurry into a boxcar. An officer pointed a gun at him and yelled, "Jump, you bozo, or we'll fill you full of lead!" A terrified eighteen-year-old boy came out. He was just trying to go west to make a few honest bucks harvesting wheat. Like all the other "bums," he was jailed as a vagrant. The fewer tramps cluttering up the rail lines, the easier it would be for the posses to track down the fugitives.

In the early days of the manhunt there was little doubt the police would soon make an arrest. How long could a fugitive last in that rough country? "We'll starve him out like a rat," one police inspector said.

The cops seemed to have every possible escape route covered. "Jiggers" full of armed men patrolled the railroads. Officers in a motor launch cruised along the Georgian Bay shoreline. Detectives disguised as hoboes rode the freight cars. In addition to watching the roads, police placed "abandoned" cars at lonely roadsides. If the bait was ever seen, it was never taken.

"There is no more thrilling hunt than when a man is the prize to be bagged," wrote a journalist for the *Toronto Daily Star*. "No single beast of the wild has had as many hunters as the present fugitive. Guns glint from the bushes on the shores of numerous lakes."

Quite possibly the hunters briefly had one of the wanted men in their hands. Near Burwash, just south of Sudbury, a posse caught a suspect they described as "a Swede." Before police officers arrived the man got away from his captors and fled into the bush. The pursuers never again caught sight of him. He might have been the elusive bandit. Or he could have been just another hobo who didn't like the idea of going to jail.

Days passed with no results. The newspapers now suggested the police had failed. Their man — or men — had made it to Toronto or Winnipeg or over the border to the United States. After almost two weeks of fruitless searching, they gave up the hunt. Blame for the robbery and the murder would fall wholly on the shoulders of John Burowski.

Burowski did nothing to help his own case. He stubbornly stuck to his ridiculous hitchhiker story. He would not tell the police anything about the other bandit. While in the Don Jail he wrote letters in Polish to people he thought could help him escape. He asked for saws and other tools to be smuggled in to him. When told he was going back to Parry Sound to stand trial for murder, he wrote letters asking friends to rescue him during the train trip. Burowski still did not seem to realize the guards were having his letters interpreted. His general behaviour begs the question: was he mentally competent?

On September 23, Burowski was taken under heavy guard from the Don Jail to Union Station for the return trip to Parry Sound. He wore handcuffs and his feet were manacled. During the drive to the train station he kept turning to look out the back window as though he expected something to happen. Extra police were on duty at Union Station to thwart any attempt at "rescue" and to keep back curious onlookers who wanted to gawk at the notorious prisoner. There was no big crowd at the station, but as Burowski was being put aboard the train someone shouted, "Where is Ellis the hangman? We are on our way to a necktie party." Burowski heard the taunt and frowned.

Burowski had his own special car. Only the prisoner, his armed escort, and a few members of the press were allowed aboard. It was coupled directly to the engine and separated from the other passenger coaches by the baggage car.

Two days later Burowski was in the Parry Sound courthouse. His counsel, J.R. Hett, tried to have the venue changed, claiming there was too much hostility against the defendant in Parry Sound for him to have a fair trial there. The request was denied.

Crown prosecutor W.L. Haight, K.C., brought forward the mail clerks who identified Burowski as one of the two bandits. Walter Laird testified that one of the first three shots Burowski fired killed Thomas Jackson. The only person Hett could call upon to speak for the defence was Burowski himself.

Burowski complained of how he had been treated in the Parry Sound jail when he was first arrested. The police questioned him, he said, until he was "driven silly." He told the court, "While I was in the jail they would ask me the same questions, first one of them and then another until I was ready to tell them anything at all … I never shoot this Jackson man. He is a farmer. He has a farmer boy with him. He is my friend pulling me from ditch. Why should I shoot my friend?"

Hett tried to convince the jury Burowski had fired in self-defence. The jurors didn't buy it. They returned a verdict of guilty. Justice Wright sentenced Burowski to hang on December 8. When the prisoner heard the death sentence passed, he gave a small laugh and said, "It isn't worrying me."

The following day Burowski admitted to the mail car robbery. But he would not tell the police anything about his accomplice. He said he would rather be hanged than be a squealer. He was returned to the

Don Jail to be held in the "death cell" until the date for the execution drew near. Hett filed every appeal available to him, but all were denied. A few days before the scheduled date, Burowski was taken back to Parry Sound, where a gallows was being constructed in the jailyard. The execution was scheduled for 12:15 the morning of the eighth.

The day before he was to hang, Burowski had second thoughts about "squealing." He told Hett he could provide the police with information about his accomplice. Hett immediately contacted the attorney general's office in Toronto, requesting a stay of execution. After some consideration, the attorney general granted the request and had one of his subordinates telephone Parry Sound. Then he went home for the night.

When the sheriff in Parry Sound received the call, he did not recognize the voice at the other end of the phone. He thought someone was pulling a hoax. He was going ahead with the hanging unless he had confirmation of an official stay of execution. By this time it was late at night, and the attorney general was home in bed. He had to be roused so he could personally, by phone and by telegram, convince the sheriff the order was legitimate. The sheriff called a halt to the proceedings at midnight, fifteen minutes before Burowski was to have climbed the scaffold.

Whatever the information was that Burowski had for the police, neither they nor the courts considered it very useful. Besides, Burowski had been tried and convicted of murder, not robbery. He would be hanged on December 21, when the stay of execution expired.

Meanwhile, local citizens had complained about the gallows, the top of which could be seen rising above the jail walls. Boys had been joking about it and playing "gruesome" games. The structure was modified in time for the twenty-first. This time there was no respite. John Burowski paid the price for the murder of his "friend."

THE CHATHAM
TRAIN ROBBERY

"NOTHING BUT KNOWING HOW"

With Bill Bovin on the run and John Burowski locked up in jail, Ontario police probably thought they'd seen the last of train robbers in their province. After all, this wasn't the American Wild West! But a strange young man was about to startle Ontarians with yet another brazen holdup, making 1928 the Year of the Train Robberies for the usually staid province. And because of his unique method of escaping from the scene of the crime, the bandit very nearly got away with it.

Norman "Red" Ryan, perhaps Canada's most infamous bank robber, once said that pulling a robbery was easy. It was the getaway that was difficult. After making the heist, the bandit had to hightail it away from pursuing policemen and even enraged citizens. This often brought about wild chases with plenty of flying lead. Wouldn't it be better for a thief if he could slip away from the scene of the crime without engaging in such potentially lethal dramatics?

On October 2, 1928, Canadian National train number 11 left Toronto at 2:00 p.m., bound for Windsor. In the mail car was about $100,000 in cash that was being shipped to banks in Windsor and the United States. The postal clerks on duty were Albert Gignac, R.H. Cromwell, and Harry E. Roos, all residents of Windsor.

The train stopped at London, then continued on to Chatham. So far, it had been a routine run for the mail clerks. At the Chatham station they opened the door so they could toss out the Chatham mail bags and take aboard mail going out from that town. Moments after the last mailbag had been thrown into the car, and just as the train started to roll and the clerks were about to close the sliding door, a man suddenly swung into the car from the ladder rungs next to the door. He leveled a .48 calibre revolver at the clerks and ordered, "Stick 'em up quick and leave 'em up!"

The intruder was not masked. He was young and dressed like any man one might see working in a railyard. He wore a cloth cap and blue overalls. He was smooth-faced and of slightly less than medium height and build. But the gun in his hand was a small cannon, and none of the clerks entertained any foolish ideas of being a hero. They quickly obeyed the gunman's order to "stick 'em up."

The bandit told the men to face the wall and then asked them if they had guns. When they replied that they didn't, he snarled that if he found a gun on any of them, "I'll splatter your guts all over the car." The robber frisked the clerks. Satisfied that they were not armed, he told Cromwell to get him the post office money packets and warned Gignac and Roos not to turn around.

The gunman evidently knew about the money in the mail car. In fact, he knew about the money shipment the clerks had made on an earlier run. He warned Cromwell not to try any tricks, or he'd kill all three of them. On the bandit's orders Cromwell sliced open a post office money bag. Then he watched as the outlaw stuffed bundles of money into his clothes.

Now the robber told Cromwell to join his pals with his face to the wall and his hands raised. He warned them again not to turn around. "There's a machine gun right behind you," he said.

The train rolled into a mail stop called Prairie Siding, about eighteen miles from Windsor. The clerks didn't see the robber leave. They heard the door slide shut as the train came to a stop, but they didn't look around, fearful he might still be there. No one else on the train knew a robbery had occurred. Ironically, the train's conductor that night, L.J. Gay, had been the conductor for the train in Toronto in June when the Boven Gang struck.

Outside the mail car, brakeman Lorne Gillan was surprised when the door didn't slide open so mail bags could be tossed inside. He banged on the door but got no reply. He later told a *Globe* reporter:

"I couldn't get into the car by the platform doors; neither could I get a reply from the clerks, and so I walked to the far side of the car and saw the clerks through the half open doors with their hands in the air and their faces turned to the side of the car. I must have been just a second or two late to meet the bandit, for the clerks told me they believed he was still there."

*An artist's conception of the Chatham train robbery. (*Toronto Daily Star*)*

Prairie Siding was said to be the loneliest rail stop in the district. There was nothing out there except the tiny station and nearby a bridge across the Thames River on a lane that led to the Wallaceburg Road. When Conductor Gay and the engineer were informed of the holdup, one of them phoned the police in Windsor. Within minutes a squad of detectives and police officers was on the way to Prairie Siding, while another group went to the Windsor train station.

At Prairie Siding the police found nothing. However, some local farmers said they had seen a strange car with American licence plates parked near the Wallaceburg Road. Soon after the train had stopped at the siding, they saw it roaring down the road at a very high speed.

Police concluded that the bandit had confederates waiting for him. They'd picked him up and made a getaway with the loot. The police didn't have much of a description of the automobile to go on, only that it had American plates. The witnesses weren't sure of which state.

The bandit who had snatched $20,500 in cash from the mail car went by the name of William Gibbs — among others. Perhaps he had indeed arranged for accomplices to wait for him at Prairie Siding in a fast car. But even if that was part of the original plan, Gibbs was not in the car the farmers saw tearing along the Wallaceburg Road in the autumn darkness. If Gibbs really did have accomplices, he had decided to double-cross them and keep all the money for himself. Instead of running from the siding to the waiting car, Gibbs crawled under the coal tender and squeezed into a space where he could ride the rest of the way to Windsor *under* the train. It was a very uncomfortable and dangerous method of hitching a ride, but it was one place the police did not think to look. Moreover, experienced hobos regularly did it as a means of hiding from railway detectives who tried to discourage them from hopping freights. Gibbs would later say dozens of people passed him before the train left Prairie Siding. He could have reached out and touched them.

Fortunately for Gibbs, the ride to Windsor was a short one because he was showered with sparks and cinders all the way. Soon the train rolled into Windsor. Gibbs apparently knew the cars would be put on the ferry for the crossing to Detroit, but the engine and the coal tender would remain on the Canadian side. He crawled along the rods underneath the cars to a position under a boxcar. This must have been a considerably more comfortable place than his hidey-hole under the coal tender because Gibbs fell asleep. When he awoke, he saw the deck of a boat beneath him. Gibbs was on the Detroit River Ferry, bound for the United States and freedom from pursuit by Canadian police.

That, at least, was one story he told. In another version he claimed that when the train stopped in Windsor, he rolled out from under the car and then strolled down to the dock and boarded the ferry. Dressed as he was, and with his grimy face, Gibbs looked as though he worked on the boat, and nobody challenged him. Whichever version was true, Gibbs might well have been better off if he'd stayed under the train.

Meanwhile, the telephone lines and telegraph wires in southern Ontario were humming as news of the holdup was spread to police stations across the peninsula. The alert went to border cities on both sides of the line. American police told their Canadian counterparts they'd heard underworld rumours of gangsters from large U.S. cities like Chicago, New York, and Cleveland heading for Canadian cities like Windsor and Toronto, where they thought the pickings would be easy. Canadian police suspected Bill Bovin, whom they were now calling a "super-criminal" and "mastermind," was behind the Chatham train robbery.

On board the ferry, Gibbs tried to conceal himself among the vehicles making the crossing. However, a deckhand saw him and became suspicious. The crewman thought Gibbs might be trying to enter the United States as a "quota dodger," the term used at that time for an illegal immigrant. As soon as the boat docked, the deck hand hurried ashore and found railway detective Chester Sylvester. When Sylvester heard there might be a quota dodger on the ferry, he quickly summoned immigration officers John Biery and Clyde Pomaville. The three officers boarded the ferry. They saw a suspicious-looking man crouched by the railing and approached him. The suspect immediately bolted through an engine room door.

After a brief search the officers found their quarry again, clinging to the ladder of a boxcar that was lined up to be rolled ashore. As the officers closed in on him, Gibbs pulled his gun. But before the outlaw could fire a shot, Chester Sylvester, a big man over six feet tall, landed a solid punch to Gibbs's jaw and knocked him cold.

Sylvester, Biery, and Pomaville hauled Gibbs off the ferry and took him to the immigration office. None of the officers were aware of the train robbery. But they were certainly startled to find their prisoner had his clothes stuffed with money. His shirt, his overalls, even his socks literally bulged with fat wads of Canadian cash. The officers also found fourteen bullets in one pocket.

The Americans contacted the Windsor police and quickly learned they had a suspected train robber in jail. Canadian detectives crossed the river to take charge of the prisoner. Gibbs freely confessed to the robbery and did not seek to resist extradition to Canada on legal grounds. The American police handed Gibbs and the $20,500 they'd found on him — along with the gun and the bullets — over to the Canadians.

In Windsor the three postal clerks identified Gibbs as the man who had robbed the mail car. Gibbs was charged with armed robbery and robbing His Majesty's Mail. He was locked in the Windsor jail to await transportation to Chatham. If found guilty of the charges, Gibbs could be sentenced to life in prison and strokes of the lash.

Identifying Gibbs would be somewhat tougher than catching him had been. The prisoner gave his name as William Gibbs of Los Angeles, California. He said he'd escaped from a mental asylum there, a place he called "the peach farm." He said he had been in Canada for about four weeks before pulling the train robbery. Gibbs said he'd been living in a shack outside Toronto, and that he also had "a nice little cave."

Gibbs behaved strangely right from the start. In the Windsor jail he clawed through the bars at other inmates "like a gorilla," as one reporter put it. When the reporter asked him if he was crazy, Gibbs replied that he was "as crazy as Chief Wigle," referring to Windsor Police Chief M. Wigle. Then he complained of having a "peculiar feeling" in his head.

The following day Gibbs was transferred to Chatham. At his arraignment the magistrate asked him if his name was William Gibbs. He replied, "That's okay with me, Chief." Asked where his home was, Gibbs said, "Wherever I hang my hat."

Gibbs boasted of the train robbery and said he'd done many others just like it. "Nothing but knowing how," he said. Gibbs claimed that he just wandered around and pulled a job whenever he needed money. He said he usually got away with it.

"Shucks, if it had not been for that damned nosey oiler at the Detroit ferry, I would be in Chicago right at this minute. I thought this idea up by myself and bought overalls so as to pass for one of the trainmen. Well, I almost got away with it."

Gibbs was asked if he had pulled the robbery alone. "I sure did. It was pretty smart work, too, if I do say so myself."

Police did not believe Gibbs had acted alone. Just who was in that strange car farmers had seen parked near Prairie Siding? Then Chatham police picked up an ex-con named Ernest Lusby for questioning. Lusby denied having anything to do with the train robbery, but he said he had seen Bill Bovin in Chatham the day of the holdup. He also claimed he had seen Gibbs loitering around the Chatham railyard before the train rolled in. That conflicted with Gibbs's claim that he had ridden train number 11 from Toronto.

The police were certain Bill Bovin was involved in the holdup. The robber had to have had knowledge beforehand of the money shipment, and Gibbs just didn't seem bright enough to have acquired that kind of information on his own. But the young bandit insisted he had pulled the job single-handed.

Because Gibbs had robbed the mail, the Royal Canadian Mounted Police were officially in charge of the investigation. They sent Gibbs's fingerprints to the Los Angeles Police Department. The LA police replied that Gibbs had done ninety days for vagrancy in that city, but that was all. They said Gibbs was "a typical hobo." Quite likely he was. He did know where to hide under a coal tender.

Then another letter arrived, this one from the Kingston Penitentiary. Gibbs had apparently done time there on a burglary conviction. He had at least one alias; the name Givis. The letter went on to say that Gibbs was from Toronto, not Los Angeles. If that information was accurate, then Gibbs must have been sent to Kingston at a very young age, because the man in the Kent County jail in Chatham was clearly no more than twenty years old.

Meanwhile, Gibbs was still behaving in an odd way. He made faces at reporters who went to interview him. He told guards he was a "cave man" and that he only had to make scary faces at people to make them hand over their money. The police were sure he was putting on a crazy act in preparation for a plea of insanity, and they weren't buying it. They told the press they expected Gibbs to be tried for his crime and then go to prison for it.

One week after the holdup a Mrs. Anna Krgich of Detroit came forward and said she was Gibbs's mother. She had seen Gibbs's photograph in the newspaper. His real name, she said, was John Grbic, and he was born and raised in Detroit.

Anna told the police and the press that she and her son's father, Steve Grbic, had emigrated to the United States from Serbia. The father, Anna said, was "a very, very bad man." He was a drunkard and a robber who finally abandoned her and their four small sons and went back to Serbia. Anna remarried, but had never been able to control her Johnny. She said he had always been bad and had a long juvenile record. Anna said her boy got into trouble because he was "weak minded."

"John was like his father. He was always acting crazy-like. He used to make faces at people to scare them. He used to tell me I didn't know what I was talking about when I tried to tell him what was right. He'd laugh at me and shove me aside. I haven't seen him in five years. I knew he'd end up something like this ... Johnny wasn't right in his head, ever! I'm sure of that."

The Canadian government evidently agreed with Mrs. Krgich's assessment of her son. Doctors examined the train robber and pronounced him mentally incompetent to stand trial. Gibbs was packed off to a mental institution. The police never did learn if that "mastermind" Bill Bovin was the brains behind the Chatham train robbery.

ALBERT DORLAND

"I WAS FRAMED!"

Under Canadian law, the duty of a police officer as a sworn protector of the public is to prevent crime whenever possible. If police officers were to actively participate in "setting up" a crime so their department could look heroic in bringing the perpetrator(s) down, they would be in violation of the law. If they were found out, there would be a huge scandal. Such a scandal shook the Toronto Police Department in 1933. This sensational story had the name of a common Canadian criminal competing for front-page headline space with that of Hitler, when the Nazis were rising to power in Germany. The outlaw in question was never more than a two-bit hoodlum, but in 1933 Canadians were rushing to buy newspapers to catch up on the latest developments in the story of this man, whose name today is all but forgotten.

Albert Dorland's name first made the Toronto newspapers in July 1924 when he and his brother Robert were caught breaking into a Toronto shop. Robert had been jailed for car theft three years earlier. For Albert, who was nineteen or twenty years old, this was the first serious brush with the law. It cost him two years in the Kingston Penitentiary. Dorland was hardly out of jail when in 1926 he was sentenced to two years less a day in the Ontario Reformatory in Guelph for stealing a car.

In April 1929 Albert Dorland was arrested again, on suspicion of involvement in the September 1928 armed robbery of a Windsor grocery store. He was also charged with the theft of the getaway car used in that holdup. Albert Dorland managed to beat both raps. But by this time the young hoodlum was well known in the Toronto underworld. Just how familiar his name was to the Toronto Police Department would become a matter of considerable debate. Would this convicted shop-breaker, car thief, and suspected grocery store robber have loomed large enough in the eyes of the Toronto Police Department that they felt they had to "get him" by whatever means possible? Or was Dorland just an unlucky punk, however unsavoury, who happened to stumble into a set-up police plan to nab some bad guys — any bad guys — in a dramatic manner and grab some glory in the process?

In 1928 the city fathers of Toronto welcomed a new chief of police, Denis (Denny) C. Draper. Born in Quebec in 1873 of United Empire Loyalist stock, Draper had a sterling reputation as a soldier. He had served with the Canadian Expeditionary Force in France during the Great War. There he had been wounded in action, decorated three times for bravery, and had risen to the rank of brigadier general of militia. His military record was certainly impressive, but General Draper (as he liked to be called) had no training or experience as a policeman, much less as a chief of police. Some of Toronto's elite felt the position should have gone to a ranking officer who had been with the force for some time and who knew both the job and the city. However, others believed Draper's military experience and discipline suited him perfectly for the job. Draper made his supporters look good when, only weeks after he'd taken the position, the Great Toronto Train Robbery occurred. Draper's men solved the crime and brought in the culprits so quickly, his detractors were silenced — for a while, at least.

Chief Draper was a man of great contrasts. He would go out in the field with his men, beating the bushes in a search for a lost child. He was the founder of the Prisoners' Rehabilitation Society and for many years its president. He had a reputation for kindness and generosity.

But Chief Draper was also a tough cop whose policies caused more than one mayor to demand his resignation. He detested gambling and believed convicted bookmakers should be sentenced to lashes. Draper hated labour unions and would send his police out with their billy clubs to break up strikes and demonstrations. He was suspicious of anything that smacked of Communism and sent "Red Squads" out to harass anyone he believed to have socialist leanings. His critics complained that no other city in Canada seemed to have as many "Communists" as Toronto. Although Draper believed in strict enforcement of the law, he was not always reluctant to bend the law if he believed the end justified the means.

Albert Dorland was released from prison after it was proven that the Toronto police had framed him for bank robbery. Within a year he was back behind bars — for bank robbery! (Kingston Penitentiary Museum)

Sometime in mid-March of 1930, Albert Dorland met a young man named William Toohey. Originally from Hamilton, Ontario, Toohey was described by the police in his hometown as "a mean little thief." Like Dorland, Toohey had done time in Kingston — two years for passing bad cheques — though it is not certain the two men had become friends there.

Dorland and Toohey were both down on their luck. Dorland had been unable to get a job because he was an ex-con. He had sent a letter to Chief Draper of the Toronto Police requesting a taxi driver's licence. At that time it was the responsibility of a community's chief of police to issue such permits. If the chief did not think the applicant deserved the licence, the request was denied. Chief Draper felt, as he later explained, that the good citizens of Toronto deserved to have their taxis driven by honest men and not by jailbirds like Albert Dorland. He refused the application. Moreover, now that he had the address of a former inmate of both the Kingston Pen and the Ontario Reformatory, he assigned officers to keep an eye on the place and see what this Dorland character was up to. That, at least, would be Dorland's claim later on. He said a fellow ex-con spotted the cops on his street and warned him that his lodgings were under surveillance. Dorland moved to a new address without letting the police know where.

After his release from prison, Toohey had found a job with a Toronto transport company. Toohey wasn't there long before police showed up and informed his employer he was an ex-con. Toohey's boss told them it didn't matter. As long as Toohey behaved himself, he would have a job there. But Toohey's eyesight was failing as the result of an injury he'd received in prison. He eventually had to give up his job because of poor vision. To make matters worse, Toohey had an ailing wife.

Toohey and Dorland decided to rob the Royal Bank of Canada at the corner of Church and Wellesley streets. Just who first proposed the idea would one day be a matter of considerable argument. Each would say the other suggested it first. They wanted a Hamilton-based car thief named Ernest Bird to join them. Bird was reluctant. He said robbing banks was not his line. But Toohey was insistent. He argued with Bird until finally the man agreed to go by bus to Toronto on Sunday, April 6, and join them for the bank raid on Monday the seventh.

Now that they had a third man, the would-be bank robbers needed guns. Both men were almost dead broke, but Toohey somehow came up with enough money to add to Dorland's few dollars so they could buy two shotguns — one single-barrelled, the other double-barrelled — for $14 in a second-hand store. Dorland sawed the barrels off them in his apartment.

The Saturday before the robbery date, Toohey was to meet Dorland at the corner of Queen and Bay streets. Dorland arrived on time, but Toohey was late. When Toohey finally arrived, he came from the direction of City Hall. Dorland thought that was a little too close to police headquarters. He asked Toohey what he'd been doing. Toohey said he'd been picked up on a minor charge involving some trouble at a garage, but the cops had let him go. The two went to a hardware store to buy shells for the shotguns. Another customer followed them in. Dorland was sure the man was a cop. They went into a restaurant for coffee. A man came in and sat at the table next to theirs. Dorland knew this man was a cop. He and Toohey left immediately.

Toohey and Dorland then pooled what money they had left to rent a car. Just when it seemed that they wouldn't be able to scrape together the right amount of money, Toohey managed to come up with a few bucks. Dorland altered the car's licence plate numbers. Toohey used the car to go for a little drive and pick up a package of cigarettes.

Sunday arrived and there was no sign of Bird. Toohey phoned him and asked why the hell he hadn't come to Toronto. They had a bank to rob! Bird said he wasn't going to Toronto. He hadn't liked the idea of robbing a bank in the first place. Toohey argued and then finally gave up. He and Dorland would have to hit the bank by themselves.

Monday morning the two ex-cons got into their rented car and set off for the Church and Wellesley branch of the Royal Bank. Dorland, who was driving, had the double-barrelled shotgun; Toohey had the single. Toohey said they should go to Hamilton and force Bird to join them for the robbery. Dorland agreed at first and turned west onto Dundas Street. But by the time they reached Bathurst Street, he'd changed his mind. He didn't think they needed Bird. In spite of Toohey's grumbling, Dorland turned the car around and headed for the bank.

Dorland parked outside the bank and waited in the car while Toohey went inside to "case" the place. It was about eleven o'clock. Toohey returned to the car and said there were too many people inside. It would be better if they came back later. On the way back to Dorland's apartment they stopped so Toohey could use a public phone to call his wife.

The two men had lunch. Toohey was a bundle of nerves. Dorland said, "Don't worry. We will be rich by night." At ten minutes to three — just before the bank's closing time — they got back into the car and headed for the bank once more. Dorland parked the car on the west side of Church Street, just below the bank. The two got out, and with the sawed-off shotguns hidden beneath their coats, they started walking toward the Royal Bank.

The plan was that Toohey would enter the bank and vault over the counter, brandishing his shotgun, while Dorland stood guard in the vestibule. But before they reached the bank door, Toohey suddenly wanted a change of plans. He said Dorland should go in and make the heist, while he waited in the vestibule. Dorland always thought he had more nerve than Toohey, so he agreed. Besides, Toohey had a tendency to stutter when he became nervous or excited. When that happened, he could struggle for minutes at a time, trying to get a word out. No doubt Dorland realized it would be better if he went in and did the talking.

Then Toohey wanted to swap guns. Dorland couldn't see any purpose in that, but he didn't want to argue with Toohey out on the street. He gave Toohey the double-barrelled shotgun and tucked the single-barrelled weapon under his coat.

The pair reached the bank door and Dorland had his hand on the handle when Toohey told him to hurry up and go in. Dorland turned around to look at his partner, and then saw something that set off his inner alarm. He saw two men watching from an apartment window across the street, and he knew at once they were detectives. Another man was standing in front of a drug store on a corner opposite the bank, trying to appear as though he were reading a newspaper. But Dorland could tell the man was watching them over the top of the newspaper. He pulled his hand away from the door and quickly said to Toohey, "Come on, let's get out of here! It's a plant! The coppers are all around the place!"

Dorland couldn't know that as he and Toohey approached the bank, one of the watching detectives had drawn his gun and said, "Let's go and knock them off now." His sergeant restrained him. The plan was to get Dorland *inside* the bank.

The two hurried back to their car, Toohey arguing all the way that Dorland was mistaken. They got in, and Dorland drove down Church Street, and then cut across to Jarvis Street. Toohey was still arguing, telling him there were no cops, and they should go back and get that money. He actually convinced Dorland, who turned the car around. On Wellesley Street Dorland saw a police car approaching. He backed into a driveway to turn around again, when two more police cars roared into view. One of them, with four detectives inside and another on the running board, screeched to a halt at the end of the driveway, blocking Dorland and Toohey's escape.

Dorland tried to shift gears, but in his panic he floored the gas pedal. His car shot forward, ramming the police car and pinning the legs of the cop on the running board. The passenger door flew open, and Toohey fell out. Then the police in the car Dorland had rammed opened fire with their revolvers and the window in front of Dorland disintegrated. A bullet creased Dorland's temple and he threw himself to the floor of the car. The police fired fifteen to twenty shots, shattering every window in the car. One stray bullet passed through the window of a nearby home, damaging a piano. Neither of the ex-cons fired a shot. Their guns were on the floor of the car. Journalists would later derisively call the incident The Battle of Wellesley Plains.

After the police stopped shooting, Dorland lay still, afraid to move. Detectives surrounded the car. A couple of them hauled Toohey to his feet, handling him roughly. "Don't you know who I am?" Toohey protested. It would be revealed later that the officers had been told, "The taller man is the informer." Six-foot-tall Toohey was much taller than Dorland.

The detectives saw Dorland cringing on the floor of the car. One of them asked, "Will I give it to him?" Another must have seen the blood from Dorland's head wound. "No," he said. "He's already hit."

The police dragged Dorland out of the car and handcuffed him. They took him and Toohey to police headquarters and placed them in separate rooms. A detective tried to browbeat Dorland into making a confession, but he wouldn't admit to anything. An inspector told him, "We are going to convict you. We have Toohey's evidence."

Toohey was brought into the room. The inspector asked him, "Toohey, what were you going to do?"

Toohey replied, "We were going to rob a bank." Then he was taken away again. Dorland still refused to talk, even after a detective threatened to break his jaw.

The police kept Dorland in a room for nine hours. They did not tell him what he was charged with. They did not "caution" him (the equivalent at that time of being told one's rights). He was given nothing to eat. For most of the time he was alone in the room. Every so often a detective came into the room to question him. One brought in the single-barrelled, sawed-off shotgun. He asked Dorland if it was the gun he'd been carrying. Dorland admitted it was. The detective told him it wouldn't have been of any use to him in a shootout. The firing pin had been broken off!

One detective did something very peculiar indeed. He entered the room with a revolver in his hand and in full view of Dorland, put it in a drawer. Then he left. Dorland could see that the drawer had no lock. Did the cops actually expect him to go for the gun and try to escape? How far could he possibly get? He didn't make a move toward the drawer.

Dorland asked one of his interrogators what was happening with Toohey. The detective replied that Toohey had been released on his own bail. That didn't make sense to Dorland. Bank robbers didn't get released on the kind of bail usually set for people arrested on minor charges. But then, he and Toohey hadn't actually robbed a bank! So why was he still at police headquarters while Toohey went free? Why had the police almost killed him in a volley of gunfire?

At last an officer took Dorland to Chief Draper's office at about three o'clock Tuesday morning. The police chief was there with Chief of Detectives Alex Murray. Draper told Dorland, "I don't want to be too hard on you. I can convict you for conspiracy to rob a bank, but there is a charge of carrying concealed weapons, and the penalty is from one to five years and if you plead guilty I will see that you get the minimum sentence of one year." Draper turned to the chief of detectives and said, "Is that right, Inspector Murray?"

Murray replied, "That is right. I will agree to it."

Dorland agreed that rather than make the law put him on trial to prove him guilty of conspiracy to rob a bank, he would plead guilty to carrying a concealed weapon and go to jail for a year. Because the sentence was for less than two years, Dorland probably expected to be sent to the Guelph Reformatory. The "joint" in Guelph was no summer camp, but it was better than the hellhole in Kingston.

In the morning Dorland was taken into police court. Presiding was Judge Emerson Coatsworth, an elderly magistrate who, by some odd coincidence, was also a police commissioner. By chance a lawyer named Harold Chaplan was in the courtroom that morning. He knew Dorland, having once defended him. He asked Dorland if he had legal counsel. Dorland said he did not. Chaplan offered to represent Dorland, but Dorland said it wasn't necessary. He was pleading guilty to carrying a concealed weapon. Chaplan told Dorland he was nonetheless entitled to legal counsel. Dorland again refused. He had cut his own deal with the cops and was getting off with just a year. Chaplan said, "All right. It is up to you," and left.

When Dorland was placed in the dock, Judge Coatsworth read the charge to which Dorland was pleading guilty. It was not one of carrying a *concealed* weapon, but of carrying an *offensive* weapon, namely a sawed-off shotgun! In the testimony of a police officer who had been present during the stakeout and the shooting, only Dorland was named. There was no mention of Toohey. The fusillade the police had fired at the alleged "bandit car" was referred to as "skirmishing around."

Coatsworth sentenced Dorland to the maximum sentence of five years in the Kingston Penitentiary. Dorland was stunned. But he noted that Coatsworth flushed as red as a beet as he pronounced the sentence and seemed to hide his face behind the papers in his hands, as though unwilling to look at the prisoner. Before Dorland could say a word in protest, he was hustled downstairs to the cells. Later that day he told a visitor, "I've been framed," before being placed on a train that would take him to the dreaded Kingston Pen.

The economic squeeze of what would come to be known as The Great Depression was starting to make itself felt, and as the unemployment rate shot up, so did the crime rate, especially armed robberies. The Toronto newspapers praised Chief Draper and his men for nipping this bank stickup in the bud. They reported that a third suspect, Ernest Bird of Hamilton, had been arrested and then released due to lack of evidence.

But how did the Toronto Police know that Bird was in any way connected with the robbery plot? The answer was simple. William Toohey was, in the underworld parlance of the time, a stool pigeon. Moreover, he had been actively working with the police to set Dorland up. Albert Dorland had in fact been framed. But he would spend three wretched years in Kingston before the story became public.

Albert Dorland's mother had died when he was seven years old. His grandmother, Elizabeth McKillop, took over the responsibility of raising the Dorland children. Mrs. McKillop, a native of Ireland, was a strong-willed woman who doted on young "Bert." In her eyes he could do no wrong. When Dorland had first been packed off to jail in Kingston and then Guelph, Mrs. McKillop had refused to believe he had been guilty of any crime. It was the police, she said, who hounded the boy.

Now Mrs. McKillop had good reason to believe her favourite grandson was a victim of injustice. She had met William Toohey once, when Albert had brought his new friend to her house to give him some of his old clothes because the young man had little more than what was on his back. If her Bert was in prison, why wasn't Toohey?

For a long time Elizabeth was at a loss over what to do to get Albert out of prison. She spent many months exploring every possible avenue, refusing to quit. Then she met a noted Toronto barrister, Frank Regan, KC. After hearing the circumstances of Albert Dorland's conviction, Regan agreed to take the case. By now it was the autumn of 1933. Toronto — and Canada — were about to endure a scandal of monumental proportions.

Regan found William Toohey in a Mimico detention centre where he was awaiting transfer to the Guelph Reformatory to serve a sentence for theft. Just how Regan persuaded Toohey to come clean is not known. But the affidavit Toohey signed and which Regan submitted to W.H. Price, the attorney general of Ontario, was a bombshell.

Toohey said that when he and Dorland agreed to rob a bank — which Toohey said was Dorland's idea — he went straight to Alfred Cuddy, former commissioner of the Ontario Provincial Police. Because the targeted bank was in Toronto, Cuddy sent Toohey to the city police. Cuddy was already aware that Toohey had a history as an informer. He had once told the Hamilton police of a planned raid on a bank in that city. A constable was sent to stand guard in front of the bank. The holdup, if indeed one had been in the works, was called off.

The Toronto police did not do things so simply. According to Toohey, he met Chief Draper and Chief Detective Murray as well as other detectives at police headquarters and in Murray's house. The police told him to "swing along" with Dorland and keep them informed. When Toohey said he did not have the bus fare to go to Hamilton to bring Bird in on the plan, the police gave him the money out of their "stool pigeon" fund. When Toohey said he and Dorland didn't have enough money to buy the shotguns and shells, the police gave him money for that, too. These were only small payments of a few dollars each, but the police were nonetheless encouraging a criminal act.

Chief Draper himself warned bank manager J. Doherty of the impending holdup and had guns sent to the bank to arm the officers who would be there, waiting for the bandits. When Toohey took the rented car for a drive so he could buy cigarettes, he had stopped at police headquarters so the detectives could get a good look at the getaway car. The police told Toohey that when Dorland entered the bank, he was not to go in with him.

That Monday morning, when Toohey went into the bank, supposedly to case it, he asked manager Doherty if there were detectives in the bank. Doherty did not know who Toohey was. He asked, suspiciously, "Why do you ask?" In nervous anticipation of a robbery attempt, Doherty had sent a memo to the senior members of his staff.

> Mr. Smith and Mr. Murphy,
>
> Do not get your cash out for a while: several men are in the office now — police; they expect we will be held up. Just hold your heads and everything will be all right. If they come in, hold up your hands right away and do as you are told.
>
> Mr. Murphy — do not go out with your drafts today; just put the clearings through. Do your work in the regular way; do not get nervous; do not say one word about the above until I say so.

Toohey wasn't sure if there were police in the bank or not, so he left. There were in fact five officers on the premises, waiting out of sight for the first sign of a holdup. When Toohey supposedly phoned his wife, he actually called the police. He told them the bank would be robbed that afternoon at three o'clock.

Toohey broke the firing pin off his shotgun and then convinced Dorland to trade guns with him so Dorland would enter the bank with a useless weapon. When Dorland placed his hand on the handle of the bank door, he did not know that inside, five policemen were waiting with drawn guns. If he had entered that bank carrying a shotgun, he might well have walked into a hail of lead.

The men Dorland saw watching from the apartment window and the man with the newspaper were three of a half dozen or so policemen watching the bank. They had their eyes on Dorland, whom they expected to enter the bank. They had instructions not to interfere with Toohey if he ran off once Dorland was inside.

Everyone was caught by surprise when Dorland sensed a trap and did not enter the bank. Then the police riddled the would-be bandits' car, and it was a miracle that neither man was killed. That had really shaken Toohey up. No one was supposed to shoot at *him*!

At police headquarters Dorland and Toohey were both charged with conspiracy to rob a bank. Then someone quietly changed the charge on Toohey's arrest sheet to "vagrancy," and he was allowed to go. Later Chief Draper paid him $25 for his work as an informer. In all, Toohey had received $43 from the Toronto police. Doherty allegedly gave Chief Draper $100 for thwarting the robbery, apparently believing the money would go to the "agent." But Toohey didn't get that money.

As soon as the press got wind of Toohey's claims, newspaper editors churned out columns damning "Wild West police methods" and the "Americanization" of Canadian police. One editor likened the incident to the type of policing that existed in New York City and Chicago, "which no sane man would want." Another observed that the "star chamber method" of law had been banished from the British Empire for two hundred years.

The newspapers were raising a lot of disturbing questions. If the Toronto police knew in advance of the planned robbery — and Doherty confirmed that they did because Draper had warned him and even put officers in the bank — why didn't they just go to Dorland's apartment and arrest him? Possession of sawed-off shotguns, classified as "gangster weapons," would have been enough to have him packed off to Kingston. Why this dramatic stakeout with armed police inside and outside the bank, waiting for a pair of armed bandits? Wasn't that placing the public in unnecessary danger? Why had Toohey been released? Did the cops really give him money to buy guns? It was true that the detective riding on the running board had a leg injured when Dorland rammed the police car, but did that justify the officers firing so many rounds into the car? Did the suspects actually have guns in their hands? Were the officers in that police car not aware that Toohey was working *with* them when they came so close to killing him? Chief Draper dismissed reporters who tried to interview him, claiming to be too busy. Just about every alderman in Toronto got his name in the papers by demanding an inquiry.

Finally Chief Draper said a police commission would investigate the affair *in camera*. Regan would have none of it. He objected to the police department investigating itself behind closed doors. He also objected to being excluded from the hearings. Judge Coatsworth grumbled that the whole issue was being blown out of proportion — and all on the word of a known criminal like William Toohey. When Regan tried to question people who had given evidence at the enquiry, Coatsworth sent the lawyer a letter ordering him not to interfere with *his* witnesses. Meanwhile, at the Kingston Penitentiary there were disturbances over the terrible conditions there. Albert Dorland was one of those involved.

Regan was finally admitted to the hearings, which were presided over by Toronto Mayor William James Stewart. Regan still wasn't satisfied. He objected to Chief Draper being allowed to listen to testimony in a hearing that was concerned with his own conduct. He objected to Chief Draper moving amongst people in the room, whispering in ears as testimony was given. Regan also wanted all testimony made public.

Coatsworth fought tooth and nail to prevent the proceedings being made public. He said it would tarnish the reputation of Toronto's police department, which prided itself on being the best on the North American continent, declaring that, "it would be a very sorry day if our confidence in them were lost." But Regan had his way, and the press covered the police commission hearings.

For weeks during the winter of 1932–33 the public followed the ongoing drama of the Dorland case. There were stories of suppressed evidence and falsified police documents. Chief of Detectives Murray testified he was out of town the day Toohey claimed to have met him in his house. Toohey responded that he could describe the interior of Murray's house. Moreover, Regan had somehow come into possession of a small notebook in which Inspector Murray had jotted down information Toohey had given him about the planned robbery. Among Murray's notes was the following:

"To strike about 10:30 a.m., have two sawed-off shotguns ten guage, double barrel; bought them on York Street yesterday for $14.00."

Officers initially denied any wrongdoing on the part of the police. Then, under cross-examination some of their stories began to crack. Finally, one of them admitted they had instructions to "get" Dorland in the bank. Told to explain what he meant by that, the policeman said they had orders not to shoot unless it was necessary, but if they did shoot, they were to "make a good job of it." Another officer testified that the policemen in the bank "joked" about what would happen to Dorland when he came through the door with a shotgun in his hands. Further testimony revealed that Chief Draper told his men to keep quiet about the Dorland set up, not to even talk to their wives about it.

Regan said of the police, "They were going to treat Dorland just as Al Capone treated his victims. They were going to bring Dorland in in a dead wagon."

There were a lot of lapses of memory among the police officers who testified and much self-contradiction. Chief Draper was no exception. At one point he said he had never heard of Albert Dorland or William Toohey until the day of the thwarted bank robbery. But the evidence proved otherwise. When Draper complained that three years was a long time for him to remember something, Regan replied that three years was a long time for Dorland to be in prison. Later, Draper made insinuations that Dorland was a communist.

At times the exchanges became heated. When Mayor Stewart said he was going to get to the truth if he had to question every detective and sergeant on the police force, Judge Coatsworth said sarcastically, "Why not call every member of the force — the whole thousand of them?"

The mayor replied, "I shall, if you wish."

Later, a detective gave what was clearly a false answer to a direct question. Mayor Stewart scoffed, "Come now, you don't expect me to swallow that and get fat on it, do you?"

In the midst of the proceedings Toohey suddenly submitted a written retraction of his affidavit. He said everything he had formerly sworn to was a lie. He said he was now afraid of the police. He was having a difficult time in jail, too. Word had spread among the inmates in the Mimico detention centre that he was a stool pigeon and had set Dorland up for the cops. The only inmates who didn't threaten Toohey were the ones who shunned him. "My lot here is bad enough," Toohey wrote, "and further publicity will make it worse, not in regards to the personal [sic], but amongst the inmates."

Toohey was moved to the Guelph Reformatory where he was kept in protective custody. Regan examined Toohey's written retraction and noted that the language was not Toohey's. He wanted to know who had actually written it. Toohey insisted that his original statement was a lie and said he didn't care if he did time for perjury. But it was too late; the cat was out of the bag.

The commission hearings shifted venue to Kingston Penitentiary so Dorland could testify. Dorland shook his fetters at Draper and blamed the chief for his troubles.

"I would not be here if it was not for you. I wanted to work and you refused me a driver's licence, by which I could have earned my living. Then I was drawn into this situation." Dorland went on to say the bank robbery was Toohey's idea, and Toohey had talked him into it.

When the police commission finally completed its interviews and all the evidence was recorded, Ontario Premier George S. Henry reached the conclusion that something was definitely amiss with the Toronto Police Department as far as the Dorland case was concerned. He called for a full Royal Commission investigation. That meant heads were bound to roll. While the *Globe* angrily denounced what its editors considered a vendetta against a hero like Chief Draper, the *Toronto Daily Star* once again raised the question of General Draper's suitability for the position of chief of police.

The new series of hearings began on April 3 under Mr. Justice Kingstone. Once again the scandal captured banner headlines across the country, pushing aside news of Nazi persecutions of the Jews in Germany. Once again the public read about the "American" tactics General Draper had brought to the Toronto police and had used to frame Albert Dorland.

Toohey and Dorland were both taken to Toronto to testify. Toohey went from the Guelph Reformatory and was allowed to wear civilian clothes. Dorland went from Kingston, standing out on the train and in court in his prison uniform. The two were kept in cells near to each other as they awaited their turns on the witness stand. Toohey called out to Dorland, saying he hoped Albert had no hard feelings. Dorland replied that he only wanted Toohey to tell the truth.

The hearings carried on through much of the spring and summer of 1933. When the inquest wound up in early August, Mr. Justice Kingstone came to some shocking conclusions:

That Chief Draper did not tell the whole truth and had tried to conceal facts.

That the Toronto Police feared Toohey might disclose information embarrassing to the police.

That Toohey instigated the crime for which Dorland was sent to prison.

That the Toronto Police tried to protect themselves.

That the Toronto Police planned to get Dorland into the bank and then shoot him.

That Chief Draper could have, and should have, arrested Dorland much earlier.

That Chief Draper contributed to crime.

Yet, Chief Draper's head did not roll. Alex Murray's did. The chief of detectives was obliged to resign. Several other detectives were demoted. Judge Coatsworth had to resign from his position on the police commission. Four officers who had fired into Dorland and Toohey's car were indicted for "shooting with intent to do grievous bodily harm." They were eventually exonerated. There certainly were cries for General Draper's head, but the Chief rode out the storm, quite possibly because he had powerful friends in Queen's Park. He remained Toronto's chief of police until 1946.

Meanwhile, there was the matter of Albert Dorland, still behind bars in Kingston for what had been proven a frame-up. Now he faced charges for his participation in the prison riot. Regan said that was not right because Dorland shouldn't have been sent to prison. Elmore Philpott, speaking for the Cooperative Commonwealth Federation (CCF) — the predecessor of the New Democratic Party (NDP) — described the Dorland case as "one of the most important in the history of British justice in Canada." Further, he said it was "scandalous to sentence Dorland to a living death."

On August 31 Ottawa sent instructions to Kingston for Dorland to be released on parole the following day. The rioting charges were dropped. Before Dorland walked through the gates a free man, the warden advised him to keep out of Toronto if he wanted to avoid trouble. One guard simply said, "You'll be back."

Dorland went to the Kingston railway station. As he awaited the next train to Toronto, his grandmother pulled up in her car. As soon as she'd heard Albert was to be released she jumped into her car and drove all the way to Kingston so she could take her grandson home personally. "They won't frame Bert again," the indomitable

Elizabeth McKillop told reporters.

Dorland was the man of the hour. Photographers took pictures of him with his loving grandmother. Reporters asked him about life behind bars. They wanted to know what his plans were for the future. Dorland swore he had turned over a new leaf and had put the mistakes of his past behind him. He just wanted to earn an honest living and get on with his life. He said he did not even feel any enmity toward Chief Draper or William Toohey.

Dorland told the press how wonderful it was to be free after all those months locked up. He said that as he and his grandmother were driving from Kingston to Toronto, he looked out at the moonlight shining on Lake Ontario and thought of all the nights he had gazed at the lake from his cell window and yearned for freedom. Memories of those nights did not prove to be a deterrent for Albert Dorland.

July 16, 1934 — less than a year after Albert Dorland, Canada's most famous wronged man, had been released from prison. Just before noon three masked men armed with revolvers burst into the Bank of Montreal at Keele and St. Clair avenues in Toronto. One of them yelled, "Lie down on the floor and don't make a sound!"

Manager W.A. Moore and his staff, two men and a woman, did as they were told. No customers were in the bank. One bandit hauled Moore to his feet, shoved him into the vault and told him to open the safe. With a gun at his head, Moore obeyed. But he was nervous, and he fumbled as he tried to get the safe open. One of the gunmen said, "Plug him, plug him! Let him have it, Mac. We can't stay here all day."

The other robber told the frightened manager, "Don't worry about that. Do what you're told and you'll be all right. Just don't stall." While the bandit covering Moore rifled through the safe, a second robber emptied the cashiers' tills. The third outlaw kept watch at the door.

The gang grabbed $25,000 and then tried to lock the bank employees in the vault. But the bolt had been "thrown" for the day and wouldn't lock. The robbers dashed out of the bank with their loot, jumped into a car, and sped away. The robbery had taken barely two minutes. Witnesses later reported seeing the getaway car speeding north out of Toronto at eighty miles an hour.

A week later Detroit police, acting on a tip, burst into the apartment of a man named Ray Alderman, an American criminal who had served time in a Canadian prison for armed robbery before being deported to the United States. In Alderman's apartment the police found a pistol and a suitcase containing over $8,000 in Canadian money.

Alderman cracked under police interrogation. He confessed to the Toronto bank robbery and named his two accomplices. One was John Volkoff, a Montrealer who had once done a stretch in Quebec's St-Vincent-de-Paul Penitentiary for armed robbery. The other bandit — the leader of the trio, according to Alderman — was Albert Dorland!

Dorland and Volkoff were both arrested. Police found $1,000 from the Toronto robbery in Volkoff's apartment. They did not find any of the loot in Dorland's residence, but Albert Dorland was once again front-page news.

Dorland protested his innocence. He said the police were trying to frame him again. Elizabeth McKillop insisted her grandson was innocent. She claimed he'd been painting her house at the time of the robbery. She said the police had been hounding him since his release from prison. Frank Regan, too, said Chief Draper had plainclothes policemen shadowing Dorland wherever he went.

But this time there was no frame-up. When the getaway car — which had been stolen — was found, Dorland's fingerprints were on it. His fingerprints were also on a can of black paint that had been used to alter the numbers on the licence plates. Dorland was known to have associated with Alderman in Detroit and Volkoff in Montreal. Alderman had visited Dorland's cottage near Bala, Ontario. (Police searched the cottage and grounds for the rest of the robbery money but never did find it.) The police also discovered a telegram Dorland had sent to Alderman in Detroit just two days before the robbery, telling Ray to join him in Toronto. The Toronto police also found inconclusive evidence that in May Dorland might have been involved in the theft of $10,000 worth of silk from a Toronto warehouse.

After a much-publicized trial that lasted for two weeks in November 1935, a jury found Albert Dorland guilty of armed robbery and auto theft. A judge sentenced Dorland and his two accomplices to twelve years each in the Kingston Penitentiary. This time he would serve the full term. Dorland would spend a lot of nights looking out his cell window at Lake Ontario.

Kingston Penitentiary was the "Canadian Alcatraz." This picture was taken in 1919 by First World War air ace Billy Bishop. (Canada's Penitentiary Museum Collection, Kingston, Ontario)

When he was released from prison Dorland looked for another way to make a living. Bank robbery had not proven to be very lucky for him, so he turned to trafficking in narcotics, particularly heroin. This led to further encounters with the law, and another four-year stretch in the Kingston Pen. Dorland again said he'd been framed! In all, Dorland spent twenty-five years behind prison walls. A judge called Dorland "a big shot in the underworld." An RCMP official said Dorland was one of the most wanted criminals in Canada. The *Toronto Daily Star* named him "Canada's top pusher." Dorland allegedly was a main operator in a dope smuggling ring that stretched from Montreal to Vancouver.

In one bizarre episode that occurred on October 7, 1947, Dorland was snatched from his brother's Rosedale home. His wife frantically called the police and reported that her husband had been kidnapped and quite possibly murdered. Reporters hurried to Rosedale to get the latest on Canada's most notorious gangster since Rocco Perri, the bootlegger known as "the Canadian Al Capone."

Meanwhile, Dorland thought he was being "taken for a ride." However, the thugs who had grabbed him thought he would be carrying a lot of money. They were disappointed to discover he had only $50 on him. Less than an hour after the kidnapping, the hoodlums dropped Dorland off in front of his brother's house. The driver told the curious reporters, "Wise up and forget everything."

Several years later, in one of his arrests on narcotics charges, Dorland's bail was placed at $200,000. Dorland paid with two hundred crisp $100 bills. It was one of the largest cash bail payments in Toronto history.

Albert Dorland died at the age of sixty in Toronto's Princess Margaret Hospital on June 13, 1965. If he had indeed made a fortune dealing drugs, the money was gone. "He did nothing," a relative told a reporter for the *Globe & Mail*. "I kept him." Dead, Albert Dorland couldn't even say he'd been framed.

JOHN "RED" HAMILTON

RUNNING WITH DILLINGER

Most Canadians with an interest in crime history are familiar with the story of Alvin "Creepy" Karpis, the Canadian-born bank robber and kidnapper who ran with the notorious Barker Gang in the early 1930s. One of very few of the "Public Enemies" to be captured alive, Karpis spent many years in Alcatraz and other American prisons before he was finally paroled and deported to his native Canada. In 1971 Karpis collaborated with Canadian journalist Bill Trent on his autobiography *Public Enemy # 1* (US title, *The Alvin Karpis Story*). Though Karpis had committed all of his crimes in the United States, his book made him one of Canada's most infamous outlaws.

Not many Canadians, however, are aware that while Karpis and the Barkers were shooting up the American Midwest, another Canadian-born desperado was right-hand man to the most legendary of all the Dirty Thirties bandits, John Dillinger. Unlike Blackie Audett, whose story is told in a previous chapter, this man actually did run with some of the most desperate criminals of his time. He was involved in brazen bank robberies, spectacular escapes from the forces of law and order, and bloody shootouts. His final demise is still shrouded in mystery.

John "Red" Hamilton was born on August 27, 1898, in Byng Inlet, Ontario, a tiny community that is only a ghost town now on the shore of Georgian Bay. He was one of eight children in a family of Irish-German background. Hamilton's father, John Sr., was Canadian, apparently from Essex County, Ontario. His mother, Sarah (née Edmonds) was from New York. One of his brothers, Joseph Foye Hamilton, was also destined to become a criminal, and his grandfather, William Hamilton, would do time in jail for bootlegging. When John was still a young boy his family moved to Sault Ste. Marie, Michigan, still very much a frontier town just across the water from the Cana-

John "Red" Hamilton sits on the front bumper of a car in his days as a bootlegger running Canadian booze into the United States. (Ellen Poulsen)

dian Soo. Though he was just a child when he left Canada, John Hamilton would never really lose touch with the land of his birth. Family members believe he held dual Canadian-American citizenship.

Young Hamilton was a better than average student and even attended Sunday school. But his father died while John was still a boy, and he began to run wild. He loved hunting and was a crack shot. He would do almost anything on a dare. In one incident involving his sled and a speeding freight train, Hamilton lost parts of the middle and index fingers of his right hand. This earned him the nickname Three Fingered Jack. But because of his hair colour he was Red to most of his friends.

Hamilton dropped out of high school after the tenth grade. (One of his jail registration forms says he had an eighth-grade education. Another says sixth grade.) He worked at a variety of jobs, including cutting timber and sailing the Great Lakes on Canadian grain ships. In 1921 Hamilton married Mary Stevenson. Mary and Red had two sons, Howard and Orville. Hamilton supported his family by hunting, trapping, and working the timber camps. But Mary had expensive tastes, and that might have been part of the reason that Hamilton turned to crime. Mary also had four brothers, Alvia, John, George, and Joseph, who were thieves.

Prohibition was in effect, and like many other men looking for fast money, Hamilton got into bootlegging. While he did work at honest jobs such as carpentry, he also ran booze over the border from Canada. He was known to be associated with the owner of a liquor warehouse in Port Lambton, on the Ontario side of the St. Clair River.

In 1924 Hamilton was arrested in Detroit on a bootlegging charge. He told the police he had money in the bank with which he could pay his fine, if they would allow him to go and get it. The trusting officers let him go, and Hamilton did not return. This was the beginning of his life on the run. It was said he abandoned his wife and children. Actually, Mary left him and took the boys with her. She would die of cancer in 1930, and Hamilton's sons were taken in by their maternal grandmother.

In addition to rum-running, Hamilton was now a member of the Stevenson Gang. On July 20, 1925, he took part in his first-known robbery when he and his brothers-in-law stole a $33,000 payroll from the Lakey Foundry Company in Muskegon Heights, Michigan. On January 3, 1927, the Stevenson Gang raided a bank in Grand Rapids, Michigan, for $25,000. On March 15 of that year Hamilton and a fellow bootlegger named Raymond Lawrence — an ex-cop — attempted to rob a bank in South Bend, Indiana. They bungled the holdup and fled empty-handed. Police soon picked them up in an apartment occupied by Red's brother William. A neighbour had become suspicious when he saw Hamilton and Lawrence changing the Michigan licence plates on their car with Wisconsin plates and called the police. When the officers burst in, the bandits were eating supper and were not armed.

To Hamilton's disgust, Lawrence confessed to everything and fingered Red for the Grand Rapids robbery. Nonetheless, Hamilton joked with the police and complimented them on the speed with which they had solved the crime. Officers searched the apartment and found a revolver and a large roll of bills. Red's nephew, Wilton Hamilton, would later claim that he saw one of the officers pocket the money. The roll of bills never made it to court to be used as evidence.

Hamilton was sentenced to twenty-five years in the Indiana State Penitentiary at Michigan City. At some point he tried unsuccessfully to be transferred to a Canadian prison. In April 1928 Hamilton suffered an attack of appendicitis and underwent surgery. On January 27, 1930, the warden received a blunt telegram: "Tell John Hamilton his former wife Mary is dead."

In prison Hamilton became part of a clique led by Harry Pierpont, one of the most notorious bank robbers of the time. His band of hard cases included Charles "Fat" Makley and Russell Lee "Booby" Clark. On the fringes of this group was Homer Van Meter, whom Pierpont did not particularly like. All of these men had been sentenced to long terms behind bars. Red Hamilton had the reputation of being one of the toughest inmates in the prison, but he was generally the quiet type. His only infraction of prison rules was skipping rope in the machine shop.

In July 1929 a young convict named John Herbert Dillinger was transferred to Michigan City from the prison at Pendleton. In convict hierarchy Dillinger, who was doing time for a bungled grocery store robbery, was little more than a punk. But Pierpont and Van Meter had met Dillinger in Pendleton and liked him. Dillinger, who was actually a talented baseball player, had schemed to get himself transferred to Michigan City with the excuse that the prison had a good ball team. In fact, he wanted to hook up with Pierpont.

Red Hamilton and the other convicts in Harry Pierpont's circle of friends also took a liking to the charismatic Dillinger. Soon Pierpont and Hamilton were giving "Johnny" professional tips on the art of bank robbery. They had learned through their own experiences and by talking shop with other jailed bandits that for a holdup to have any chance of success it had to be timed, rehearsed, and planned down to the last detail.

John Dillinger, Public Enemy Number 1. (Tony Stewart)

Hamilton and Pierpont had a good reason for sharing their expertise with the relatively inexperienced Dillinger. He would be the first of the Pierpont clique to be eligible for parole. His friends wanted him to be their contact man on the outside once he was free. (Van Meter was actually scheduled to be released before Dillinger, but Pierpont didn't trust him and thought Dillinger was more reliable.)

Dillinger's most important assignment was to rob a string

of small-town banks selected by Pierpont and Hamilton to finance a major breakout from the Michigan City prison. Jail breaks usually worked only when bribe money was placed in the right hands and therefore tended to be costly. Moreover, the criminals who assisted in getting their "friends" out of the slammer and then hid them usually expected to be well paid for their help.

Dillinger had his own motive for going along with Pierpont and Hamilton. Aside from deserting the United States Navy, Dillinger had not had any serious confrontations with the law until he and another man tried to rob that grocery store. Dillinger's partner, a man with a long criminal record, had been given a light sentence. But the judge decided to make an example of young Dillinger and threw the book at him. He sent him into the hellish world of the Indiana prison system for ten to twenty years. As far as an embittered Dillinger was concerned, the state of Indiana owed him.

After serving nine brutal years for a petty crime, Dillinger was paroled in May 1933. If he had not been a hardened criminal when he went into prison, he was one now. It did not help Dillinger's anti-social attitude that authorities would not release him in time to see his ailing stepmother before she died.

Dillinger visited his father at the family farm, then went straight to work collecting the funds he needed to spring his friends. On June 10 he and two or three other men — one of whom might have been Van Meter — scooped $10,600 from a bank in New Carlisle, Ohio. Dillinger's first bank robbery went off without a hitch.

Dillinger discovered that the list of banks Pierpont and Hamilton had prepared for him was out of date, many of the banks having failed and closed their doors because of the Depression. In his quest to build up the escape fund he knocked over any business that was likely to have a cash register: a supermarket, a sandwich shop, a soda fountain. But Dillinger was learning the trade of banditry well. With the help of various accomplices, in a three-week period he held up ten banks in five states. The press began to take notice of the flamboyant, nattily dressed outlaw who vaulted over bank railings, was courteous to frightened female tellers, and seemed to gleefully thumb his nose at the police as he made his escape in a (stolen) fast car.

Dillinger's first attempt to break his pals out of prison failed. He wrapped three loaded guns in newspapers and tossed them over the prison wall. They landed in the athletic field where Pierpont was supposed to pick them up. But two other inmates saw the package. Hoping to gain favour with the prison administration, they told a deputy warden.

Dillinger then bribed the foreman of a Chicago thread-making factory to allow three automatic pistols to be hidden inside one of several barrels of thread being shipped to the prison's shirt factory. The top of the barrel containing the guns was marked with a crayon. Quite likely additional bribes prevented the barrels from being inspected as they entered the prison. Around September 24 an inmate named Walter Dietrich removed the guns from the thread barrels and hid them in the basement of the shirt factory. This, at least, was the version of the breakout story accepted by Dillinger biographer G. Russell Girardin. In another version, Walter Dietrich picked up the guns Dillinger tossed over the wall, and it was the guns in the thread barrel that were turned in to the guards.

However Dillinger managed to get the weapons into the prison, on September 26 just after 2:00 p.m., Pierpont and Clark told George H. Stevens, superintendent of the shirt factory, that he was wanted in the basement. When the unsuspecting Stevens went into the tunnel that led to the basement, Red Hamilton jammed a gun into his ribs and two other men seized him.

"Turn around, Stevens," Hamilton ordered. "We're going home and you're going to lead us out. There won't be any rough stuff if you just come along and mind your own business."

Minutes later Walter Dietrich lured assistant deputy superintendent Albert E. Evans into the same trap. He was followed by foreman Dudley Triplett. Almost at the start the breakout came close to being marked by tragedy.

Pierpont hated Evans because the official had been the cause of him being harshly disciplined. Now

Red Hamilton, the only bandit who belonged to both Dillinger gangs. (Tony Stewart)

Pierpont had the man at his mercy and wanted revenge. "Here's one that I settle with before I go," the convict said menacingly.

Evans no doubt thought he would be dead before another minute passed. But Hamilton grabbed Pierpont and said, "No killings! One shot and the whole penitentiary will know what's going on. We've got enough trouble ahead of us. Let's not make anymore for ourselves."

Pierpont snarled a few curses but decided not to murder Evans.

The three hostages were forced to walk with a group of ten prisoners who were in on the escape plot. Besides Pierpont, Hamilton, and Dietrich, whose guns were hidden by bundles of shirts, the escapees included Makley and Clark. The group walked the whole length of the prison yard without arousing the suspicions of the guards or other inmates.

At the first of the steel gates the jailbreakers had to pass through, Stevens told Frank Swanson, the guard, "Open the gate. These men are armed and they will kill us if you don't."

Swanson opened the gate and then was forced to join the procession of convicts and hostages. The same thing happened at the second gate, guarded by Guy Burklow. However, at the third and last gate where Fred Wellnitz was on duty, there was trouble. Wellnitz refused to co-operate, so the convicts beat him senseless. Evans protested this violence and was given a working over himself. The convicts took the keys from Wellnitz's pocket and unlocked the gate.

Now the escapees and their captives were in the prison administration building. The convicts rounded up eight clerks, including two women, and locked them in a vault. When seventy-two-year-old Finley Carson did not move quickly enough, one of the gunmen shot him in the stomach and the leg. Fortunately the old man was not killed. The convicts tried to force Lawrence Mutch, superintendent of prison industries, to open the door to the prison arsenal. Mutch would not co-operate and was given a savage beating. The escapees did not see chief clerk Howard Crosby, who was under his desk with a telephone. He called the local police station, whispering, "There's trouble out here at the prison. Send policemen and guns."

It was now pouring rain. The ten escapees fled through the prison's main entrance. Dietrich and three other men commandeered the car of a sheriff who was just entering the prison. Pierpont, Hamilton, Clark, Makley, and two other cons named Ed Shouse and James

Jenkins ran across the street to a gas station where they pointed guns at proprietor Joe Pawleski. "Give us the keys to your car or we'll blow your brains out!"

The startled Pawleski turned and ran. One of the convicts yelled, "Give it to him, give it to him!" One or two of the others fired three shots at the running man. Pawleski later told the *Indianapolis Star*, "They acted like crazy men, and I guess that's why their aim was so poor.

"They fired three shots. One went through the sleeve of my overall jacket. The other two went past my head, or else I outran them."

The jail breakers flagged down a passing car, forced a man and two women out at gunpoint and then roared away.

Only now was a general alarm raised at the prison. Police converged on the area and roadblocks were set up everywhere. Panic swept through Indiana as bulletins spread the unbelievable news of the breakout. One radio station did not consider the news dramatic enough by itself. Using stock sound effects of gunfire and sirens, the station presented "live" bullet-by-bullet coverage of the event until police put a stop to it. Vigilantes patrolled the highways and byways. Several of the escapees were soon recaptured, and Jenkins was shot dead. But Hamilton, Pierpont, and friends made their getaway.

In the days immediately after the breakout the gang kept on the move, hiding out in various towns and cities, including Chicago, Cincinnati, and Indianapolis. They needed money, lots of it, and fast. They had not only their own expenses to cover — and life on the run could be costly indeed — but they also owed a favour to the author of their liberty. John Dillinger himself was back in jail.

In Dayton, Ohio, Dillinger had met Mary Jenkins Longnaker, a divorcee and the sister of the late James Jenkins. Dillinger was smitten by the young woman and hung around Dayton a little more than he should have. Captain Matt Leach of the Indiana State Police, a dedicated officer who would prove tireless in his pursuit of Dillinger and his gang, got wind of this. He passed the information on to the Dayton police. The cops in Dayton raided the Longnaker house on September 25 and caught Dillinger completely by surprise. The bandit was heavily armed but had no chance to use any of the six guns he had on him.

Captain Leach had hoped Dillinger would be returned to Indiana. But Ohio wanted him for bank robbery. Dillinger had pulled one of his jobs in Allen County, so he was transferred to the jail in the town of Lima. He would not remain there long.

On October 3 Hamilton, Pierpont, Makley, Clark, and Shouse robbed the First National Bank in St. Mary's, Ohio (Makley's hometown) of $14,000. On October 19 Hamilton, Pierpont, Makley, Shouse, and a hoodlum named Harry Copeland who had met Dillinger shortly after the latter's parole, raided the little county jail in Lima and sprang Dillinger. Sheriff Jesse Sarber was unarmed when the outlaws entered his office, but Pierpont shot him in the stomach. Then Makley pistol-whipped him hard enough to lay his skull bare. Sheriff Sarber died the next day. Mrs. Sarber, who had been in the sheriff's office when the gang burst in, identified a police photo of Pierpont. It did not take the police long to figure out who his accomplices were. On November 3 Harry Pierpont, Ed Shouse, Harry Copeland, and Red Hamilton were indicted for the murder of Jesse Sarber. It was the blow to the head Makley had given the sheriff, rather than Pierpont's bullet, that proved fatal. Newspaper editors with a flair for sensationalism dubbed the outlaws "The Terror Gang." To crime historians they would be "The First Dillinger Gang."

Cool Professionalism

At this point John Dillinger was not actually the leader of the gang, though he certainly displayed leadership qualities that could have been put to better use in more legitimate endeavours. According to Dillinger biographer Jeffery S. King in *The Rise and Fall of the Dillinger Gang*, "Dillinger was able to promote trust, loyalty, and confidence among the gang's members, as well as restore calm when they became angry." This was of vital importance in a gang that included a man like Pierpont, who was daring, but dangerously impulsive.

If anyone could be singled out as the leader at this stage, it would be Pierpont. (Matt Leach thought he could create jealousy in the bunch by having the newspapers call it "the Dillinger Gang," but the ruse didn't work. Pierpont didn't care what the papers said.) But for advice, the bandits turned to the eldest of the group, Red Hamilton. For a man with such a reputation as a tough guy, Hamilton was quiet, easygoing, and generally well-mannered. He was somewhat more stable and mature than the others and seemed to get along with just about everybody he met. J. Edgar Hoover believed Hamilton was the "brains" of the gang.

This was the heyday of the "automobile bandits"; a relatively brief era when gun-toting crooks like Charles "Pretty Boy" Floyd, the Barker/Karpis Gang, and Lester Gillis — alias "Baby Face Nelson" — stuck up banks and then roared out of town in fast cars. The world was in the grip of the Great Depression, and financial institutions like banks were thoroughly hated. For this reason many people regarded the bank robbers as modern-day Robin Hoods, which they certainly were not.

One man who saw the automobile bandits from a different perspective was J. Edgar Hoover, head of the Federal Division of Investigation, which would soon be renamed the Federal Bureau of Investigation (FBI), with considerably expanded powers. What Hoover saw in the likes of Dillinger, Floyd, Nelson, and the rest of the bank-robbing fraternity was opportunity.

At the time Hoover's department was small, and there were relatively few crimes that would bring federal agents onto a felon's trail. Major offenses like bank robbery and even murder came under state jurisdictions. But Hoover was a megalomaniac with an insatiable hunger for power, and he knew how to manipulate the situation so he could get it. By seeing to it that the bank robbers got much more publicity than they deserved and by building up a bunch of gun-toting hoodlums into masterminds of crime who threatened the very security of the nation, Hoover would make himself and his department look like crime-fighting heroes, if and when he got the chance to go after them.

Also, by turning the public's attention toward the bank robbers, Hoover kept it from focusing on the considerably larger problem of organized crime. Hoover publicly denied that organized crime existed in America, even though the loot taken by bank robbers was small change compared to the millions of dollars that disappeared through graft and corruption. It was convenient for Hoover to dismiss the existence of organized crime, because he was incapable of doing much about it. It was easier to go after the bank robbers, especially since his agents, and not he, were the ones who would be shot at. John Dillinger would become the first criminal to have the dubious honour of being called "Public Enemy Number One." The names of men like Red Hamilton became household words because of their association with this highly publicized outlaw.

Nonetheless, the Dillinger gang approached the art of bank robbery with cool professionalism. Not for them the poorly planned, blood-soaked antics of Bonnie and Clyde, whom Dillinger criticized as rank amateurs who gave bank robbery a bad name. A Dillinger gang stickup was usually well-thought-out and well-timed. The men studied the banks and getaway routes. They would have substitute cars waiting at strategic locations. While pulling a robbery they would — as far as it was possible — avoid unnecessary violence. Some of their jobs, in fact, were "set up," meaning bank managers were in on it.

Between jobs the gang kept a low profile. If the men drank at all, they drank beer, abstaining from hard liquor. As crime historian Ellen Poulsen explains in *Don't Call Us Molls: Women of the John Dillinger Gang*, the wives and girlfriends of the bank robbers were essential in helping them live their day-to-day lives. The women rented the houses and apartments they used as hideouts. They bought food, clothing, and other necessities. Besides being the outlaws' lovers, they were cooks, nurses, and liaisons between their men and other underworld figures.

Dillinger's girlfriend was Evelyn "Billie" Frechette, daughter of a Menominee Native mother and a French-Canadian father. Patricia Cherrington, a nightclub dancer whose husband was in prison for mail robbery, was romantically involved with Harry Copeland. Later she would be attached to Red Hamilton. Mary Kinder, also married to a man who was serving time, was hopelessly in love with Harry Pierpont. Following the jailbreak, Russell Clark was soon reunited with his wife, Opal — who was also Pat Cherrington's sister.

After liberating Dillinger, the gang established headquarters in Chicago. They had several bank robberies planned, but first they wanted to increase their firepower. They did something that not many bandit gangs would even consider. They robbed not just one but *two* police stations!

On October 14 the gang hit the police station in Auburn, Indiana. They locked the two officers on duty in a cell, then cleaned out the gun cabinet. Seven days later they raided the Peru, Indiana, police station. Harry Pierpont held a gun on the four surprised officers and coldly said, "I haven't killed anyone in a week, and I'd just as soon shoot one of you as not. Go ahead and get funny." None of the policemen tried to be a hero. The bandits locked them in the basement and then helped themselves to the cops' weapons and other equipment. From the two robberies the outlaws got an assortment of pistols, rifles, shotguns, machine guns, bulletproof vests, badges, and enough ammunition for a small army.

On October 23 the gang swept into Greencastle, Indiana. Their target was the Central National Bank, which Dillinger and Pierpont had scouted out a few days earlier. Now, with Clark waiting at the wheel of the getaway car and Red Hamilton posted as a lookout at the door, Dillinger, Makley, and Pierpont went in to make the withdrawal. (Shouse might also have been with them.) Fat Charlie held a stopwatch. Pierpont hauled a machine gun out from under his overcoat. "Keep your hands at your sides and don't move. We're not advertising," he said. When the bank staff and customers had been crowded into the vault room, Dillinger made his trademark dramatic leap over the railing separating the lobby from the tellers' area. Pierpont was right behind him. The pair filled a sack with $18,428 in cash and $56,300 in bonds. There was still money on the counter when Makley shouted, "It's five minutes!"

Dillinger and Pierpont immediately stopped grabbing loot and vaulted back over the railing. Police would be bewildered that the robbers had left so much money behind. But the Dillinger bunch knew that getting greedy and taking too much time got bank robbers caught.

A little incident that occurred during the holdup became part of the gang's legend. Dillinger saw a farmer standing by a teller's cage, with a small amount of money on the counter in front of him. He asked, "That your money or the bank's?"

"Mine." The farmer replied.

"Keep it," Dillinger said. "We only want the bank's."

The story would add to the myth that John Dillinger was an American Robin Hood. Years later the scene would be re-enacted in the 1967 film *Bonnie and Clyde*, with Warren Beatty's Clyde Barrow replacing Dillinger as the bank robber with a conscience. The real Clyde Barrow, in a similar situation, in all likelihood would have taken the farmer's money.

Another incident was probably somewhat embarrassing to Red Hamilton. In the confusion of the early moments of the stickup, an elderly woman, unnoticed by the bandits inside the bank, went out the front door. Hamilton stopped her and told her to go back inside. In a thick foreign accent the old woman told the bandit, "I go to Penney's and you go to hell." Then she went on her way. Had it been a man, Hamilton might have slugged him to the ground, as one of the robbers did to an unfortunate male customer who started to enter the bank just as they were leaving. But Red didn't quite know what to do when an old lady refused to be intimidated. Perhaps the woman was fortunate that it was Hamilton, and not Pierpont, standing watch at the door.

By the time police arrived at the bank, the bandits were long gone. Using back roads they had already scouted, they easily avoided roadblocks and made a clean getaway. The Greencastle robbery was the biggest haul any of them had ever made.

The gang's next big robbery came on November 20. By this time Ed Shouse, never really "in tight" with the others, had been kicked out of the gang. He had allegedly made a play for Dillinger's girlfriend, Billie Frechette; had tried to talk the loyal Hamilton into striking out with him on a bank robbery of their own; and in a dispute over money had made the almost suicidal mistake of pulling a gun on Pierpont. The other gang members tossed Shouse some cash and Dillinger told him, "Get your ass out!"

On this occasion the target was the American Bank and Trust Company in Racine, Wisconsin. Dillinger, Makley, Pierpont, Hamilton, and Clark all went into the bank. They came out with $27,789. This time the robbery was not without bloodshed. Makley shot an uncooperative teller, wounding him in the elbow and hip. Then he shot and badly wounded police sergeant Wilbur Hansen, who had responded to an alarm that the bank was being robbed. The gang seemed to have forgotten the policy of keeping violence and bloodshed to a minimum.

A crowd formed outside the bank, so the bandits exited with several hostages to discourage police from shooting at them or giving chase. When the hostages were released a few miles from town, Pierpont gave his coat to a woman who complained of the cold. Evidently, he could be as gallant as he was vicious.

The Dillinger gang is believed to have been responsible for the December 13, 1933, robbery of Chicago's Unity Trust and Savings Bank (though in this case the identity of the thieves was not certain). The bank itself had been closed for some time, a victim of the Depression, but the safety deposit boxes were still in use. Makley allegedly stood watch out front, disguised as Santa Claus, with a pot in which passersby even dropped some charitable donations. Hidden in the bottom of the pot was a pair of .45 pistols. Dillinger, Hamilton, and Pierpont, armed with hammers and cold chisels, went inside. They trussed up the lone attendant, then went to work on the safety deposit boxes. Just how much they got in cash, bonds, and jewellery is uncertain. Estimates have ranged from $8,700 to more than $200,000.

If the safety-deposit box heist had been something of a lark, what happened the following day was not. It would be a sharp reminder to the public that the Dillinger bunch were not folk heroes, but desperate men. Red Hamilton had been seeing a waitress named Elaine Dent. She had just lost her job and believed herself lucky to meet this "businessman" named John Smith. He put her up in an apartment, made a down payment on a shiny green roadster for her, bought her presents, and seemed to have loads of spending money. He told her he came from a wealthy family. The new car needed to have a fender straightened, and on December 14 Hamilton and Elaine took it to a garage on Chicago's Broadway. Then they went to a movie.

The police had their ears to the ground, trying to get a lead on the Dillinger gang. Some hangers-on, like Harry Copeland, had already been arrested. That December 14 Chicago police got a tip that one of the bandits had left a green roadster at a Broadway garage. Detective Sergeant William Shanley, recipient of a hero's award for bravery in the line of duty, was sent to investigate. With him were patrolmen Martin Mullen and Frank Hopkins. Shanley and Hopkins entered the garage, while Mullen waited in the patrol car. They found the green roadster but no sign of any desperadoes. It was nearing the end of their shift. Shanley sent Hopkins to tell Mullen he could take the car back to the station so it would be available for the night squad. Mullen had just left when Hamilton walked in with Elaine Dent on his arm. Shanley did not know who the man was, but considering that he had been warned his quarry might be a member of the Dillinger gang, he did not act wisely.

"Is this your car?" the detective asked.

"No," Hamilton said. "It belongs to my wife."

Elaine pulled the licence receipt from her purse and gave it to the officer. Then Shanley told Hamilton, "Keep your hands out of your pockets."

He began to pat Hamilton's pants pockets, searching for a gun. Hamilton swiftly grabbed a pistol from a shoulder holster and shot the detective twice point-blank. Shanley collapsed in a pool of blood, gasping, "I'm shot! Call the police." He would be dead within twenty minutes.

Officer Hopkins heard the shots and rushed back to the garage. He saw a man running from the garage, dragging a woman with him. Immediately the officer gave chase. The man released the woman, who was clearly slowing him down, and sprinted across a vacant lot. He got away, but Hopkins caught the woman.

Elaine Dent tearfully told the police she had no idea her gentleman friend was a criminal. "He was good to me, bought me this coat and the car … I thought he was a rich man's son … He used to take two baths a day, and he never said any swear words."

At first the police thought the killer was Pierpont. But when Elaine Dent told them the man had three fingers on one hand, they knew it was Red Hamilton. Chicago suddenly became too hot for the gang.

The bandits fled Chicago by separate routes, agreeing to meet in Chattanooga, Tennessee. From there they made their way to Daytona Beach, Florida, where they rented cottages by the ocean. Chicago, meanwhile, was in an uproar over the murder of William Shanley, one of a dozen Chicago cops to be slain in the line of duty that year.

The Chicago Police Department formed a special Dillinger Squad, whose sole purpose was to bring the gang to bay, by any means possible. It was made up of forty picked men led by Captain John Stege. These officers practically turned the Windy City upside down in their hunt for the outlaws. They nabbed a few hoodlums who were known to have associated with the Dillinger gang, and they bagged ex-gang member Ed Shouse.

Acting on a tip that Dillinger, Hamilton, and Pierpont were in an apartment on Farwell Avenue, Stege and men from his Dillinger Squad raided the apartment. They burst in with guns blazing and riddled the three male occupants. The dead men were in fact criminals, but they were not Dillinger, Hamilton, and Pierpont. Even so, Chicago Mayor Edward J. Kelly praised Stege and his men for a job well done.

On December 28 the state of Illinois issued a list of the twenty-one most wanted Public Enemies. The first five names were John Dillinger, Harry Pierpont, John Hamilton, Charles Makley, and Russell Clark. Pierpont's girlfriend Mary Kinder was number nine. Dillinger associate Homer Van Meter was eighteen. Number twenty-one was Baby Face Nelson.

Meanwhile, the Dillinger bunch were enjoying a vacation in Florida. They fished, swam, rode horses, went to movies, and shopped. They listened to the radio and read newspapers and laughed at reports that had them sighted all over the country. On New Year's Day the men allowed themselves the luxury of getting drunk. They celebrated the arrival of 1934 by firing their machine guns at the ocean. The noise just blended in with the fireworks their neighbours were setting off.

During the first two weeks of January the bandits left Daytona Beach, departing at different times and taking different routes. They arranged to rendezvous in Tucson, Arizona. It was around this time the robbery that is still a source of dispute among crime historians took place. On the afternoon of January 15, two bandits armed with machine guns entered the First National Bank of East Chicago, Indiana. They were identified as John Dillinger and Red Hamilton. They looted the bank of $20,376. Outside they got into a gunfight with police. An officer named William Patrick O'Malley hit the man identified as Dillinger four times, but the bandit was wearing a bulletproof vest. The robber returned fire and put eight machine gun slugs through O'Malley's body, killing him. The killing might even have been unintentional. The bandit seemed to be shooting at O'Mally's legs, and the officer either fell or dove into the stream of machine gun bullets.

Before the outlaws could reach their car, Hamilton was shot seven times in the hand, arm, shoulder, and pelvis. The other outlaw could have abandoned him, but did not. He helped the wounded man into the car and then sped away.

The police wanted that other outlaw to be John Dillinger. J. Edgar Hoover certainly wanted the public to see Dillinger as a murderer as well as a thief. But Dillinger and other gang members would always deny he was in East Chicago that day. Billie Frechette and Mary Kinder, who had no reason to lie, would swear to the end of their lives that Dillinger was not in East Chicago. It is not certain just when Dillinger left Florida, but if he was still there on the fourteenth, as some claim, could he have driven all the way to East Chicago overnight, on 1934 roads, and in an automobile of that period?

Some crime historians believe the robbery was pulled by Red Hamilton and an unidentified accomplice, and that it was Hamilton, not Dillinger, who shot Officer O'Malley. Nonetheless, the killing was officially laid to Dillinger's charge. For all the violence associated with Dillinger's criminal career, this was the only killing for which he was personally held accountable.

Whoever the bandit with Hamilton was, he got the wounded man to Chicago and wired Pat Cherrington to meet them. After a lengthy search they found a doctor who was willing to treat Hamilton's wounds and ask no questions — for $5,000! Then they got rooms in an apartment hotel where Pat could nurse the injured man back to health. Thus it was that Red Hamilton was not with the gang when disaster struck in Tucson. It was also at this time that Pat began to fall for the red-headed bandit.

Disaster in Tucson

The outlaws had decided to extend the vacation they'd been enjoying in Florida, and the nightclubs and gambling dens in Tucson and across the Mexican border in Nogales looked inviting. Charles Makley, Russell Clark, and his wife, Opal, arrived about January 10. They attracted attention by being a little too free with their money. Someone tipped the police about the suspicious big spenders.

Then on January 23 a fire broke out at the Congress Hotel where they were staying. Afraid that firemen or police would look in the big box containing their guns, Makley and Clark convinced a couple of fire fighters to rescue their property. Once the box was safely out of the hotel, Makley gave the obliging firemen a $50 tip. The firemen were immediately suspicious. There was a depression on! Who could afford to give a tip that was more than many people's weekly paycheque? The following day one of the firemen saw pictures of the

Dillinger gang in a detective magazine and recognized Makley and Clark. He called the police.

That same day, the twenty-fourth, Dillinger and Billie Frechette rolled into town and checked into the motor court Pierpont and Mary Kinder had been staying at since January 16. No one had any idea that the Tucson police had been alerted and were on the move. In a series of well-orchestrated raids the policemen surprised and arrested the outlaws one by one. There was no gunfire and little bloodshed. Clark was roughed up when he resisted arrest. One policeman suffered a broken finger when Opal slammed a door on his hand. Dillinger was the last to be taken. He was in his car when officers surrounded it. He moved his hand toward his gun, but stopped when a cop ordered, "Reach for the moon, or I'll cut you in two!" Dillinger expressed embarrassment that he had been captured by "hick" policemen.

This was the end of the line for Pierpont, Makley, and Clark. In the Lima, Ohio, courthouse, which was protected by sandbag defences, machine guns, the National Guard and even patrolling aircraft, they were tried for the murder of Sheriff Jesse Sarber and found guilty. Pierpont would die in the electric chair. Makley was also condemned but was shot dead in a failed jail break. Lucky Boobie Clark escaped the death sentence but was packed off to prison for life. He died at the age of seventy on Christmas Eve 1968, five months after being paroled.

For John Dillinger the story was far from over. He was flown to Indiana to stand trial for the murder of Officer O'Malley. He was lodged in what was supposed to be an escape-proof jail in the town of Crown Point. The outlaw had achieved celebrity status in the media, not only in the United States, but in Canada, Britain, and other countries around the world. News of his arrest made headlines everywhere and his picture was all over the front pages of newspapers. Dillinger was even "captured" in a few moments of newsreel film that would become famous as the only footage known to have been taken of the notorious bank robber.

Reporters flocked around Dillinger. Among other things, they wanted his comments on other members of the gang. When someone asked him about John Hamilton, Dillinger (knowing Hamilton was alive and convalescing in Chicago) said:

"Poor Red! He died from the wounds he received in East Chicago. Caught a whole flock of bullets in his stomach. I wasn't with him when he got it, but one of the boys told me about it. I think they dumped his body in the Calumet River. Hamilton has some kids, and before he died he sent me some money to take to them. That was the dough that was in the sacks that the Tucson police took away from me."

It was in Dillinger's best interest to let the police think Red Hamilton was dead. He did not intend to stay in the Crown Point jail for long. Once he was out he would need help so he could grab enough loot to enable him to skip the country. With Pierpont, Clark, and Makley beyond reach, Dillinger's best hope lay with the trusty Canadian outlaw.

On March 3, 1934, John Dillinger made one of crime history's most sensational escapes when he broke out of the Crown Point jail using a wooden gun. He stole the sheriff's car and headed for Chicago. When Dillinger crossed the state line from Indiana to Illinois in a stolen car, he broke a federal law. Now J. Edgar Hoover's agents would be after him.

The escape stunned the nation and brought about a massive investigation. Dillinger undoubtedly had help, and somebody on the jail staff was almost certainly bribed. But who was responsible officially remains a mystery. In discussing the escape with his lawyer, Louis Piquett, Dillinger said it was Red Hamilton who set things in motion. He convinced Homer Van Meter, Dillinger's old pal from the Indiana State Prison, and Van Meter's bank-robbing partner Baby Face Nelson to advance the money needed for bribes. Hamilton and Dillinger would repay them with loot from future bank robberies.

While authorities seethed over the jail break, and people were "sighting" Dillinger all over the United States and in places as far apart as Montreal and Mexico's Yucatán, the outlaw was in St. Paul, Minnesota, attaching himself to another gang. This group, often called "The Second Dillinger Gang," included Homer Van Meter and two other experienced bank robbers, Tommy Carroll and Eddie Green. Red Hamilton had recovered enough from his wounds to go back to work. Then there was Baby Face Nelson!

At five foot four and with boyish features, Nelson was one nasty little man. He believed a gun made him a big shot, and he did not hesitate to use it. Men like Dillinger and Hamilton would shoot in self-defence or if they were cornered. Baby Face killed because he liked it. Dillinger detested Nelson as a trigger-happy punk. But he needed the diminutive killer to help him loot a few banks. Nelson, for his part, resented the fact that Dillinger, and not he, was the bandit the newspapers called Public Enemy Number One.

On March 6, only three days after the spectacular escape, the outlaws hit the National Bank and Trust Company in Sioux Falls, South Dakota, and made off with about $49,000. Nelson was delighted because he had shot a policeman (not fatally). On March 13 the gang struck again, but this time things did not go smoothly.

The First National Bank of Mason City, Iowa, had a quarter of a million dollars in the vault, and Dillinger and company planned to clean it out. But when the bandits burst in with shouts of "Hands up! Everybody on the floor!" bank president Willis Bagley locked himself in his office. He had the only key to the vault. Then a guard in a bullet-proof cage above the lobby fired a tear-gas grenade that struck Eddie Green in the back. Green machine-gunned the cage and the guard was wounded by bullets that went in through his gun slot.

Outside, Baby Face Nelson stood guard. A man named R.L. James approached on the sidewalk, and Nelson told him to stop. James apparently did not hear, so Nelson shot him in the leg twice. The whole town's attention was now on the bank.

Tear gas was swirling through the bank. Dillinger, Van Meter, and Green were cleaning out the tellers' drawers. Hamilton pushed a cashier named Harry Fisher toward a steel gate leading to the vault and told him to open it. Fisher stepped into the vault, but before Hamilton could follow him, Fisher clanged the gate shut. Hamilton told Fisher to open the gate again, but Fisher said he didn't have the key and could not open the gate from his side. He began to pass Hamilton bundles of $1 bills through the bars. Hamilton could see stacks of bills of larger denominations and told Fisher to give him those. Fisher kept handing him the bundles of ones.

Finally Van Meter shouted, "Let's go!"

Hamilton told Fisher to give him the big bills or he'd shoot him. Fisher responded by passing out more singles. Van Meter was getting frantic now, anxious to get out of there. Hamilton finally had to give up on Fisher (who was lucky he wasn't dealing with Baby Face Nelson). "It's hell to leave all that money in there," Hamilton said, as he joined the others with his sack full of about $20,000 in $1 bills.

Dillinger exited the bank with a line of hostages. When he saw Mr. James bleeding on the sidewalk, Dillinger growled at Nelson, "Did you have to do that?" Baby Face replied with a shrug.

Waving his machine gun, Dillinger herded his captives toward a car in which Tommy Carroll was waiting at the wheel. From a third-floor window of the bank building, a local judge named John Shipley aimed an old pistol and fired. The bullet struck Dillinger in the right shoulder. The bandit wheeled around, ready to cut loose with his tommy gun, but Shipley had ducked out of sight.

Dillinger made the hostages move in closer around him as Green, Van Meter, and Nelson dashed for the car. Then Hamilton came out of the bank and hurried to join the others. The judge fired again and wounded Hamilton in the right shoulder.

With Dillinger and Hamilton both bleeding, the outlaws forced the hostages to stand on the car's running boards and back bumper, making it impossible for the police to shoot. The car moved slowly through town, watched by hundreds of people. When a police car began to follow at a distance, Nelson shot at it with a high-powered rifle, forcing the officers to turn back. At the edge of town the outlaws released a few hostages, coated the road with carpet nails to flatten the tires of pursuing police cars, and continued on. Two hours and many miles later, they released the last hostages and headed for St. Paul. They had come away with a tidy $52,000, but as far as the robbers were concerned they were $200,000 short. "I should have killed that man," Hamilton grumbled. In St. Paul they forced a reluctant doctor to patch up the holes in Dillinger and Hamilton. The wounds, it turned out, were superficial.

The bandits now decided to split up for a while. Nelson went off to kill a man as a favour to some hoodlum friends — for which he was also being well paid. Dillinger allegedly made a secret visit to Canada, crossing the border somewhere along the St. Clair River. Wherever he'd been, by mid-March he and Billie Frechette were at an apartment they kept in Minneapolis. They were often visited by Eddie Green, Homer Van Meter, and Red Hamilton and Pat Cherrington. These visits by suspicious-looking men, often at strange hours, worried the building's landlady. On March 30 she called the police. That night two of Hoover's agents staked out the building. In the apartment were Dillinger, Billie, Hamilton, Pat, and Charlie Makley's wife, Opal.

In the morning Hamilton left to take Pat and Opal grocery shopping. At about ten o'clock one of the agents entered the building and knocked on Dillinger's door. At the same time Homer Van Meter arrived. What followed was a wild gun battle, with cops and robbers blasting away at each other while Billie tried to throw a few things into a suitcase. Dillinger, Billie, and Van Meter escaped. The only casualty was Dillinger, who'd been shot in the leg. Once again he had to seek out a doctor who would patch him up and keep his mouth shut about it.

When Hamilton and the other women returned from their shopping trip, they saw a crowd in front of the apartment building. Pat got out of the car and asked people what was going on. As soon as she learned the news she hurried back to the car and Hamilton drove away.

Red and Pat sent Opal to Detroit, then scurried from one hideout to another before landing at a tourist camp near Nashville, where they shared a cottage with Van Meter. On the night of April 10 the men went into town to buy a few things. They were sitting in their car drinking soda pop when a police officer approached and asked them to identify themselves. They gave false names, and the cop asked for credentials. Red Hamilton shoved the muzzle of a machine gun in the policeman's face and said, "Here's our credentials! You better get in your car and get away."

The startled officer made a hasty retreat. So did Hamilton and Van Meter. They picked up Pat Cherrington and got out of Nashville. That was what outlaws on the run called being "jumped up."

Meanwhile, Hoover's agents had tracked down Eddie Green in St. Paul, Minnesota. The bandit was unarmed when he walked into their ambush, but the agents shot him down without warning. They had orders from above that the men in the Dillinger gang were not to be taken alive!

On April 7 Dillinger visited his father's farm at Mooresville, Indiana. He told his father that he would soon be going on a long trip, and the family would not have to worry about him anymore. Amazingly, agents watching the farm knew nothing of the visit.

On April 17, Dillinger, Hamilton, and Pat Cherrington showed up at the home of Hamilton's sister, Mrs. Anna Steve, in Sault Ste. Marie. The men wore bulletproof vests and were armed to the teeth.

The fugitives had something to eat, showed off their guns and bullet wounds, then drove off into the night. Not until the following day did a neighbour inform the local sheriff. Hoover's men soon showed up, and though they had no search warrant, they ransacked Anna's house.

On April 20 Dillinger, Hamilton, Nelson, Van Meter, Carroll, and a hood named Pat Reilly drove to an isolated Wisconsin lodge called Little Bohemia. With them were their girlfriends (except Billie Frechette, who had been arrested) and Nelson's wife Helen. They were looking forward to a few days of rest and relaxation before they pulled their next big job. A full account of the debacle that occurred at Little Bohemia would require a lengthy chapter on its own, so in short:

Hoover received a tip that the Dillinger gang was at Little Bohemia. A squad of agents led by Melvin Purvis went there in hopes of bagging the lot of them in one fell swoop. They struck on Sunday, April 22, pouring a fusillade of lead into the building. Not only did the agents fail to kill or catch a single bandit — all of whom fled into the woods and escaped — they also killed an innocent man and seriously wounded two others. Baby Face Nelson, in the course of his escape, killed one agent and wounded another agent and a local policeman. Little Bohemia was one of the most badly bungled assignments in the history of American law enforcement. The only people arrested were the outlaws' women, with the exception of Pat Cherrington, who had gone into town that day. J. Edgar Hoover, who had announced to the press that his department was about to nail the Dillinger Gang, looked like a fool.

The morning after the Little Bohemia fiasco, Dillinger, Hamilton, and Van Meter were in a stolen car, heading for St. Paul. Van Meter was driving, Hamilton was sitting by the passenger door and Dillinger was in the middle. The countryside was crawling with police looking for them, so it was probably inevitable that they would be seen.

Near Hastings, Minnesota, Deputy Sheriff Norman Dieter and three other officers spotted the bandits and gave chase. Dieter opened fire on the outlaws' car. Dillinger smashed out the back window and returned fire with his pistol. Van Meter floored the gas pedal. The policemen, who had rifles, fired about a dozen shots at the fleeing car. Suddenly Hamilton jerked and said, "I'm hit!" A rifle bullet had pierced the car seat and buried itself in the middle of his back, just to the left of his spine. The car seat was soon saturated with blood.

Van Meter managed to lose the cops. Then he and Dillinger stole another car. St. Paul was out of the question now, so they headed for Chicago. There they learned that the Chicago underworld wanted no part of the Dillinger gang. They were bringing down too much heat. Dillinger and Van Meter did the rounds of doctors who usually looked after wounded criminals, but nobody would touch Hamilton, for any price. They finally took Red, who was in agony, to the town of Aurora, Illinois, where a hoodlum friend named Volney Davis tried to make the suffering man as comfortable as possible. On April 26 or 27 Hamilton died. Dillinger and Van Meter secretly buried the body. That, at least, was the story Dillinger told later, regarding the death of Red Hamilton. Dillinger had lied once before about Hamilton being dead, and quite possibly he was doing so again.

During the spring of 1934 many robberies were blamed on the Dillinger gang, and perhaps Dillinger and Van Meter actually were involved in two or three of them. But the loss of Eddie Green and Red Hamilton had severely weakened the gang. Another blow came on June 7 when police caught up with Tommy Carroll in Waterloo, Iowa. Carroll pulled a gun and went down in a hail of bullets.

On June 30 the Dillinger gang pulled its last robbery, this time with the assistance of the notorious Pretty Boy Floyd. The gang hit the Merchants National Bank in South Bend Indiana, the town in which Red Hamilton had botched a bank robbery seven years earlier. Dillinger's bunch got away with $50,000, but it was a messy operation with a lot of shooting. One policeman was killed and six civilians were wounded. Floyd and Van Meter were also injured.

For several weeks nothing was heard of Dillinger, though the nationwide "sightings" continued. Rumours had him in Canada, Mexico, and dozens of places in between. Hoover even received a tip that he was on a Canadian ship heading for Britain. Then on July 22 came the earth-shaking news. John Dillinger had been gunned down outside the Biograph movie theatre in Chicago. He'd been betrayed by a woman named Anna Sage, who would enter the Dillinger legend as the Lady in Red. Melvin Purvis led the team that finally brought Dillinger down, and in all likelihood the bandit's death was an execution without benefit of trial.

Baby Face Nelson, Homer Van Meter, and Pretty Boy Floyd would all soon be dead, too — shot full of police bullets. Nelson, for a short period, got to enjoy the notoriety of being Public Enemy Number One, but even then some newspapers gave the title to Floyd. The women of the Dillinger gangs (including Pat Cherrington, who by this time had been arrested) were sentenced to prison terms for aiding and harbouring their fugitive husbands and boyfriends.

John Dillinger and most of the men who had robbed banks with him were dead. Many people saw the bodies. Their burial places are known. All but one! The fate of John "Red" Hamilton, the Canadian in the Dillinger gang, is not so certain.

Arthur O'Leary, Louis Piquett's assistant, said in a statement that Dillinger told him how he and Van Meter had disposed of Hamilton's body. At a place near Oswego, Illinois, in the Aurora vicinity, "Van and I dug a good, deep grave, and after we put Red's body in it we poured four cans of lye over it, so they can never recognize him even if they do find him." He went on to say that the only other person besides himself and Van Meter who knew the location of the grave was Baby Face Nelson.

On August 28, 1935, federal agents dug up a shallow grave outside Oswego. The body in it was badly decomposed and there was evidence it had been soaked with lye. The face was beyond recognition and no flesh remained on the hands for fingerprinting. Some teeth were removed from the corpse, and the dentist at the Michigan City Penitentiary identified them as John Hamilton's.

Identification by dental records was still rather primitive at that time, but J. Edgar Hoover was anxious to stamp "Closed" on the files of the Dillinger gang, with no loose ends dangling. He and his "G-Men" were national heroes now, and the "discovery" of the body of a notorious outlaw in a crude, lonely grave — dumped there like so much rubbish — suited Hoover's purposes very well. He saw to it that the discovery of the body was reported in every newspaper in the country.

Some parts of the story, however, did not fit. How had the federal agents managed to "find" that unmarked grave out in the sticks? They claimed local workmen had noticed "stunted growth" in one spot and became suspicious. But there were areas of stunted growth everywhere. And stunted growth does not necessarily indicate a grave site. One possible explanation lay with Dillinger's alleged statement that Nelson knew where the grave was. Neither Dillinger nor Hamilton had liked the pint-sized homicidal maniac, but Dillinger might have passed the information on to Nelson for use as a bargaining chip, not for Nelson's benefit, but for that of his wife, Helen. Little Lester Gillis didn't have many socially redeeming virtues, but he was devoted to his wife, and he would surely have shared the information of Hamilton's burial site with her. It is interesting to note that one day after the body was found, Helen Gillis was released from jail. Her probation included a condition of secrecy.

There was more. Dillinger said he and Van Meter had buried Hamilton in a *deep* grave. The corpse the federal agents exhumed was in a grave only about two feet deep. It was well known that in a childhood accident Hamilton had lost two fingers from his right hand. During the gun battle at East Chicago, Hamilton was wounded again in the right hand and lost part of yet another finger. The federal report on the body found near Oswego apparently made no mention of damage to a third finger. (It's even possible the corpse was missing one or both hands.) Curiously, the American federal government was very close-mouthed about the body Hoover's agents found in that grave, aside from their conclusion that the dead man was Red Hamilton.

Louis Piquett did not think the body was Hamilton's. From information the lawyer claimed Dillinger had shared with him, Piquett believed that Hamilton's body had not been buried at all, but hidden in a flooded mine shaft neat Platteville, Wisconsin. In Piquett's story, Dillinger and Van Meter weighed the body down with a heavy chunk from a big stone bull wheel. Volney Davis also gave an account of Hamilton's death and burial. But Davis's story changed every time he told it.

Was Red Hamilton really dead? The FBI received reports that Hamilton was alive and hiding in northern Indiana. He was even briefly listed as Public Enemy Number One. But with the discovery of the body near Oswego, and the confirmation of a dentist (who might never have actually worked on Hamilton's teeth) that the body was indeed Hamilton's, Hoover decided the outlaw was dead and that was the end of it.

At least two members of Hamilton's family publicly acknowledged that he was dead. His brother, William J. Hamilton, said John was the "brains" of the Dillinger gang. "He was a good scout who got a bad break from the law. All his troubles came from being too bull-headed." Hoover countered this by describing Red Hamilton as "a cold calculating rat." John's brother Joseph S. Hamilton said he was relieved that it was all over but: "The government which hunted and found the body of John Hamilton will have to bury it … I haven't seen or heard from John since I went to the prison (at Michigan City) to see him six months before he escaped. I won't see him again, I guess — I'm not able to take care of his burial." Joseph and Red had not been on friendly terms for years.

Bruce Hamilton's Story

But *was* it all over for Red Hamilton? Bruce Hamilton, a resident of New Mexico, is Red Hamilton's great-nephew. He was born in 1936 to Wilton and Harriet Hamilton. Wilton was John Hamilton's nephew. Bruce Hamilton has a rather intriguing story, which is included in the Miscellany of the expanded edition of *Dillinger: The Untold Story*, by G. Russell Girardin and William J. Helmer, with assistance provided by Rick Mattix — all authorities on the lives of the men in the Dillinger Gangs. Bruce Hamilton also shared the story with this author by email, the post, and telephone.

As a boy, Bruce heard family conversations about his great-uncle, John Hamilton. Though the conversation was generally guarded because Red was the Hamilton family's black sheep, Bruce had the impression that this uncle he had never met was still alive. In 1945, shortly after the end of the Second World War, Wilton Hamilton began making trips to northern Wisconsin, supposedly to go deer hunting — even though deer abounded in the Indiana woods. Bruce later learned that his father and relatives were searching for loot supposedly buried by the Dillinger gang before the Little Bohemia debacle. There was a story, allegedly vouched for by Patricia Cherrington, that the robbers had stuffed a suitcase with $200,000 in cash — money they'd got through the black market sale of over a million dollars' worth of stolen securities. Then they'd hidden the money somewhere in the triangle formed by the northern Wisconsin towns of Eagle River, Tomahawk, and Mercer. "People are still searching for that money," Bruce says, "but they won't find it, because my dad found it in 1947."

In 1947 Wilton suddenly paid off the mortgage on his home in South Bend, Indiana, and then sold the house. He bought a twenty-seven-foot-house trailer and took his family West. Bruce had asthma, and his parents hoped the dry western climate would be beneficial. It was a rough journey that took the Hamiltons through Texas, California, and Oregon. In Roseburg, Oregon, Wilton parked the trailer and his family for a week while he went off somewhere on his own. When he returned, he took his family to Phoenix, Arizona, where he considered buying a house for $8,000. Bruce, who was eleven at the time, heard his father say that if he spent the $8,000, he would still have $2,000 left. Bruce says he actually saw $10,000 in his father's possession.

Wilton decided to go back to South Bend, where he bought a house in 1948. Two years later he bought a brand new Ford — the first new car he'd ever owned. In 1950 or 1951, Wilton took his wife, fifteen-year-old Bruce, and Bruce's brother and sister on a trip to Sault Ste. Marie, Michigan, to visit Anna Steve, Red Hamilton's sister. They crossed the border to the Canadian side of the Soo. Bruce remembers going down a dirt road to a house in a wooded area. There Bruce Hamilton met the man he had heard about but had never seen before. Only later did his father tell him the man was his great-uncle, John Hamilton. Plenty of family photos were taken during the visit, but Red would not allow any pictures to be taken of him.

About this time Foye Hamilton, Red's brother (not long out of jail), suddenly came into a large sum of money. He set himself up with a machine shop in Rockford, Illinois. Then, according to Bruce Hamilton, Foye bought an island in Turtle Lake in northwestern Ontario. If Bruce's information is correct, this must be Turtle Lake which is near the town of Atikokan. That was rough, isolated country in the 1950s and it remains so today. Bruce says Foye built a large cabin on the island and purchased boats and seaplanes for transportation.

Wilton Hamilton told Bruce not to discuss the trip to Canada with anyone. In later years, other members of the Hamilton family were unwilling to talk about Red with Dillinger biographers, making the story rather difficult to pin down. Bruce Hamilton believes — and William J. Helmer says at least one other family member supports him in this — that the log cabin on an island in a Canadian lake, far from the reaches of the FBI, was the last hideout for Red Hamilton. The story Bruce Hamilton heard from his father is a rather credible account of what might actually have happened.

Dillinger could not find medical help for Red in Chicago, probably because by this time the Dillinger gang was drawing too much heat. The mob put the word out to underworld doctors to have nothing to do with Hamilton. Dillinger took Red to the home of Hamilton's brother, Sylvester, in East Gary, Indiana. Sylvester found a doctor who saved Red's life. This might have been Dr. Harold Cassidy, who did plastic surgery on Dillinger. Then Sylvester took Red to Bruce Hamilton's grandfather, William, in South Bend. William hid Red in an old Dillinger hideout called Rum Village Woods. Bruce's grandmother would send Wilton out to Rum Village Woods with food for Red. He was particularly fond of her spaghetti. Soon after, the family took Red to Sault Ste. Marie, Ontario, where he received further medical aid. At the time

Bruce Hamilton (right), great nephew of John "Red" Hamilton, claims that his father, Wilton (left), located a stash of Dillinger Gang loot and turned it over to Red. Wilton was rewarded with $10,000. (Bruce Hamilton)

the body near Oswego was found and identified as the remains of John "Red" Hamilton, says Bruce Hamilton, John was safe on the Canadian side of the Soo.

Red recuperated there until he was fit enough to work as an electrician in a family-operated bowling alley. Wilton Hamilton saw him there from time to time. However, he did not speak to him, not wishing to give him away. Bruce believes that on July 26, 1934, Red Hamilton and a man named Tony Marchetti, along with Homer Van Meter and Baby Face Nelson, robbed a bank in Henderson, Kentucky. They got away with over $33,000. (A teenaged girl in the Hamilton family had a baby, believed to be Marchetti's, and the child died under mysterious circumstances.)

As late as the summer of 1936 an informant who identified himself as "Happy" wrote to J. Edgar Hoover, telling the head of the new FBI that for a price, he could give him information on John Hamilton. "There are three people who know that he is still living and I happen to know the most details about him." Hoover ignored the letter. He had now turned his attention to hunting down Communists.

In 2003 a ninety-year old Florida woman, Bruce Hamilton's aunt, supported the story that Red had survived the bullet wound and escaped to Canada. She also claimed that he died in Canada in the 1970s and that she knew where he was buried. Bruce was never told the location of the grave.

In the summer of 2006 Red Hamilton's granddaughter told Bruce a similar story, that her grandfather recovered from the gunshot wound and fled to Canada. He occasionally crossed back to the United States to visit family, but apparently made his home in the cabin on Turtle Lake. Red would have been right at home there, says Bruce, because he always had been an outdoorsman. The granddaughter, who prefers not to be named, also confirmed to the author by phone that Red Hamilton lived to a ripe old age in Canada.

Bruce believes Wilton retrieved the stash of hidden loot, and was rewarded with $10,000. Red took the bulk of the money but gave Foye enough to open the machine shop. Then he gave Foye the money to buy the island in Turtle Lake.

If Hamilton did in fact survive and escape to Canada, whose body was found in that shallow grave near Oswego in 1935? Rick

Mattix suggests it could have been the body of Dr. Joseph P. Moran, an underworld doctor who had refused to treat Hamilton's bullet wound. Dr. Moran was believed to have been murdered by the Barker Gang, and his body disposed of in secrecy. If Dillinger directed the FBI to that body through an unwitting Helen Gillis, or by any other ploy, he could have been making sure that Red would get away. The outlaw had meanwhile escaped to Canada, possibly with a large amount of loot, and quietly thumbed his nose at J. Edgar Hoover.

It would appear, then, that while Alvin "Creepy" Karpis was counting the days, weeks, and years in his prison cell in Alcatraz, John "Red" Hamilton was living in a free, if somewhat restricted retirement, in his home country. "He spent his time fishing," says Bruce Hamilton. Of course, justice demanded that Red Hamilton pay for his crimes. But it seems just possible that in the end, the Canadian in the Dillinger Gang got away with it.

From the Fort Wayne, Indiana, *News Sentinel*, August 29, 1935

DILLINGER FAVORITE
HAMILTON WAS CHIEF AID OF
NOTORIOUS GANG LEADER
Indianapolis – Aug. 29 – (INS)

John (Three-Finger-Jack) Hamilton, Canadian born outlaw, whose body has been located at Oswego, Ill. by Federal "G" men, was John Dillinger's favorite lieutenant in bank robberies, local authorities said here today.

State police said it was with Hamilton that Dillinger negotiated sending button boxes loaded with automatic pistols into the Indiana State Prison to effect the big September 26, 1933 break.

It was reported that Hamilton had administered the oath to the members of the proposed break in the prison that they would in turn free Dillinger from the Lima, O jail where he was incarcerated after arranging the Indiana prison break.

The police credit Hamilton with executing, with the aid of other freed convicts, the delivery of Dillinger from the Lima jail in which Sheriff Jess Sarber was slain October 21, 1933.

First definite word that Hamilton had been wounded fatally was said to have been received from his one-time girlfriend, Patricia Cherrington. A former henchman of the gang gave to federal authorities a letter in which Dillinger wrote his regrets over Hamilton's death to Miss Cherrington.

EDWARD McMULLEN

DEATH OF AN OUTLAW

On the night of May 29, 1936, one of Canada's most notorious desperadoes lay unconscious in a hospital in Seattle, Washington, barely clinging to life. A bullet from his own gun was lodged in his brain, but he was not an attempted suicide. In the town of Blaine, Washington, on the Canadian border, the body of an American border guard named Charles Flachs was in the hands of the local undertaker. Flachs had been brutally murdered when the Canadian outlaw tried to cross into the United States.

Doctor Walter Kelton, a Seattle surgeon, was about to perform a delicate operation to remove the bullet from the wounded man's head. Doctor Kelton told reporters he had a strange duty. As a doctor he was obliged to do everything in his power to save the patient's life. But on a personal level, considering who the patient was and what he had done, the doctor wished the man would die because it would be a justly deserved end and would spare the state the expense of trying him for murder and executing him.

In Canada, where the wounded man was also wanted for bank robbery and murder, and had a $1,200 price on his head, authorities hoped he would live. It was not for his own sake that the Canadians wanted this man to survive. As far as they were concerned, he was gallows bait. But he was the only man alive who could provide information on one of the biggest mysteries in the annals of Canadian crime.

Just a few days earlier Norman "Red" Ryan and an accomplice named Harry Checkley had been shot dead in a blazing gun battle with police while trying to rob a liquor store in Sarnia, Ontario. A police officer named John Lewis had also been killed in the fight. Ryan's demise had stunned the Canadian public. He was the "Canadian Jesse James" whose criminal exploits had made headline news. His apparent reform in prison, and his parole after many years behind bars, had been

Edward McMullen looks more like a bank manager than a bank robber in this photo. Yet this associate of the notorious Red Ryan was labelled the most dangerous man in the Kingston Penitentiary. (Kingston Penitentiary Museum)

well publicized. Ryan was held up by liberal-minded people as a shining example of a bad man turned good. If *Red Ryan* could become a good citizen, then *any* criminal could.

Then Ryan committed his great act of betrayal, and died for it, less than a year after he had been paroled from the Kingston Penitentiary. Canadian authorities wondered what criminal activities Ryan had been up to in those months between his release from prison and his death in Sarnia. The Canadian public, who had made something of a hero of Red Ryan — not for his crimes, but for his apparent redemption — had been let down with a resounding thud with the news that Ryan had killed a man while committing a crime before being slain himself. Now the newspapers were full of stories that the police had evidence that Ryan had been involved in other crimes since his parole, perhaps even murder. Canadians wanted to know the truth. Vital information was locked in the bullet-shattered brain of Edward "Wyoming" McMullen.

The series of events that would link McMullen's fate to that of the notorious Ryan began fifteen years earlier. On the night of Tuesday, October 18, 1921, the train from Toronto stopped at the little village of Thorndale in southwestern Ontario. Three strangers stepped onto the platform. These men did not know anybody in the tiny agricultural community. They had no legitimate reason for being there. They did, however, know about the brand new McLaughlin car in the garage of automobile dealer R.T. Wright. The following morning, Mr. Wright reported his car stolen.

The car thieves would later be suspected of being the same men who on that very Tuesday had robbed the Bank of Hamilton on College Street in Toronto of $3,000. (This was never proven.) Now, with two more confederates they had picked up along the way, they

The older Red Ryan seems more like a prosperous financier here. Was Edward McMullen responsible for Ryan's return to crime? (Metropolitan Toronto Police Museum)

were heading for the little town of Wyoming, southeast of Sarnia, to hit the branch of the Bank of Toronto there.

The McLaughlin pulled into Wyoming a little after 2:30 on the afternoon of October 20. It stopped about a hundred yards from the bank. Four men got out, while the driver stayed at the wheel. The four strolled around as though they were exploring the village. Then they went into the bank.

Inside, one of the men approached teller E. S. Taylor with a $5 bill and asked for change. Suddenly the man pulled a revolver and stuck it in Taylor's face. The other three hauled out guns and covered the rest of the bank staff and a few customers. They told everybody to lie down on the floor. When manager E. Lambert was slow to obey, a bandit jammed a gun in his ribs and said, "Get down and stay down, or I'll plug you!"

One robber locked the front door and stood guard there. Two kept the people covered with their guns. The other emptied the cash drawers. Then he told Taylor to open the vault. Taylor said he couldn't. The robber kicked him viciously, stuck the barrel of the gun into his side, and threatened to kill him if he didn't do as he was told. At the same time a junior teller named Ronald Brown somehow managed to slip out the back door, unseen by the bandits. He had one of the bank's revolvers. Brown ran to the street and cried out that the bank was being robbed. People came running from all over the community to see what all the excitement was about.

Inside the bank, Taylor decided the bank's money wasn't worth dying for. He opened the vault, and the robbers cleaned it out. Their loot bag now had about $14,000 in it. One thief said they should look for more. But the others didn't like the look of the crowd gathering on the street in front of the bank. "Let's get out of here," the one who seemed to be the leader said.

The robbers locked the people in the vault and then dashed out the back door. Brown was waiting for them. From the cover of the corner of a building, he opened fire with his revolver. One robber fell and got up again. Brown wasn't sure if the man was hit or if he'd slipped in the mud. The robbers shot back, forcing Brown to pull back out of sight. Then they ran for their car.

Some of the village men hurried to the hardware store to arm themselves. As the McLaughlin roared down the street several men shot at it. The robbers replied with a fusillade from the car windows. The people scattered, diving behind telephone poles and into doorways for safety. Fortunately, no one was hit. The big car sped out of Wyoming.

Several armed men piled into a Ford to give chase. The roads were not paved, so it was easy for the posse to follow the tracks the getaway car left in the mud of a recent rain. But the Ford had no chance of catching the powerful McLaughlin. Later several people — unaware of the robbery — reported seeing the big car racing along country roads at high speeds. Police from London combed the region in cars and on motorcycles but found no trace of the robbers. Two days later the McLaughlin was found in the Niagara River a short distance from the mouth of Chippewa Creek. The thieves had evidently fled to the United States.

From all appearances the thieves had made a clean getaway. Police speculated the holdup might have been the work of Bill and Sid Murrell, who had recently escaped from the London jail where they were being held on charges of bank robbery and murder. Police thought the Murrells had pulled the Wyoming job and the earlier Toronto robbery to get money for their flight to the United States.

For months investigators found no clues to the identity of the bandit gang. Then in May 1922 a woman named Olive Koehler went to the police in London. She said a man with whom she had been involved bragged to her back in January that he had pulled the Wyoming robbery. His name was Edward McMullen. She said she did not report this earlier because she was afraid of him. She had met

*A newspaper sketch visualizes the Wyoming, Ontario, bank robbery that Edward McMullen participated in. (*Toronto Daily Star*)*

three of his friends who she said had been in on the robbery: George Anderson, William Ayers, and Frank Yohn. McMullen had boasted to her, Olive said, that he had not given them their fair shares of the loot. Evidently, they were too scared of him to do anything about it. McMullen also allegedly told Olive the name of the fifth robber was Muggsy Lafortune, but she had never met him. (Police never found any suspect of that name.)

McMullen, Anderson, Ayers, and Yohn were all residents of London. All were involved in the local bootlegging business. Three of the men were arrested without incident, but McMullen tried to pull a gun and had to be subdued. About twenty-eight years old at the time of his arrest, McMullen had a record going back to 1913 when he'd been convicted of a robbery in Vancouver. At that time he was using the name George Baldwin. Police soon found that Edward McMullen's fingerprints matched those of George Baldwin.

The trials were held in Sarnia. The first jury to hear McMullen's case could not agree on a verdict and was dismissed. On September 2, while he awaited a second trial, McMullen made a desperate attempt to escape from Sarnia's Lambton County jail. He somehow carved a pistol out of wood and covered it with silver paper from tobacco packages. When two guards named Burns and Forbes were taking him for his weekly bath, McMullen suddenly pulled the gun and ordered them to put up their hands.

Facing what they thought was a loaded gun, Burns and Forbes obeyed. McMullen forced them into a room where he took their keys and left the men on the floor, their hands and feet bound with strips of cloth. Back in the corridor where the cells were, McMullen opened the door of Anderson and Yohn's cell and told them to make a run for it with him. (Ayers had already been convicted and sentenced to twelve years in Kingston.) To McMullen's disgust, the two wouldn't leave the cell.

Then McMullen stuck a key into the lock on the office door of the jail's governor, James Dodd, intending to lock the governor in. Just at that moment Dodd, who had heard a noise, opened the door. McMullen told him to put up his hands. Dodd was sixty-four years old, but he ignored the wooden gun and tackled the would-be jail breaker. There was a fierce struggle before Dodd laid McMullen out cold with a blow to the head with a billy club.

Guards searched McMullen's cell but could not find whatever tool he had used to carve the gun. When the prisoner regained consciousness, he was surly and uncooperative, refusing to speak except to utter threats against Dodd. Because of the escape attempt, McMullen was told he would now have to wear a jail uniform instead of the street clothes all of the prisoners had been allowed to wear. He defiantly refused to put it on until Dodd told him his meals would be withheld until he complied.

McMullen realized his failed escape attempt wiped out any chance he might have had of an acquittal. Rather than go through the motions of a trial, he pleaded guilty to armed robbery. The judge sentenced him to twelve years for the robbery and two more for trying to escape. Anderson got ten years. Yohn, to the surprise of all, was found not guilty.

On the train that took him to Kingston, McMullen met another man who had just been convicted of armed robbery. This was Red Ryan. He was making his third trip to the Kingston Pen, this time for a stretch of twenty-five years. The guards who escorted them said that Ryan and McMullen became very chummy.

According to Tim Buck, the Canadian Communist leader who had been imprisoned because of his political views, the prison world was a topsy-turvy place in which bank robbers like Red Ryan and Ed "Wyoming" McMullen were the elite. They were the role models other inmates respected and hoped to emulate. But neither Ryan nor McMullen intended to stay long, basking in the admiration of their peers.

The Kingston Pen was a fortress, but men had escaped its stone walls in the past. Ryan and McMullen somehow overcame the obstacles of long hours of isolation and enforced silence to formulate a plan and recruit a band of jail breakers. They were Arthur (Curly) Sullivan, a Toronto burglar; Gordon Simpson, doing time for robberies in Guelph, Toronto, and Hamilton; and Thomas Bryans, a Sault Ste. Marie youth who was in for manslaughter. Their escape would be the most spectacular in the grim history of the Kingston Pen.

On the morning of September 10, 1923, near the prison's east wall, several inmates grabbed and bound an elderly convict who had duties in a barn there. With the old man tied up and out of the way, they set fire to a pile of straw. A billow of thick smoke obscured the wall from the view of the guards in the watch towers. Five convicts bolted from the barn and made straight for the wall. One of them carried a long board fitted with spikes for climbing, which he leaned against the wall. Curly Sullivan, carrying a coil of rope, scurried up first. He secured the rope, then slid down the other side. McMullen, Simpson, and Bryans quickly followed. Red Ryan, standing guard at the foot of the improvised ladder, was the last to go. But not before he stabbed guard Matt Walsh in the leg with a pitchfork and then knocked him cold with one slug.

Once they were over the wall, the convicts sprinted for the home of H.W. Richardson. He was a millionaire whose property was adjacent to the prison. The escapees hoped to steal Mr. Richardson's fast car. But the Richardsons were not home. The only car on the property was a battered old Chevrolet owned by a painter who was doing some work on the house. The men piled into the car and sped away, with McMullen at the wheel.

Prison guards pursuing on foot opened fire on the Chevy. One bullet pierced McMullen's hand. He was in pain and was bleeding heavily but still managed to drive the car through the streets of Kingston, as fast as the jalopy would go. Meanwhile, prison guards commandeered a rattling old Ford to give chase. That car was soon joined by twenty other vehicles full of guards, police, and civilian volunteers.

Just short of about three miles east of Kingston, McMullen became faint from loss of blood. He lost control of the car and crashed it into a farmer's gate near a place called Kemp and McAdoo's Woods. The convicts abandoned the wrecked car and ran into the woods, taking McMullen with them. It soon became obvious, though, that McMullen could not keep up. He had lost a lot of blood, leaving him ashen-faced and weak. Ryan sat McMullen down under a tree with his back against the trunk. He was fairly well hidden by brush and long grass. Then the other four convicts pressed on deeper into the bush, after telling McMullen they'd be back for him.

Soon man hunters were beating the bushes looking for signs of the runaways. They passed McMullen's hiding place about twenty times before one of them spotted him. McMullen was too weak to put up any kind of a fight, though he'd sworn he would never again be taken alive. "I'm through," he said when he realized he'd been found. "Leave me alone."

A guard pulled him to his feet and said, "Well, are you going to try and run, McMullen?"

The convict looked at the dozen or so armed guards around him and said, "What do you think I'm going to do, commit suicide?"

McMullen's captors took him back to the Pen. No doubt he was subjected to time in the hole, bread and water, and the paddle. Ryan later said that as soon as he and the other escapees were in the clear, he'd worked out a plan to bust McMullan out. But if Ryan did come up with such a scheme, he didn't put it into action.

For Ryan, "freedom" lasted a little more than three months. He and the other fugitives robbed a bank in Toronto to get some traveling money, then split up. Ryan and Sullivan crossed into the United States, while Simpson and Bryans headed for Quebec. Bryans would eventually be hanged for murder. Simpson's ultimate fate is uncertain.

Ryan and Sullivan knocked off a few banks in the Midwest. In December, Canadian detectives traced the pair to Minneapolis and passed the information to the Americans. On December 15, Minneapolis police cornered Ryan in a post office. He tried to shoot it out but was wounded in the shoulder and captured. The next day two Minneapolis detectives ambushed Curly Sullivan in his girlfriend's apartment and shot him dead. The Canadian government began extradition proceedings, and in January 1924 Ryan, manacled hand and foot, was on his way back to Kingston. This time he faced a life sentence.

The decade that followed was a long one for McMullen and Ryan, but they bore it all stoically. Neither played a significant part in the disturbance of 1932, when so much public attention was focused on Sam Behan, whose story is told in the following chapter. Ryan so impressed the prison administration with his new persona of nobility, he was promoted to the cushy position of nurse in the prison hospital. He was the convict who was getting attention all across the country as a truly reformed man. McMullen, silent and morose, just served his time and kept out of trouble.

In April 1934 McMullen was released from Kingston on a "ticket of leave," a conditional release similar to parole. Any breach of the conditions would land him back in prison. Curiously, though he had to report to a parole officer regularly, McMullen did not have to do that in person. He could mail in his report.

McMullen and a woman named Mary McGill (who called herself Mrs. McMullen) moved into a house in the Toronto suburb of East York. Neighbours would later say they'd never met a friendlier man. None of these people were sure what Good Neighbour Ed did for a living. He'd said at various times that he was a mechanic, a professional wrestling promoter, a landscaper, and a businessman in the oil industry. People noted that he took quite a few business trips and seemed to do a lot of night driving.

The neighbours all knew McMullen as a dapper man who liked to dress well, even when he worked on his car — which he did often. Children on his street called him "The Count" because of his immaculate clothes and appearance. McMullen was very fond of hats and was known to buy a new one almost every week. He had, in fact, gone bald in prison, and was self-conscious about his naked dome. He never ventured outside without a hat on and even wore one indoors.

While the neighbours liked Mary and "Teddy," they weren't sure about the visitors who came to the couple's house at all hours of the day and night. Many of these visitors were tough-looking characters who just didn't seem to fit in a quiet residential neighbourhood. Quite a few of them arrived in cars with American licence plates.

The neighbours knew that Teddy and Mary had a radio, just like many other families in the neighbourhood. They didn't know that Teddy also had a device (smuggled in from Detroit) that he could use to listen in on police radio communications. The neighbours hadn't a clue that Teddy McMullen was Edward "Wyoming" McMullen, recently a resident of the Kingston Penitentiary. Nor did they have the faintest idea that he made his money by robbing banks.

In July 1935 Red Ryan was released on parole after getting a recommendation from the prime minister himself, R.B. Bennett. Ryan spoke to cheering crowds everywhere, lectured on the foolishness of living a life of crime, and told everyone he would never go back to prison. On that last point, he would prove to be absolutely correct.

Of course, Ryan was leading a double life. By day he was the new, reformed Norman Ryan. By night he was Red Ryan the outlaw, up to his old larcenous tricks. He was certainly in cahoots with Ed McMullen. How long the two were partners in crime, and how many unsolved heists could be laid to their charge no one could absolutely prove. But McMullen would eventually be fingered as the most likely perpetrator of one particular outrage, and Red Ryan was in all probability his accomplice.

Early in the morning of February 28, 1936, two men tried to steal a car from the garage of Markham automobile dealer Edward Stonehouse, age fifty-eight. They set off an alarm that alerted Stonehouse and his twenty-two-year-old son, James, who'd been asleep in the house. Father and son rushed outside to stop the thieves. James had a .22 calibre rifle.

The car thieves were just backing the vehicle out of the garage. Edward Stonehouse jumped on the driver's side running board and reached in for the key in the ignition. James jumped on the passenger side running board but had to drop the rifle in order to hold onto the moving car.

The elder Stonehouse managed to get hold of the key. He pulled it out of the ignition and tossed it into the snow. Suddenly he was literally blown off the car by a gunshot to the head. He would die in hospital a week later. James Stonehouse fell with a bullet wound to one hand and a pistol bullet in his abdomen. He was seriously injured but would survive.

The thieves fired half a dozen shots at a constable who arrived on the scene. The car they'd been trying to steal rolled to a stop. The two men got out and climbed into another car that a third man had kept waiting. They took off and were soon out of sight. Police followed the tire tracks in fresh snow but lost them in Toronto. James Stonehouse got a good look at the men in the car, but it would be some time before he would be well enough to be of assistance to the police. Meanwhile, a police guard was placed at his hospital door in case the killers came back to silence him for good.

There was a great public outcry over the murder of Edward Stonehouse. Police in Toronto and other cities took steps to restructure their departments so they could more effectively protect the public. In the weeks following the shootings, police hauled in suspects but then had to let them go due to lack of evidence. The dragnet did snare one felon who'd been evading the cops since 1928. Red Ryan, in a further show of what a model citizen he'd become, offered to help the police in any way he could to catch the murderer of Mr. Stonehouse.

Meanwhile, there was a rash of armed robberies and major burglaries across southern Ontario. Banks and businesses were hit in Toronto, Hamilton, St. Thomas, Collingwood, and Markham. The outlaws also paid a visit to Quebec. On April 15 armed bandits robbed the Bank of Nova Scotia in the town of Lachute. They pistol-whipped the manager, grabbed $3,500 and escaped in a fast car with guns blazing from the windows to discourage pursuit.

Canadian police felt besieged. In the United States lawmen had rid their country of the likes of John Dillinger, Baby Face Nelson, the Barker Gang, Pretty Boy Floyd, and Bonnie and Clyde. While those desperadoes had been on the loose, Canadians had rather smugly assured themselves that such villains could never thrive in *their* country. Now the shoe was on the other foot, and Canadians had a crime wave on their hands, even though Canada's most notorious bad man, Red Ryan, was now living on the straight and narrow.

The whole thing was blown wide open on May 25, when Red Ryan and Harry Checkley were killed while trying to rob the Sarnia liquor store. The stolen car in which they had driven from Toronto to Sarnia was identified as the same car the bandits had used in the Lachute robbery. Police searched property Ryan had rented in Toronto, and found guns and explosives — the kind of explosives that had been used to blow safes in recent burglaries. They also found solid evidence — including a suitcase packed with clothing and medical supplies — that Ryan intended to go to Vancouver after the Sarnia job. In an unmailed letter to McMullen, Ryan said he was leaving behind his family and all the people who had befriended him. After he and Checkley knocked over the liquor store in Sarnia, he said, he was going to tell everyone he was going fishing in northern Ontario for a few weeks. That would give him a head start on the police.

Then an informant told the Toronto police that Ryan and McMullen were responsible for the Stonehouse shootings. Harry Checkley drove the getaway car. They had no doubt planned to use the stolen Stonehouse car in a robbery. The informant said he had it straight from Ryan himself that if it had not been for the presence of the constable, they would have gone back and finished James Stonehouse off as he lay helpless on the ground. (Other evidence suggested that McMullen would have gone back and finished young Stonehouse off, but Ryan wouldn't agree to the murder.)

Police showed James Stonehouse pictures of Ryan and McMullen. He identified McMullen as the man who had shot him and his father, and Ryan as one of the other would-be car thieves. Now Ryan was dead. Where was Edward "Wyoming" McMullen?

While Red Ryan's corpse was on public display in a Sarnia funeral home, Ed McMullen was setting things up out West. After the Stonehouse shootings, he and Mary had finally been obliged to clear out of their Toronto house. Even as witnesses looked at pictures of McMullen and identified him as one of the Lachute bank robbers, an informant told Toronto police that McMullen had a bottle of nitroglycerine. He would blow up himself and any police who tried to arrest him.

Most Canadians were shocked by the news of Ryan's sordid death. Ed McMullen panicked. Leaving Mary in Vancouver, he climbed aboard a bus for the United States. On May 28 the bus pulled into the Washington border town of Blain and stopped at the customs and immigration check point. The passengers had to get out and the driver opened the cargo bay so that luggage could be examined. Inspector L.J. Pike and Immigration Officer Charles Flachs asked McMullen his name.

"John Arthur Fraser," McMullen answered. He said he was taking a little holiday in the United States. Something about "Fraser's" manner aroused the border officials' suspicions. Flachs said he would have to search his clothing. McMullen suddenly pulled a .38 calibre revolver and snarled, "No one's going to search me!"

His first shot struck Flachs in the chest, killing him on the spot. McMullen fired three more shots, slightly wounding another immigration officer. Then Inspector Pike grappled with him. Several other officers rushed to help. McMullen still had the gun in his hand. Just as he was about to fire another shot, Pike twisted his arm up so the muzzle of the gun was pointed at McMullen's face. The weapon discharged, and the bullet struck McMullen just below the left eye and travelled up into his brain. The outlaw collapsed.

The American officials found no identification on the man, but there was $780 in Bank of Nova Scotia notes in his pockets. They opened his suitcase and discovered a .44 calibre revolver and over two hundred rounds of ammunition. Whoever the mysterious Canadian was, he was no ordinary working man going on a little vacation.

An ambulance took McMullen from Blain to the larger community of Bellingham where there was a hospital. If McMullen regained consciousness, he would be charged with the murder of Charles Fachs. The Americans contacted Canadian authorities. When they described the man's tattoos: a lantern, a flag, a train engine, and a naked woman, the Canadians knew they had at last found Ed McMullen. A team of detectives from Vancouver hurried down to Bellingham to check the man's fingerprints, just to be sure.

McMullen was moved to a hospital in Seattle, where Dr. Kelton removed the bullet from his brain. When the operation was completed, the doctor said there was a chance McMullen would recover. But no one could predict what his mental condition might be.

Back in Vancouver, police located the east-end house McMullen had rented under an alias. They questioned Mary McGill. There had recently been a sudden outbreak of armed robberies in British Columbia's lower mainland, and they suspected McMullen was responsible. Mary claimed to have known nothing of Ed's criminal activities. She asked permission to visit him in Seattle. Permission was granted, but Mary did not go to McMullen's bedside. In the suburb of Burnaby, police also found an elaborate hideout McMullen had prepared in case of an emergency. In the hideout was a newspaper, folded open to an article about Red Ryan's death.

On May 31, barely a week after Ryan met his end, Edward McMullen died. He had never regained consciousness. Toronto police collected strong evidence, including a statement from Ryan's own brother, that the "reformed" criminal had indeed been involved in robberies — and (by his own confession) the Stonehouse shooting. But with McMullen's death went the last chance for Canadians to learn the absolute truth. A few days later Mary claimed the body. McMullen also took to the grave the secret of where the loot from the robberies and burglaries was stashed. Police tore apart the outlaws' residences — even slashed open the tires of Ryan's car. They found nothing.

Ironically, the only person in Canada to offer at least a token word on behalf of the infamous Ryan was one of his former jailers, Deputy Warden R.R. Tucker of the Kingston Penitentiary. Tucker had worked at the prison for many years and knew both Ryan and McMullen well. He speculated that the real leader of the last "Ryan Gang" was not Red Ryan but McMullen. Tucker told the *Toronto Daily Star*:

> I think Ryan would have gone straight had he not met McMullen after his release on parole. Ryan was volatile, easily led. McMullen was cold as ice, silent, immovable as a gypsy's curse. Ryan had a bright future when he left the penitentiary. McMullen had

none but crime. He was the most dangerous man I knew in Kingston.

"I'm sure Red intended to go straight when he left the penitentiary. But McMullen must have got after him. He was the stronger [one]. It wouldn't have mattered if Ryan had been making $50,000 a month; he would still have followed McMullen if that arch criminal had exerted enough pressure.

How accurate Deputy Warden Tucker was in his speculation is something we will never know.

SAM BEHAN

BURIED ALIVE

There was a time during the early 1930s when Sam Behan's name made the front pages of Canadian newspapers. When he died the news was the front-page banner headline of, among others, the *Toronto Daily Star*. This now largely forgotten man was a crook, to be sure. But it was his activity as a stand-up guy trying to get humane treatment for his fellow convicts that caught the public's attention, and for which he deserves to be remembered.

Sam Behan was born to a Jewish family about 1892. He claimed to be from Boston but was more than likely born in the United Kingdom and immigrated to the United States as a child. According to his own account, he first got in trouble with the law at the age of six. He was bundled off to reform school for stealing bottles of soda water. As a young man Behan went to England, where he was jailed on eight separate occasions. When he returned to the United States, he said, he went to work for the Al Capone mob in Chicago. But he had some sort of falling-out with the gangsters and fled to Canada. Behan also claimed to have fought with the Canadian Expeditionary Force during the First World War. There are problems with this story. Behan said he enlisted in the Canadian Army in Connecticut. While several thousand American boys and men did travel north to sign up with the Canadian Army before the United States got into the war in 1917, the American government did not encourage its citizens to serve in foreign armed forces. Behan would not have been able to enlist in Connecticut because the Canadians would not have been permitted to recruit there. Moreover, the records do not show a Sam Behan in the Canadian Army. It is entirely possible that Behan enlisted under an assumed name. "Sam Jackson" was a favourite alias of his. The records show a number of Sam Jacksons in the CEF, but none of them seem to have been Behan.

Behan evidently did some border hopping in the 1920s. His name first appeared in Toronto newspapers in February 1924 when he and five other men, including Montreal hoodlums Joe Serafini and Ciro Niegro, were arrested on weapons charges. Behan took the rap, claiming a suitcase containing several handguns as his own. The other men were off the hook, though a Toronto judge ordered them out of town. However, authorities learned that Behan had a $1,000 price on his head in the state of New York. He was an escapee from Sing Sing prison and was wanted in connection with a $10,000 fur robbery in New York City. Indeed, when Behan was arrested in Toronto he was wearing a sharp-looking coat trimmed with beaver fur. A pair of American detectives travelled to Toronto to take Behan back. As he left the courtroom with his hands cuffed, Behan called out, "Won't he let me have the guns back?"

Months later it was revealed that Behan, Serafini, Niegro, and the others had been planning to rob a bank messenger car in Toronto. They were going to load a stolen car with bricks to give it weight and then use the car to ram the bank vehicle. With the guards either dead or injured, the pickings would be easy. The Toronto police had thwarted that scheme without even being aware that it was in the works.

It might have been just as well for Behan that he was taken to jail in New York rather than going to Montreal with his pals. A year later a gang that included Serafini and Niegro robbed a bank messenger car in Montreal. They killed the driver, and one of the bandits was shot dead by a policeman. Four of the robbers, including Serafini, were hanged for murder. Niegro escaped the noose by turning king's evidence against his friends.

Sam Behan did not remain in American custody for long. He was evidently paroled and in August 1927 Montreal police were looking for him following a $40,000 jewellery heist. On October 2, 1930, several gunmen robbed two messengers of Montreal's Banque Canadienne Nationale of $7,400. A woman who witnessed the robbery through a window from a distance of seventy feet later identified Behan as one of the bandits.

Behan was arrested in New York City, and this time it was the Canadians who had to do the extraditing. Behan was certainly keeping the bureaucrats in the departments of justice in Washington and Ottawa busy. He denied having anything to do with the holdup. In court his defence counsel pointed out that the woman said the man she identified as Behan had a scar on his right cheek. Behan had a scar on his *left* cheek, and at seventy feet it was not even discernible. But Behan also had the Montreal jewellery heist to answer for, though he said he had nothing to do with that one, either. His long record worked against him, and he was convicted. Behan's wife Mary was also arrested on suspicion of being an accomplice, but charges against her were eventually dropped.

Sam Behan had the bad luck to be convicted at a time when Montreal's crime rate was on the rise, and local magistrates had decided a crackdown was in order. The judge presiding at Behan's trial felt that this man who had come to Canada to plunder at the point of a gun was just the right villain of whom to make an example. He sentenced Behan to life imprisonment for armed robbery, *plus* seven years for conspiracy to commit armed robbery.

Behan was shocked. No doubt he'd expected to get ten years, twenty at the most. But *life!* For a miserable *stickup!* Behan bitterly said that the extra seven years wouldn't bother him.

At first Behan was sent to the St.-Vincent-de-Paul Penitentiary in Quebec. Then on February 9, 1932, he was transferred to the Kingston Penitentiary.

Sam Behan was registered at Kingston as convict # 2505. His registry form shows he had been imprisoned in Sing Sing and Dannemora in New York, in addition to St-Vincent-de-Paul. Behan was not a big man, standing just five feet seven inches and weighing 137 pounds . But his body bore the marks of a hard life of outlawry. He had a four-and-a-half-inch scar on his left cheek, courtesy — he said — of one of Capone's thugs. He had another scar on the bridge of his nose and yet another on his forehead. He had the scars of bullet wounds on his left wrist and right knee. Nobody could say Sam Behan wasn't tough; and tough he would have to be now that he was behind the grey walls of the Kingston Pen!

The Kingston Penitentiary was founded in 1835. After almost a century the institution's main purpose was virtually unchanged. It was a place of punishment where the wicked were kept segregated from decent society. Kingston offered little in the way of rehabilitation or reform.

A new arrival at Kingston was stripped naked and had his head shorn and rubbed with acetic acid. He was given a prison uniform of blue denim and then was locked in a cell. Most cells were five feet wide, eight feet long, and ten feet high. The cell had a table, a chair, a seatless toilet, and a cot that folded against the wall in the daytime. There was a wash basin and tap, but the water that came out of the faucet was not fit to drink.

The prisoner's day was regulated by a bell. The bell told him when to get up, when to eat, when to work, and when to go back to his cell. Meals were eaten in the cell. A rule of silence was strictly enforced. The prisoner spent most of his waking hours in the lonely quiet of a dimly lit cell. He was allowed outside for twenty minutes a day (except Sunday) for exercise. Talking was not allowed in the exercise yard.

Some prisoners had the privilege of working a few hours a day in one of the prison shops or with a work gang outside the prison walls. The rule of silence was still in effect, but working was preferable to the monotony of sitting in a cell. On Sunday the prisoner got out of his cell to pick up meals and to attend church services. Aside from that, he spent the entire day in his cell. If it were a long weekend, the boredom continued on Monday. There was nothing to do but read something from the rather limited selection of books in the prison library. For those who could not read — and many inmates were illiterate — there was not even that bit of escape from the crushing monotony.

Any breach of the rules brought on punishment, and there were so many regulations — most of them petty in the extreme — that remembering them all was next to impossible. It was very difficult indeed for a man to go through a term at Kingston without at least occasionally breaking a rule.

Punishments were handed out by a Warden's Court. It could put a man on bread and water for a few days or have him handcuffed to the bars of his cell. A difficult prisoner could be "paddled." This spanking of a grown man was humiliating and extremely painful. In a room called Keeper's Hall, the prisoner was blindfolded and had his pants and undershorts removed.. He was then made to bend over a modified medical examination cot and had his hands and feet secured. A guard would administer to the man's bare buttocks whatever number of strokes —usually ten — the Warden's Court had ordered. The paddle was a leather strap about two feet long and two inches wide.

It was perforated with small diamond-shaped holes so that when it struck, it tore the flesh and drew blood. The victim often passed out from sheer agony before the flogging was over. Some guards refused to participate in paddlings. Others took sadistic pleasure in it and would even soak the strap in water overnight so it would deliver blows that were even more excruciating. The prison doctor was supposed to be present whenever an inmate was paddled, but many paddling sessions were carried out without his knowledge and went unrecorded.

Although paddling was painful, what convicts dreaded most was solitary confinement in the Prison of Isolation (P of I). There were two levels of isolation. One was P of I itself, in which the men in the cells were isolated from the main prison population but could still hear what was going on in other P of I cells, though they could not see fellow inmates. Then there was "the hole." This was a dungeon below Keeper's Hall. Time in the hole could drive even the toughest con to the verge of madness. Before going into the hole, the prisoner had his hair clipped short. Though the cell was usually cold, he was allowed only light clothing. He spent his time in silent darkness, forbidden to have books or tobacco, and living on bread and water. A stay in the hole was often accompanied by frequent paddlings. All it took was an accusation from a guard, even if the accusation were false, to land a man in the hole. While many of the guards at Kingston were decent, honest men, dedicated to a difficult job, there were always a few who were sadistic brutes. Those guards would go into a cell in the P of I with billy clubs and beat and kick the occupant senseless.

Nobody expected a term in the Kingston Pen or any other prison to be a vacation. But for many inmates the over-regulated world of Kingston — a world of numbing monotony punctuated by episodes of violence — was too much to bear. The list of grievances was a long one. Inmates were not allowed visitors on Saturday and Sunday. For many those were the only days on which family members were free to travel to Kingston. Prisoners could have books from the prison library and a few heavily censored magazines but no newspapers. The small amount of mail they were allowed was also severely censored. Church attendance on Sunday was compulsory. Medical and dental facilities were poor. The men were allowed little recreation in the open air. They were not permitted personal grooming items such as combs and mirrors. They were fed a constant, monotonous diet of steam-cooked food. (The person in charge of the kitchen was allowed a budget of 19¢ per man per day and not a penny more.) But for all these issues, the matter that brought things almost to the breaking point had to do with cigarette papers.

Inmates were issued a ration of tobacco. In fact, tobacco was the currency of the underground prison economy. But the men were not issued cigarette papers. Inmates had to either smoke a pipe (which used up too much tobacco) or roll their tobacco in toilet paper. Toilet paper was a very poor substitute for proper rolling papers. Again and again the inmates asked for cigarette papers and were refused. If a man should be found in possession of smuggled cigarette papers, he would have sixty days docked off his "good time" (time earned toward early release). The cigarette papers would not have cost the government a cent because the tobacco companies provided them for free.

The Kingston Pen was laid out like spokes radiating from the hub of a wheel, all of it surrounded by high stone walls. The main gate was in the north wall. This was where the administration offices were, as well as the armoury. Only guards on the walls carried rifles. Guards on the ground carried no firearms at all, out of concern that inmates might overpower a guard and take his gun.

From the north gate stretched an empty wide yard. On the other side of the yard was the main building. It was capped with a large dome. The tiered wings of cells radiated out from this centre.

To the south of the main building there was another yard. Beyond that was the industrial building. It had a smaller dome, and the various shops were in wings that ran out from the hub. It was here that the "riot" of 1932 began.

Rumours had been circulating for months that the inmates were planning something. Whether it was to be a general uprising or a big breakout, officials did not know. Whatever it was, they suspected Sam Behan of being a ringleader.

The main reason Behan had been transferred from St.-Vincent-de-Paul to Kingston was to thwart a breakout plot. Informers had told the warden that Behan and a black inmate named Chester Crossley (or Crosby) were conspiring to lead a major breakout. Whatever plans, if any, Behan and Crossley might have had were thwarted by the transfer.

What the prisoners in Kingston had planned was not a "riot" or a mass escape. It was, rather, a demonstration; a stop-work action to protest the administration's refusal to give them cigarette papers. It began quietly enough.

At three o'clock on the afternoon of October 17, some five hundred inmates working in the industrial block put down their tools and headed for the doors. Prison administration under Acting Warden Gilbert Smith had been anticipating something happening that day. They quickly ordered the shop doors locked. However, convicts in the mailbag room got out through a window. They used acetylene torches and hammers to destroy the locks on the other shop doors. Soon a mob of convicts had congregated in the room under the big dome. They had taken a few guards hostage, but their leaders had warned them not to hurt anybody.

Now Warden Smith decided he would go down and talk to the men. Smith was a bespectacled smallish man who looked more like a schoolmaster than the warden of Canada's toughest prison. A senior guard warned him, "If you go in there, they'll grab you and hold you. God only knows what will happen."

In spite of the risk, Smith went in. Immediately the convicts began to hoot and jeer. Smith advised them to go back to work or face serious consequences. He was approached by Sam Behan, a convict named Albert Garceau, and the notorious Tim Buck. Tim Buck was not a criminal at all, but a man who had been jailed because of his politics. Buck was the founder of the Communist Party of Canada. He had been sentenced to four years in prison on a contrived charge of sedition. Behan and Garceau were two of the ringleaders of the protest, and Smith was under the impression that Buck was one also. In fact, he was not.

Behan told Smith the men wanted cigarette papers, more recreation time, and newspapers and magazines. Smith admonished Behan and the others for their rash action and said they should just get back to work. Behan later testified that Smith said, "If I had cigarette papers here now, I would not give them out."

So far the protest had been peaceful enough. No one had been hurt. Little damage had been done, except to the locks on some doors. Behan stayed close to Warden Smith to discourage any young hotheads among the inmates from doing him any harm. Then Smith said he wanted to use the telephone. Behan apparently thought the warden was going to phone Superintendent of Penitentiaries General D.M. Ormond in Ottawa and pass on their grievances. Actually, Acting Warden Smith was calling in the army. The time was now 3:55 p.m.

Smith put a call through to Tête de Pont Barracks, urgently requesting troops. Within minutes ten trucks loaded with officers and soldiers of the Royal Canadian Horse Artillery, commanded by Colonel J.C. Stewart, roared out of the military base and headed for Kingston. The soldiers were armed with rifles, but not bayonets. When they reached the penitentiary, they took up positions on the walls.

The soldiers had no orders to attack. Their job was to hold the perimeter and prevent a mass escape while the guards went in to put down the "mutiny." They endured volleys of curses and foul language from the prisoners, but nothing more.

When they saw the soldiers, some of the men became panicky and began to grab hammers and other tools from the workshops to use as weapons. They closed the doors and barricaded them with large stones from the stone-cutting shop. Someone smashed up a couple of sewing machines in the mailbag room.

There was a cry of "Rush the bastards!" Another voice called for putting the "screws" (guards) in the front line so they'd be the first to be shot if the soldiers opened fire. One inmate — possibly Behan — told Smith and the guards, "Don't try any monkey work, and you won't be harmed."

Tim Buck told the men he doubted the soldiers would shoot them. But he advised filling buckets with water in case of fire. Some of the more violently natured men threatened the hostages and wanted to use them as human shields in a bid for escape. But Behan and some others called on the men to keep their heads and not resort to violence.

For a tense hour there was a standoff. The convicts on one side of the barricaded doors had their hostages. On the other side the guards and soldiers waited nervously with guns in their hands. Then, shortly after five o'clock a ten-ton truck loaded with rock from a nearby quarry was brought into position. Rolling in reverse, it pushed against the main doors of the domed building and forced them open. The driver then moved the truck out of the way. The guards now poured in, firing rifles and revolvers as they went. Behan cried, "This is murder!" Smith said, "Well, you brought it on yourselves." Prisoners and hostages dove for cover as bullets whistled and ricocheted around. Someone cried, "All right! We'll go to bed! Don't shoot!"

Amazingly, no one was hit by gunfire. There were but three injuries. One young inmate had hurt his hand while moving rocks to the barricade. Another inmate had cracked ribs, possibly from being struck down by guards. One guard had a slight head wound after being bashed with a spittoon. By 6:00 p.m. all of the prisoners were accounted for and in their cells — still with nothing but toilet paper to roll their cigarettes in.

For the next couple of days a sullen mood gripped the inmate population of the Kingston Pen. Once again the rumour mill was turning out tales. On the prison grapevine it was whispered that the leaders of the "riot" would be singled out for punishment. They might be tried in open court, or their punishment might be left in the hands of the warden. Of the two possibilities, the convicts feared the latter more. "It is just as well that women's organizations don't know what can be done," an anonymous prison official told a *Toronto Daily Star* reporter who had asked what kind of punishment might be dealt to the "mutineers."

Reporters sought out ex-convicts who told horrific tales about what went on behind Kingston's walls. They described men being "tied to the gate." That meant the prisoner was handcuffed to the door of his cell, so that his hands were bound to an iron bar above his head, sometimes with only his toes touching the floor. He would be left in that position from 8:00 a.m. to 5:00 p.m., being taken down only for his meals of bread and water.

The former inmates said some of the guards were okay, but others were bullies who goaded inmates into rash acts so they could be hauled off to P of I, or to Keeper's Hall for paddling or a stint in the hole. The worst guards, they said, were new young rookies who were eager for promotion and would report the slightest infraction of the rules to demonstrate their diligence and enthusiasm. These new guards would have a man on the carpet in the Warden's Court for such crimes as turning one's head while walking, having a collar button undone, not wearing trouser braces, or having a handkerchief tucked anywhere but a trouser brace. Of course, such small-minded meanness earned the guards the undying hatred of the inmates.

The ex-prisoners also said there was a lot of resentment over the matter of the penitentiary at Collins Bay. (Collins Bay was a small community just outside Kingston that has since been overgrown by the city.) This new facility was supposed to be much less oppressive than the Kingston Pen, and according to the government it was for "preferred inmates." The government said that term meant juvenile offenders whom it did not want locked up with the hard cases in the Kingston Pen.

If that were the case, the ex-cons asked, why were boys as young as sixteen still being sent to Kingston? And why were wealthy crooks — men who had made fortunes through corruption, embezzlement and graft — being sent to Collins Bay? The cons in Kingston had a catch phrase: "Steal a million and see Collins Bay."

At the best of times, the reporters were told, the Pen was a powder keg about to explode. There was always *somebody* who had reached the breaking point and needed only the slightest provocation to push him over the line. Of such a man the other convicts would whisper, "Keep away from him. He's on the meat today." To be "on the meat" was to be on the edge of murderous fury.

While former prisoners were regaling reporters with their stories, fresh news was breaking in the Kingston Pen. On October 20, after being confined to their cells for almost three days, the inmates were again on the verge of eruption. It began with a few men and then spread throughout the prison. Men began to shout out their rage. They smashed their bunks and the few bits of furniture in their cells. They used pieces of metal twisted off the frames of their bunks to smash the porcelain toilets.

The prison was overcrowded. Almost one hundred inmates did not have cells. Those men had to sleep on cots outside the cells, but still on the ranges — the corridors outside the cells. While the prisoners in the cells ranted and destroyed whatever they could get their hands on, the other men smashed their cots and used the pieces to try to force open their fellow cons' cell doors. A few actually succeeded. Convicts who were not in cells, however, were still confined to their own ranges. A curtain of iron bars prevented them from getting into the central area under the dome. Guards waited there, but they did not try to enter the ranges to force the prisoners back into the cells.

Once again the call went out to the army, and once again troops were called in to patrol the walls. Spotlights were brought in to illuminate the yards and walls at night. Police blockaded all roads leading to the prison gates. Prison officials kept telling reporters there was nothing amiss in the penitentiary. But people in the streets could hear the din coming from the main building. Mixed with the howls and curses of the men were the shrill-sounding shrieks that came from the house where female inmates were confined.

General Ormond was in Kingston to investigate the disturbances that had happened earlier in the week. When he was asked what he thought was the cause of all the trouble, Ormond said he believed the Reds in Moscow were behind it. Then, when a reporter asked him if he held Tim Buck responsible, Ormond said that in his opinion, Tim Buck was getting a lot more publicity than he deserved.

Ormond insisted that everything in the prison was under control. But when smoke could be seen rising from the prison's power station and the sound of gunfire could clearly be heard, alarmed citizens demanded to know what was really happening. Ormond repeated that all was well, and would say no more.

Kingston Mayor G.C. Wright, frustrated at the government's veil of secrecy, told the press, "After what occurred yesterday and what is occurring today, anybody except a moron can realize that things are

not quiet." He said he had been given no information and knew "only the alarming rumours in the newspapers."

In this newspaper artist's conception, firemen fight the blaze at the Kingston Penitentiary during the "disturbances."
(Toronto Star)

For want of hard facts, the newspapers *were* printing the rumours: that the convicts had taken control of the power plant and set it on fire, that there had been a gun battle in which convicts and guards had been killed and wounded, that a massive breakout was imminent. People in neighbourhoods near the prison kept their children off the streets.

A fire had in fact broken out in the power station but that facility was not in the hands of the convicts. Nor was there much of a chance of a big escape. Most of the inmates were still in their cells, and those who were loose on the ranges were not going anywhere. The prison was ringed by soldiers in full battle gear, armed with rifles, bayonets, and machine guns. There had been no gun battle because the convicts had no guns. But there had been shooting.

Guards had fired shotguns into ducts to discourage inmates from using them as a means of escape. From strategic locations guards had fired into the cells of prisoners who continued to act in what was considered a disturbing manner. It was reported later that the guards who fired the shots into cells were not trying to hit anyone, only make them settle down and behave. But one inmate was shot in the shoulder and had to wait over twenty-two hours before he received medical aid. There were two more minor injuries among the convicts. No guard received as much as a scratch. And no one could explain why seven shots were fired into Tim Buck's cell. Buck's friends believed this was an attempt to assassinate him under the cover of a prison riot. Fortunately for Buck, the layout of his cell provided him with a bit of wall to hide behind.

By October 22 the hungry, thirsty, exhausted inmates had settled down. General Ormond took reporters on a tour of the prison — on the condition that they ask no questions. The place was eerily quiet. Aside from the wreckage in the cells, the damage was minimal. General Ormond brushed off the stories reporters had heard from ex-convicts as "Lies, lies, lies!" He said there was no "hole" in the Kingston Penitentiary. When one brave reporter did venture a question as to why the men had suddenly rebelled, Ormond replied, "Just foolishness, nothing more that I can see. I have no opinion as to the cause; not the faintest idea."

But men who had experienced the Kingston Pen told reporters

they had no doubt that once order was restored, the cells in the P of I would be full, and there would be a steady parade of inmates to Keeper's Hall.

In the investigation that followed the "riots," Sam Behan and Tim Buck were two of the five men fingered as being the ringleaders behind the disturbances. They were charged with a variety of offences related to rioting and destruction of property. Some two dozen other men faced lesser charges.

One might think that with a sentence of life plus seven years hanging over him, Sam Behan had nothing to lose by involving himself in the troubles in Kingston and then facing charges in court. But he did, in fact, stand to lose something if the trial did not go well. Behan was in jail for robbery, not murder. In spite of the harsh sentence he'd been given, there was always the possibility of parole. Other "lifers" had been granted parole. Even as the prison troubles were being investigated, authorities were considering parole for Red Ryan, who was far more notorious an outlaw than Behan had ever been. Behan also had to consider the fact that if he never did gain parole, he would spend the remainder of his life in the Kingston Pen. If conditions in that place were to improve, Behan and the others would have to make a good impression in court.

The hearings, which began in mid-April 1933, were held in the Frontenac county courthouse in Kingston. Behan appeared as a witness for some of the other accused convicts — one of whom was a young man whose sentence had expired since the October disturbance, but who was in danger of being sent back to the Pen if found guilty. The very idea terrified him.

Behan was blunt and straightforward with his testimony. "Life was unbearable," he told the court. "We couldn't stand it any longer. We were reported for the most ridiculous little breaches of the regulations.

"If I were sitting in my cell reading, a guard would sneak up on hands and knees and say, 'What are you talking about?' If I said I wasn't talking, I'd be reported both for talking and for insolence — that is, for talking back to the guard. I'd be paddled or thrown in the hole. For smaller infractions you might get five or seven days on bread and water; one slice of bread for each meal."

Behan demonstrated the position in which a man had to stand when he was tied to the gate. "Some men have been there for seven days, to my knowledge," he said. "It leaves you almost dead."

Regulations said the men were supposed to have fifteen to twenty minutes exercise in the yard each day (except Sundays when there was no exercise period). Often, Behan claimed, they got only five or six minutes outside, "walking around and around like dumb animals in a circle, not allowed to talk."

Another grievance, Behan said, was that a prisoner named O'Brien had been kept in solitary confinement for nineteen months. (This was John "Two Gun" O'Brien, a bank robber who was also an American citizen. Behan's testimony would cause the American government to look into O'Brien's case.) "If they could do that to one man," Behan asked, "why couldn't they throw me in the hole for seven years, or eleven years?"

Red Ryan, much younger in this picture, got to know Sam Behan well in prison. "He was a tough boy," Ryan said. (Metropolitan Toronto Police Museum)

Behan admitted he had been "one of the active spirits" in organizing the protest. Then he took a packet of tobacco out of his pocket and a couple of sheets of toilet paper. That, he said, was what the men had to use to roll a smoke. "Don't try it," he said to W.F. Nickle, KC, who was defence counsel for the convicts. "It gags you, stifles you, hurts your throat so that you couldn't talk if you wanted to … We wanted an immediate answer about cigarette papers. We had been getting promises and promises, nothing but promises, and if you make too many requests you're put in the hole as an agitator."

When a man was taken to the hole, Behan said, "They

(the guards) do what they like — jump on a man, punch him, kick him and everything else."

The newspapers printed every word Behan said. Prison officials said Behan was exaggerating and asked reporters if they could really take the testimony of a convicted criminal seriously. But even if many people did think Behan's accounts were somewhat embroidered, a growing number of sympathizers called for a full investigation into penitentiary policies. Behan's credibility with the public increased after an incident that occurred on April 27.

A number of inmates refused to go to their cells at supper time in protest over a man being given thirty days in the hole for swearing at the warden. They in turn were given an ultimatum: go to the cells or else. Sam Behan and Tim Buck tried to talk the men into obeying the order. But the more hotheaded among them would not listen. Guards waded into the rebellious inmates with fists flying (but no billy clubs). After a short fight they subdued the protesters and hauled them to their cells.

On June 15 Behan had an exchange with Colonel J.K. MacKay, the assistant to Crown Prosecutor T.J. Rigney, KC.

"Where were you at the time of the riot?" MacKay asked.

"There was no riot, as far as I am concerned," Behan replied.

"When you saw the accused, where was he?"

"Standing inside the closed door of the change room. As we stood there the door swung open and I told him to come out but he remained behind."

"He didn't like the company?" MacKay quipped.

"He didn't like the shots," Behan answered.

After Behan told of how he went to prevent one of the guards from being mistreated, Colonel MacKay asked Behan if he had done all in his power to prevent violence.

"I certainly did," Behan said. "But if I'd had my way, the walls would have been broken down."

MacKay said sarcastically, "You've had experience in that before."

Behan shot back, "Prove it!"

MacKay said, "You're a pretty bad man. I must read your record to his honour and the jury."

"Call me as bad as you like," Behan answered.

Soon the newspapers were calling Behan "the picturesque and

nimble tongued New York and Montreal gunman." The reporters had initially referred to Behan as "Samuel" and then "Sam." Now they used the name by which he was known to his friends in jail, "Sammie."

Although W.F. Nickle provided counsel for the inmates in the preliminary hearings, the government would not allow the inmates to use their earnings from prison work to hire a lawyer for the actual trial. Those funds, Ottawa decided, would go towards the cost of dental care. Tim Buck and Sam Behan helped several of the convicts defend themselves in court and actually won some acquittals. Ray Boven was one of those whom the jury found not guilty of participation in a riot. So was the young man who had served his sentence and was afraid of being sent back. On June 26 Sam Behan's turn came. He had decided to defend himself. His performance in court over the next five days had the Canadian legal community wondering why this man had chosen to lead a life of crime.

In a legal duel that heavily favoured the prosecution, Behan conducted himself like a professional. He drilled the very guards who were his jailers with questions, knowing full well they might later make him pay for it. He pounced on inconsistencies and contradictions in their statements. It was clear that several of the guards had little regard for Behan as he questioned them. Behan was questioning a guard named John Gilley about his (Behan's) entry to the scene of the so-called riot.

"How were they [the doors] opened? Did you do it?" Behan asked.

"That's best known to you," Gilley snapped.

"You must be a better burglar than I," Behan said. "You can't say how I got into the shop dome."

"Yes, you came through the door."

"You just said the door was closed."

"Then you must have come through the keyhole."

When Gilley said that Behan had urged the rioters on, Behan cried, "You're lying!" Gilley told the court, "I tried to persuade Behan to desist and put the demands through the proper channels." Behan repeated, "You're lying!"

The presiding judge, Justice E. H. McLean, told Behan he couldn't say that in court. Behan replied heatedly, "I can't keep quiet! The truth is bad enough. I've suffered too much from these dogs to keep quiet!"

McLean finally prevailed upon Behan to hold his tongue, and the following day Behan apologized for the outburst. Then he requested that the paddle, a set of leg irons, and the "paddling machine" (the table to which the victim was strapped) be brought into court as exhibits for the defence. He wanted to show the kind of provocation that had led to the disturbances. Colonel MacKay objected. He said such exhibits would only appeal to the sympathy of the jury. Moreover, he said, there was no such thing as provocation to rioting. His objection was sustained.

Some of the guards who took the stand would not give Behan straight answers. When Behan complained about this to McLean, the judge told him he would have an opportunity to make an address to the jury, "I'll make one, too," Behan promised.

The following exchange took place between Behan and a guard named J.K. Hull.

"All you heard was I'll take the punishment," Behan said. "You didn't hear me say, 'Men, there's no use in all being punished. I'm doing life and seven years and will take whatever punishment is meted out.' You don't remember hearing that?" pressed Behan.

"No. I don't remember."

"The only thing that you remember was that they barricaded the doors. Machines were broken. Those are the only things you remember. Is there not one good thing done by those 350 men that day that you can remember?" The witness refrained from answering.

"Were you nervous?" asked Behan three times. Each time the witness evaded answering. Finally he admitted that he was because the convicts "were in complete control."

"If they were in complete control, they could have done anything."

"They could."

"They had no cause to love any of the officers in the dome?"

"You'll have to decide that for yourself."

"I will not!" Behan shot back.

"We were not great favourites. Some of the guards were hated by the convicts."

"Did any of those convicts who hated the guards take revenge?"

"No, I don't think so."

Behan wanted to call convicted murderer Joseph Chartrand to

the witness box. Chartrand had spent most of the last twenty-three years in solitary confinement. MacKay objected. "Whether this man has been in solitary confinement for 1,000 years has nothing to do with what Behan is accused of doing on October 17."

"It has everything to do with it," Behan argued. "What has happened to this man could happen to me."

Chartrand was allowed to talk about his own experiences but was not permitted to talk about the treatment of other inmates.

Then Behan charged that two of the broken sewing machines the prosecution had brought into court as evidence of the destruction wrought by the convicts were in fact old machines that had been in a storage room at the time of the disturbances. He questioned Deputy Warden George Sullivan about them.

"When were these machines broken?"

"Just before the riot ..."

"Be careful of that word 'riot,'" Behan said. "What is a riot?"

Sullivan gave his definition of the word.

"You don't know what a riot is," Behan scoffed. "If you saw one, you'd drop dead."

Behan then called a convict named Cecil Smith. He was the young man who had badly injured his hand while carrying a large rock to the barricade. Smith testified that the prison doctor had refused to treat his injury. He claimed the doctor said it was part of his punishment.

One convict after another testified that on that October day, Sam Behan had made a speech to the men urging them to do nothing violent. He had told them not to destroy prison property. He had told them not to smoke in the mailbag room because of the danger of fire. These men all insisted there had been no "riot" but said there might well have been one had it not been for Sammie Behan. It had been a peaceful demonstration, they said, until Acting Warden Smith called in the army.

Finally Deputy Warden Matthew John Walsh admitted he had heard Behan tell the inmates, "Men, use no violence."

"Thank you very much, Mr. Walsh," Behan said. "You are the first witness (for the prosecution) that heard me say that." On the fifth day of his trial, Behan made an impassioned plea to the jury:

It doesn't matter much if you find me guilty. I am serving a term of life and seven years for a crime I didn't commit.

I don't care what your verdict is as far as I personally am concerned. My life means nothing to me, for I can't live long enough to get out: but I want to show you men there has not been humane treatment in the penitentiary.

We are not humans. We are dogs. It is a living hell. A living grave. At the age of six years I was sent to school where I learned to steal, where I learned everything ... I am not here to discuss prison reforms. The court rules against it. But I say any public court is a court of inquiry. The public must know and ought to know.

They won't stop a man from stealing at the penitentiary. If God won't stop me from stealing, no one else will. Yet they think this life and seven years isn't enough for me. They want to make sure I'll never walk the streets again a free man. I'm in my early forties now. Perhaps in the ordinary course of events I would get a chance for parole in 1961, but if they tack seven more years on me, which is the penalty for rioting, I'll be there forever.

Humane treatment? Walk into Sing Sing Prison anytime, and you'll hardly know you are in a penitentiary. You see men smoking and talking: they have all they want except their liberty. Only a couple of reports a month are made against men, and they must be serious. Inmates themselves discipline the place, and a new man coming in is warned by the convicts not to do anything to cause them to lose their privileges or it will be just too bad for him.

The affair at Kingston Penitentiary last October was a mole hill out of which they made a Mount Everest ... If that was a riot at the Kingston Penitentiary, what was it at St. Vincent de Paul, where $1,000,000 damage was done and men were wounded? What about Dorchester, where convicts fought the officers? What about Auburn Prison in 1928, where officers and convicts were killed? What about Nevada, where convicts shot down officers like dogs, and then shot themselves? In St. Vincent de Paul some got life for their part in the trouble. Why? Because they were like the little child in 'Oliver Twist': they asked for a little more porridge.

It was the same with us. We asked for humane treatment and they locked us up ... Was it a riot? Right here in the city of Kingston you had a riot of unemployed a few weeks ago ... they smashed windows and broke into a meeting. Were there charges laid? No, there were not, because the city had more sense and they had no one to whitewash with a waste of money. Why didn't the Crown say it would be better to save the money being wasted on their trials to help the unemployed and needy, and instead take the matter before the Warden's Court?

In the penitentiary, they are making it a veritable fortress. Even in the chapel where the Lord's Gospel is preached, bristling rifles are to be seen. If there was a riot, and you find I was a rioter, every man in the penitentiary is guilty.

Don't consider me, gentlemen. I'm speaking for thousands asking you to give them a chance. Do away with the rotten system. Give them a chance for something to live for. Give the convict a break, and you'll not be making another criminal. I am not asking for sympathy from the jury. I merely want justice. Give me a chance to tell men there were people who did their duty and gave men a chance.

Then Behan added, "I'll be buried alive in solitary confinement for this, and until the present social system is changed, there will be thousands that follow me. Maybe some of you will be there. Maybe some of your children, though God forbid."

It took the jury only seventy-five minutes to find Behan not guilty of rioting. Behan wept as he thanked the jury members. He said those were the first tears he had shed in over twenty years.

Behan's address to the jury was printed in the newspapers. Veteran criminal lawyers read it and told colleagues they wished they had that kind of eloquence. Archdeacon F.G. Scott of Montreal, an influential clergyman, issued an open "thank you" to Behan for telling the country what was going on behind the walls of the Kingston Pen. People wrote letters to the editor, offering Sam Behan work if he could be released. One magistrate commented on how sad it was that a man of Behan's obvious talents should become a thief, when he could have been a doctor, lawyer, or anything else he wanted to be. Behan's words also drew the attention of social reformers like Agnes Macphail, Canada's first female Member of Parliament. With the conditions in Canadian prisons being lambasted in the press as a national shame, the federal government was forced to act.

General Ormond had conducted an investigation and described his findings in a twenty-nine-page report. He placed much of the blame on Acting Warden Smith and on the failure of the prison administration to provide proper training for guards. Ormond interviewed convicts and noted their complaints but made no recommendations for changes. He stated, as well, "I am also of the opinion that two or three convicts, whose identity has not been disclosed up to the present time, are the principal organizers of the outbreak."

One of those "two or three convicts" was Sam Behan. In his report, Ormond did not identify the inmates to whom he had spoken by name but gave each man a letter. Behan was convict F. Of his interview with Behan, Ormond wrote:

> Convict F's first complaint was against the officers, stating they were petty tyrants and persecuted the convicts at every opportunity. This incited the men to talk back and they were reported and punished without having the officer appear in evidence against them or without their evidence being given any consideration whatever. F boasted that he had been born a thief, had always been a thief and intended to die a thief; that he was undergoing a sentence

of life and seven years; that he did not expect to get out of the penitentiary alive and his life meant nothing to him and he was willing to sacrifice it, if by losing it he would make things easier for the future generation of convicts in Kingston Penitentiary. His range of complaints extended to include the cooking of food. He stated the food was the finest in any prison in the world but that it was badly cooked. He also complained that visits allowed to convicts were conducted under inhumane conditions and were not of sufficient length; that letters and magazines were too severely censored, and stated that censored portions of magazines and periodicals were sold by the officers to convicts. The exercise period was too short, he said, and the amount of time in the fresh air with no freedom of movement. There were also, he said, no recreation and nothing that would divert the introspective mind of a convict.

This was followed by a lengthy description of Behan's own version of what had happened during what he referred to as a "demonstration." Ormond's report was not enough to satisfy the critics. The federal government was obliged to appoint a Royal Commission to investigate. The result was the Archambault Report, which called for major reforms. Unfortunately for Sam Behan, he did not live to see them implemented.

For months after the "riot" trials, the public heard little about the Kingston Pen. Things in the Big House had apparently settled down. All that time, however, trouble was smoldering. The inmates were finally getting cigarette papers with their tobacco. Lieutenant Colonel W.D. Megloughlin, who had replaced Gilbert Smith as warden, allowed the men to play softball as a form of recreation. But discontent was still rife. Many of the guards who had been considered unfit for the job were still working at the penitentiary. There were 105 American convicts in the prison, and they complained that in American prisons they were allowed to have radios in their cells, newspapers, and a larger ration of tobacco. Canadian inmates joined the Americans in demanding these things. The shift to daylight savings time also caused grumbling. It meant that the men were locked in their cells well before dark, making sleep difficult.

Then, early in May 1934, without any explanation, the warden cancelled the softball games. Seventeen men who became disruptive because of this were hauled off to Keeper's Hall to be paddled. With rumours flying around that the prisoners were planning a major disturbance, the prison administration placed more armed guards on the walls. Then, any convicts who might assume leadership roles in an uprising were thrown into solitary. One of them, of course, was Sam Behan.

The P of I was so overcrowded that the cells were divided in two by partitions. This meant not only that the prisoner was confined to a much smaller space, but also that while the man on one side of the partition had a toilet, the man on the other side had only a bucket. The smell in the P of I became unbearable. An anonymous guard told the *Toronto Daily Star* that giving the men softball and then taking it away from them was just asking for trouble. He said he didn't think the prison administration ever intended to make the game a permanent form of recreation. "It was just a sop to get the men back gradually to the old system."

Some of the men in the P of I — including Behan — went on a rampage in their cells. They tore down the partitions, smashed the few furnishings, and then turned on the taps in the sinks, allowing the water to overflow and flood the place. More than a dozen men were paddled. However, the initial report stated that Behan was not subjected to this punishment because the prison doctor had diagnosed him as having heart trouble.

Then on the afternoon of May 15 fire broke out in the carpentry shop. Prison staff quickly extinguished it. No sooner had they doused the flames than three more fires suddenly flared up in the building known as the change room. This was a combination barber shop, laundromat, and bath house. With heaps of clothing and bedding, there was no shortage of flammable material. The flames were soon out of control and the Kingston Fire Department had to be called in. Armed guards patrolled the perimeters of the penitentiary in case someone tried to escape under the cover of smoke. But the convicts went to their cells in a quiet and orderly manner when told to do so. However, once they were locked in they began to ring their tin cups on the bars and sing "The Prisoner's Song" very loudly. This was a folk song that had become very popular in the 1920s. The final verse went:

> Now if I had the wings of an angel
> Over these prison walls I would fly
> And I'd fly to the arms of my poor darling
> And there I'd be willing to die

It took the firemen about four hours to extinguish the blaze, and by that time the change room was a smoking ruin. There was no doubt the fires had been deliberately set. Ten days after the news of the fires, Canadians read headlines about an even more stunning event.

For weeks it had been falsely rumoured that Tim Buck had died in the prison. The federal government refused to comment on the story one way or the other. Then on May 26 the Canadian public was shocked to read that Sam Behan had died suddenly. Again, Ottawa was keeping close-mouthed about it. So was Warden Megloughlin. But Kingston residents living in the vicinity of the penitentiary could hear the loud din of the convicts shouting their anger and banging cups and other objects on the bars and stone floors.

At 8:30 on the morning of the twenty-sixth, Behan's lawyer, Frank Regan, received a telegram from Warden Megloughlin: "Regret to have to advise Sam Behan died very suddenly here this morning. His wife has been advised. Instructions regarding disposition of remains awaited from her."

Regan had been hard at work trying to arrange a new trial for Behan that they hoped would clear him of the Montreal robbery charge. Eerily, at the same time Regan received the telegram from Megloughlin, he received a letter from Behan, written three days earlier. In it Behan wrote of his confidence that a new trial would exonerate him. He also expressed appreciation for help he was getting from Agnes Macphail.

Sam Behan did not die in the hole, as was reported in the newspapers. But he was in the P of I, and his surroundings were squalid enough. His half-cell had a bucket for a toilet. His bed was a wooden platform three inches off the cold stone floor. It had a mattress and some blankets, luxury items in that place. A coroner's jury visited the cell and reported that Behan had been kept in a clean and acceptable cell. The prison doctor said Behan had been laid low by coronary thrombosis, and there was nothing anybody could have done for him. The condition, the doctor said, was undetectable (though earlier the same doctor had diagnosed a weak heart). The jury was told that at 6:30 on the morning of the twenty-sixth, Behan said good morning to a guard making the rounds of the isolation cells. Shortly after that, other prisoners began shouting for help, that something was wrong with Behan. The doctor arrived in time to hear Behan's last breath. Red Ryan carried the body out of the cell. Behan's remains were sent to his widow, Mary, in Brooklyn. The coroner's jury took only fifteen minutes to conclude that Behan had died of natural causes. Inmates swore he had been poisoned.

Perhaps Behan did die of natural causes. But why was he in the P of I, two weeks after the doctor had diagnosed heart problems? Surely an oppressive and emotionally and physically stressful place like the P of I was no fit environment for a man with a weak heart! Then there was the question of the paddling after the uproar in the P of I. At first it was said that Behan had not been paddled because of poor health. But weeks after his death the story came out that he *had* been paddled, in violation of the doctor's orders. Apparently Behan was supposed to get twenty strokes — twice the usual sentence. But after four he either passed out or pleaded to be given no more. According to the story, the warden cancelled the remaining sixteen. Behan allegedly said it was the only "break" he'd ever had in prison.

Still, a mystery remains. Doctor W.P. May, Assistant Professor of Pathology at Queen's University, did the autopsy. He said he found plenty of old scars on the body but no fresh wounds. If Behan had indeed been paddled less than two weeks before his death, would there have been sufficient time for the abrasions to heal? Or did Dr. May simply not turn the body over? Or, was the doctor part of yet another penitentiary cover-up?

In December 1934 Tim Buck was released from prison following the repeal of the law that had been used to put him away. He told a cheering crowd of supporters in Toronto, "We know there was cruelty to Sam Behan. And sooner or later we'll have the opportunity of asking why the truth has not yet been told in connection with Behan's death."

In February 1937 the Royal Commission investigating prisons interviewed Tim Buck and asked him about Sam Behan. "Behan was a sick man," Buck told them. "He was paddled on orders from Ottawa. Behan said that at the third stroke he fainted, but there is a dispute over whether the punishment was stopped then."

In the weeks following Behan's death newspaper editorials commented on the "ugly reports" about him being flogged by official order and contrary to the prison physician's instructions. According to these reports, Behan struggled with the guards and had to be dragged to Keeper's Hall and strapped to the table by overpowering force. Editorial writers wanted to know why the government had spun such a "web of secrecy" around Behan's death. Why did the inquest into that lonely death deep in the bowels of a prison not include a lawyer representing Behan's family, they wanted to know. Why did the people conducting the inquest not interview the prison doctor? Why did they not interview the other inmates who were also in the P of I at the time Behan died? In spite of the efforts of a few conscientious people like Agnes Macphail, those questions were never answered.

In July 1935 Red Ryan was released on parole. Within ten months he would be shot dead while attempting to rob a liquor store. But before that fateful day Ryan would give many interviews. In one discussion with a *Globe* reporter, Ryan talked about Sam Behan and said the words that could have been a fitting eulogy.

"He always wanted to have the last word and make a speech. He was a tough boy, but he made a lot of trouble for himself; made things unnecessarily hard. But he was never beaten, in the hole or out of it."

PHILLIPS AND LUND

"NOW BOYS PLEASE TAKE A WARNING"

Dorchester Penitentiary in New Brunswick was for many years the maximum-security dumping ground for hardcase criminals from all over Atlantic Canada. It was in that grim institution in 1939 that Fred Sterling Phillips, twenty-three, met Earl Lund, twenty-seven. The two Prince Edward Islanders were an unusual pair to strike up a friendship. Perhaps the smallish Phillips needed someone like Lund to watch out for him in a rough place like Dorchester. Lund wasn't exactly a hulk of a man, tipping the scales at 150 pounds. But he was muscular, strong and tough. Philips was more of a joker than a fighter.

Born in Summerside, Phillips was the grandson of the town's chief of police. He was orphaned at an early age, and in his mid-teens he moved to Charlottetown. At that time the population of the provincial capital was about fifteen thousand — a big city to a kid like Fred Phillips.

It didn't take young Phillips long to run afoul of the Charlottetown police. At age seventeen he was arrested for breaking and entering and sent to reform school. Most Canadian reform schools of the 1930s were strong on punishment and not much given to actual reform. Phillips left the institution no better a young man than he had been when he went in. His hero was the notorious Ontario bank robber Red Ryan.

Phillips continued to get into trouble for things like petty theft and breaking and entering. He did marry and father two children, but the marriage did not last very long. Then Phillips stole a truck and served a stint in the Queen's County jail. He was doing nothing except making himself an all too familiar nuisance to the Charlottetown police.

In September 1939 Canada declared war on Nazi Germany and young Canadian men rushed to enlist. Fred Phillips was one of them.

He applied for the Royal Canadian Air Force. But before he could actually be enlisted, Phillips was arrested for burglarizing houses. Instead of being shipped off to fight the Luftwaffe in a Spitfire, Phillips was bundled off to the Dorchester pen. Had Fred Phillips kept his hands clean long enough for him to go overseas, destiny might have had a very different role for him.

Earl Lund was already a longtime resident of Dorchester when Phillips landed there. Lund was a laconic man of mixed white and Native background. He had piercing dark eyes and a rather prominent hooked nose. He looked like a "heavy" from the Hollywood gangster films that were so popular at the time. Lund had very little formal education. He was a bachelor, and when he wasn't in jail he lived with his widowed mother.

Like Phillips, Lund first ran into trouble with the law at the age of seventeen. The year was 1929, and he was charged with breaking and entering. That was followed by a long series of liquor-related charges. Thirty-five of them! This was the age of Prohibition, and like many Prince Edward Islanders, Lund got into the bootlegging business. The Island was a major way station for booze on its way to American ports like Boston and New York, and the "dry" provinces of Canada's east coast. But Lund wasn't the brightest of the rum-running fraternity. He kept getting caught and jailed for it. In 1933 he escaped from jail, and a year later he was arrested for armed bank robbery. A judge sentenced him to ten years in Dorchester.

The taciturn Lund and the wisecracking Phillips became such good buddies that they decided to get together when they were both on the outside. Thus it was that in January 1941 the two small-time outlaws became the principal players in a crime drama that would stun wartime Prince Edward Island. Phillips and Lund were well known to the Charlottetown police as thieves. Now they would go into the arrest books as murderers.

On the night of January 30, 1941, Phillips and Lund were in Charlottetown's Capitol movie theatre watching *G-Men*, a gangster movie starring James Cagney. Lund had been back in Prince Edward Island just sixteen days, out on parole after serving seven years of his ten-year bank robbery stretch. He and Phillips were swigging moonshine whiskey from a bottle in a brown paper bag. The PEI version of white lightning was like the homemade booze brewed anywhere else. It packed twice the wallop of the legal stuff. By the time the gangster movie was over the pair had polished off the bottle and were feeling no pain. They decided they didn't want to stay for the second feature, a cowboy shoot-'em-up called *The Marshal of Mesa City*. They staggered out of the Capitol and went reeling down King Street, near Charlottetown's waterfront.

It was after eleven o'clock, and not a soul was to be seen on the snow-clogged streets. Fred and Earl wanted to get another bottle so they could continue their celebration of Lund's newly gained freedom. They weren't likely to find one at that late hour, but perhaps they could get some two-percent beer, or even just some soft drinks to kill the dryness left by the high-octane hooch they'd been swilling. But would any store still be open?

Soon they were in front of Trainor's Meat Market at the corner of King Street and Pownal Street. This was a combination butcher shop and convenience store run by seventy-eight-year-old Peter Trainor. The store was on the ground floor, and Trainor lived alone in the second-floor apartment. He had been a widower for fifteen years, and his only child, a daughter, lived with her husband in Nova Scotia. Old man Trainor was ordinarily in bed by 10:30, but Lund and Phillips could see that a light was on behind the drawn curtains. In their inebriated state, it probably did not occur to them that a light burning in Trainor's store at that hour was unusual. Nor did they give much thought to a man whom they later claimed they saw running from the store. They were too set on finding something to drink. The door was not locked, so they went inside. Accounts of just what happened next would be clouded by alcohol-fogged memories, and a magistrate's opinion of the characters of Earl Lund and Fred Phillips — ex-cons!

Shortly before midnight two Charlottetown plainclothes officers approached the corner of King and Pownal. One of them, Anthony Lund, was Earl Lund's cousin. His partner that night was Sterns Webster. At that time Prince Edward Island police officers did not carry firearms. Like the English bobbies who were their models, they had billy clubs and handcuffs. The two policemen saw the light on in Trainor's Meat Market. In a small community like Charlottetown, anything out of the ordinary warranted investigation. The officers decided they'd better take a look. As they walked toward the establishment they caught a glimpse of a man who darted around a corner of the store and vanished in the darkness. Because of the high snow banks all they saw was the man's head and hat. The policemen did not pursue him but went straight to the storefront. They encountered another man who was just passing by and sent him to a nearby house to phone the police station. Minutes later Constables George Gregory and Charles Poole arrived in the patrol wagon.

The curtains were drawn and the policemen assumed the door was locked. Anthony Lund peered through a crack between the curtains. The light within was dim, but Lund could see a man standing behind the counter near the cash register. He recognized his cousin Earl. He heard Earl speak to someone else but couldn't see the other person nor make out what Earl said. Suspecting his cousin was up to no good, Anthony Lund tapped on the window with his billy club. There was no response, so the policemen smashed the glass with their billies and leapt inside. Then the lights went out!

The officers heard the racket of falling boxes and smashing glass. They groped their way through the darkness and found that a back window had been smashed. Anthony Lund and Constable Poole climbed through it, and in the small yard behind the store they captured Earl Lund and placed him under arrest. Then Webster and Gregory heard a voice from the top of the stairs cry out, "Come on up and get me, too!"

Constable Gregory raced up the stairs, but Fred Phillips struck him with a bottle of ginger ale and sent him tumbling back down. Webster started up the stairs and then saw the man at the top pointing Peter Trainor's .32 calibre Smith & Wesson revolver at him. Fortunately for the policeman, when Phillips tried to fire the gun, the trigger stuck. As Webster advanced on him, Phillips threw the gun at him, and then pelted him with pop bottles. Webster reached the top of the stairs and grappled with Phillips. The two men fell down the stairs, where Phillips was subdued and handcuffed. Webster later testified that Phillips told him, "If the gun had worked, you wouldn't have gotten up the stairs." The officers tossed the pair into the patrol wagon and the constables took them to jail. Then Anthony Lund and Webster turned on the light so they could inspect Trainor's store. What they saw shocked them.

The place was a shambles, as though a violent struggle had taken place. Spattered blood was everywhere. A city official named Ivan Y. Reddin had been at the police station when the call came in, and he had walked over to Trainor's store to see what was going on. Reddin helped the police search the premises, and it was he who found Peter Trainor's body in a back room. The old man had been hacked to death!

The autopsy would reveal twenty-two stab wounds in Trainor's body, mostly to the head, neck and hands. One had completely severed his spinal cord. The victim had almost been decapitated, with only a shred of skin still attaching the head to the torso. Trainor's skull was fractured in two places. His nose and jaw were broken. His false teeth had been knocked right out of his mouth and lay on the floor near a fish barrel. When Reddin found the body, the eyes were still hauntingly open.

The following morning Earl Lund and Fred Phillips woke up in jail with massive hangovers. Police Chief Albert Bertwhistle said to Lund, "Aye there, Lund, nice fix you got yourself into."

Lund replied, "Hello, Chief. How's she going?"

Both men expressed disbelief when told they were charged with the murder of Peter Trainor. They thought the police were joking, trying to scare them into sobriety. They said they had gone into Trainor's Meat Market looking for something to drink. They were trying to find the proprietor when the police suddenly burst in. They explained that as soon as they saw police, they realized there must be some kind of trouble. They tried to run, because they were afraid that with their records, they would be blamed for it.

But the police were not joking. And Phillips and Lund could not explain why they had the victim's blood and hair on their clothing. Phillips couldn't satisfactorily explain how he came to be in possession of Trainor's gun, nor why he had threatened a police officer with it.

As the police saw it, the two ex-convicts had tried to rob Trainor, and the old man had resisted. Though neither man had a history of savage violence, the brutal assault on Trainor could have resulted from the effects of rotgut whiskey. It was hardly surprising to the police that the pair seemed to have no memory of their foul deed.

Nonetheless, the evidence the police had was all circumstantial. Two police officers had seen another man running from the store. Moreover, none of the knives or other butcher's tools in Trainor's shop could be identified as the murder weapon. And one of Trainor's knives was missing! The chances for an acquittal were not good, but neither were they impossible. In a life-or-death trial, guilt had to be established beyond the shadow of a doubt. A good lawyer just might be able to plant enough doubt in the minds of the jury members to gain a verdict of not guilty.

No one could say that Lester O'Donnell was not a good lawyer. The problem was that he was inexperienced. Since Phillips and Lund could not afford to hire a lawyer, the court appointed O'Donnell to defend them. Young O'Donnell had only recently been admitted to the bar. This was his very first jury trial.

The rookie counselor was up against a formidable opponent. Arguing the case for the Crown was none other than Thane A. Campbell, who was both the premier of Prince Edward Island *and* the province's attorney general. Campbell decided to prosecute Lund and Phillips himself because he did not think anyone else in the province was qualified. That was hardly surprising, since Prince Edward Island had not had a murder in almost forty years. However, the fact that the premier himself was handling the prosecution was not lost on the jury. Would so significant a person risk his political reputation prosecuting innocent men?

Lund and Phillips were also unfortunate in the choice of a judge to preside over the trial. Albert C. Saunders was a former PEI premier and a former mayor of Charlottetown. He was also Thane Campbell's mentor. As a young man Campbell had studied law under Saunders.

The trial began in the last week of June. O'Donnell did manage to prevail on two important points. He was able to prove that a knife presented by the Crown as the possible murder weapon could not, in fact, have inflicted the wounds Trainor had suffered. He also prevented the Crown from showing the jury photographs of Trainor's mangled body. When O'Donnell was successful with his motion regarding the pictures, Phillips slapped him on the back and said, "Attaboy, Lester!"

But Phillips and Lund did not do well on the witness stand. They spoke poorly. Their testimonies sounded contrived and coached. They did not sound convincing when they said they must have gotten blood on their clothing when they stumbled over boxes in their haste to get out. Under Campbell's cross-examination they gave the impression of being guilty men.

Campbell asked Phillips, "If you were in the store not doing anything improper, why didn't you open the door and let the policemen in?"

Phillips replied, "They would have arrested us if there was anything wrong."

"What gave you the idea there was something wrong?"

"Well, by the cops hitting the window."

"In other words, your minds were rather prophetic."

"I heard of lots of fellows that were innocent of things they were convicted of."

"So you were perfectly innocent?"

"Certainly, sir."

"But you were afraid to be caught in the building?"

"Certainly."

"Why were you afraid if you weren't doing anything?"

Phillips pointed at Campbell and replied, "It's all right from someone of your social standing, but not in mine."

O'Donnell based his defence on the fact that another man had been seen hurrying away from the store. That unidentified person, O'Donnell said, was the real murderer. His clients simply had the bad luck to stumble onto the scene of a ghastly crime.

If O'Donnell had succeeded in planting any doubts about Phillips and Lund's guilt in the minds of any jurors, Judge Saunders swept those doubts aside when he made his address to the jury. In one of the most bizarre episodes ever to take place in a Canadian court of law, Judge Saunders stated several times that he was not saying the defendants were guilty, and then went on to demonstrate his belief that they were guilty as hell. In his three-hour address Saunders harped on the disreputable characters of the accused, and then actually *acted out* his version of what happened in Trainor's store. "I need not remind you that prisoners so situated when guilty will naturally cling to any straw in order to save themselves," the judge said. "They will manufacture any story to suit the occasion. An oath means nothing to them. I am not saying the prisoners are guilty. I will say without hesitation I was not greatly impressed with the evidence of the prisoners. The suffering that poor old man must have endured

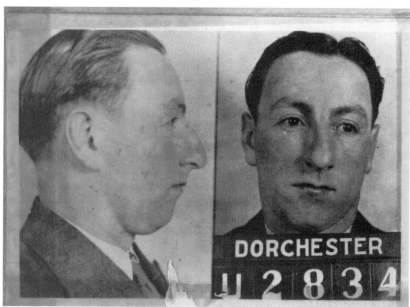

Fred Phillips and Earl Lund, the last men to be hanged in Prince Edward Island, are shown here in their mug shots. Did the judge have them convicted before the trial even began? (Library and Archives Canada, Brechin Group, C-143254 and C-143255)

when he was so brutally attacked by some ruffians, is probably the most outrageous thing that ever happened in this province. Twenty-two wounds! So severe that the injury almost severed that poor old man's head! I tell you gentlemen! So horrible that it's hard to imagine what must have happened to that poor, unfortunate old man."

Then Saunders pointed at the pair in the prisoner's box. "And *they* ask for mercy and sympathy! What sympathy did they show that poor old man! What sympathy do they deserve!"

At that point, to the astonishment of all, Judge Saunders left the bench and went into his performance. A blackjack had been found in Lund's pocket when he was arrested. Saunders now produced that item and a handkerchief from under his robes and used them as props in his demonstration. Changing his voice to indicate the roles of the killers and the victim, Saunders engaged in theatrics that certainly did not belong in a courtroom. After he had finished stabbing his imaginary victim, Saunders said:

"I will tell you what happened in my opinion. These men went there for the purpose of holding up this old man. Not for the purpose of murdering him, no. What evidence is there for a holdup? The strongest evidence possible that I could imagine. There, I say, is the blackjack. They took this skull cracker or blackjack and they had it for a purpose; they did not go there, I am satisfied, to murder the man. Why do I say that? Because they would have taken the real thing, a gun, and shot the man, or else a knife or a dagger."

Saunders returned to his bench and continued:

> I think it must be clear to anyone that the accused were caught in the store under circumstances which do not admit any doubt regarding their guilt. Remember, these are only my ideas, which may or may not be correct. I am not saying these men are guilty. As I see it, it is not within the realm of reasonable probability that some other person was in that store between 10:30 pm on January 30 and 12:10 am on January 31. Many things in this world are possible, but to me it is beyond all reasonable probability that such a strange co-incidence would possibly happen. It seems to me, the accused, who have penitentiary records, planned

a holdup. I think they tried the holdup game and it miscarried or got out of control. I am convinced the man the police saw was their lookout man or an accomplice. I am convinced that the story told in court was a clear invention.

Then Saunders looked directly at the jury and said, "I fear it would strain your consciences to find them not guilty." Clearly the judge expected the jury to reach a guilty verdict. After less than two hours of deliberation, the jury did just that. Judge Saunders sentenced Fred Phillips and Earl Lund to be hanged on August 20. Speaking for both condemned men, Phillips said he was satisfied they had been given a fair trial, but he still denied killing Peter Trainor.

Lester O'Donnell sent a letter to Ottawa requesting an appeal and complaining about the conduct of Judge Saunders. "This demonstration without evidence to support it must have had a strong effect upon the jury." Letters from the two men's relatives went to the Minister of Justice Ernest Lapointe and Prime Minister Mackenzie King. Matilda Lund, Earl's mother, said that Judge Saunders was "not all there." Ottawa would neither grant an appeal nor commute the death sentence to life imprisonment.

Phillips's sister Olive wrote to King George VI. "I know you are busy in time of war and I am sure you are in sympathy with our young men who have lost their lives in fighting, and I am sure you wouldn't want them to take the life of my brother who would give anything to be in your fighting forces now. I don't blame the jury for having convicted them. It was Judge Saunders. It's the first time I ever heard a judge talk like that ... he's not supposed to stick up for either side, but he was against my brother from the start. Him and I are orphans ... he's all I have left."

The letter would never even have reached King George's desk. His staff would have forwarded it to the governor general of Canada, who in turn would have passed it on to the Minister of Justice. Moreover, the British monarchy is not permitted to interfere in matters of civil law.

The execution was carried out as scheduled on August 20. Officer Sterns Webster witnessed what he would later call the "cruelest darn thing I ever saw." The gallows was erected in an enclosure outside the prison walls. Both condemned men walked to the gallows calmly. "They were really tough characters," Webster said. He recalled Phillips saying, "I feel a little queer, but I'm not afraid."

John Ellis, the official Canadian hangman, dropped them both at the same time. Phillips's execution went off without a hitch. But Lund's neck was so thick and muscular, he was slowly strangling. The hangman had to stand on Lund's shoulders to hasten death.

After sentencing Lund and Phillips to hang, Judge Saunders had urged them to make a written confession of their crime, to purge their souls and leave a warning for other would-be criminals. They never did write out a confession, maintaining their innocence to the end. But Phillips wrote a poem titled "A Warning," which appeared in the *Charlottetown Patriot* on the day of the hanging.

> I'm sitting here waiting
> My time is growing nigh
> And soon I'll be with my Master
> Away up there on high
>
> My dear old dad and mother
> And little sister too
> Are away up there in heaven
> High up there in the blue.
>
> It will be a happy reunion
> When I arrive up there
> And through God's divine mercy
> His heavenly home I'll share
>
> My life has been so empty
> Of God and all things good
> But I know that he loves me
> For look at the pains he took
>
> He died on Calvary's Cross
> For sinners just like me
> And if you will heed this little poem
> You'll make Him happy, you'll see

Now boys please take a warning
For crime it does not pay
And if you are on the crooked path
You are sure to land here some day

Now take for instance Dillinger
He was from the U.S.A.
And take our own Red Ryan
In a Canadian grave he lay

These are only instances
That what I say is true
And if you will not listen
It will surely happen to you

I'll not say any more boys
You all know what I mean
There's just one thing to remember
"Look" what happened to me

Fred Phillips and Earl Lund were the last men convicted of murder to be hanged in Prince Edward Island.

MARGARET GOEDE

KIDNAPPER

For centuries criminals have seen kidnapping as an effective way to force the wealthy to part with large sums of their money. In the days of ancient Rome, pirates regularly abducted Roman patricians travelling by sea and held them for ransom. One such victim was the young Julius Caesar. During the bandit-plagued early years of the 1930s, American hoodlums like the Barker boys, their Canadian pal Alvin "Creepy" Karpis, and George "Machine Gun" Kelly turned from robbing banks to kidnapping rich tycoons. Probably the most infamous kidnapping in American history was that of aviation hero Charles Lindbergh's baby son in 1932. Sadly, the child was found dead. One suspected kidnapper was executed.

Canada, too, has had incidents of kidnapping. In August 1934 Canadian beer baron John Labatt was waylaid on a lonely road near Sarnia, Ontario, and held for ransom. After being blindfolded and chained to a bed for three days and two nights, Labatt made a deal with the kidnappers, who subsequently released him unharmed. The criminals did not receive a cent of the promised ransom money.

In 1958 another wealthy Canadian family, the Reitmans of Montreal, were targeted for a kidnapping. The victim was a small boy. The kidnapper was not a notorious gangster, but a woman.

She was born Margarete Zablowsky in Tilset, Germany, in 1912. Family and friends just called her Greta. In 1933 she married Gerhard Goede. Both survived the Second World War, but in 1950 Gerhard died. Greta had no money and no skills except those of a housekeeper. She went to work as a cook.

Greta immigrated to Canada in 1954. Her life in the new country was lonely. She drifted from job to job, working as a waitress, cook, and housemaid. She left one job at a Toronto restaurant without notice and with pay still owed to her.

Greta went west, working in a variety of communities in Alberta and British Columbia until illness struck in April 1956. Greta was living alone in a shoddy dwelling in Dawson Creek, British Columbia, when a strange malady laid her low, causing temporary paralysis of her right leg. She was bedridden for two days before neighbours found her almost frozen to death. She was removed to Coquitlam where she did not fully recover until October.

Greta returned to Toronto. On April 21, 1958, she was hired as nursemaid in the home of Mr. and Mrs. Arthur Cobham. That very day when Mrs. Cobham brought in the mail, she found among the letters an unstamped envelope. She opened it and was stunned to find it contained an extortion letter.

Written in oddly phrased English, the letter demanded $2,500 that was to be left in a sanitary box in the women's washroom of a Bloor Street restaurant. If this was not done, the note threatened, the Cobham's small child would be killed and their house burned down. Mrs. Cobham phoned the police.

The Toronto police put a "money" envelope in the ladies' washroom of the restaurant in question and then kept watch. Nobody tried to pick it up. Over the next month eight more anonymous letters arrived at the Cobham house, all demanding money and threatening the child. The police laid traps, but no one took the bait. On May 21 Greta quit her job, saying she was going to Montreal.

Greta stepped off a bus in the Montreal depot on June 2. She went to an employment agency and said she was looking for domestic work. One day later she was hired as a nursemaid in the home of Cyril Reitman.

Sam Reitman, patriarch of the family, owned the largest chain of women's clothing stores in Canada. His son Cyril, in charge of purchasing, lived in a fine big house in Montreal's exclusive Mount Royal district with his wife and little son. Two-and-a-half-year-old Joel, "Jo Jo" to the family, was a curly-haired, blue-eyed boy who was the apple of old Sam's eye.

The little boy quickly took to his new nurse, and within a couple of days the child's parents had no doubt they'd made a good choice in the kindly German woman. Greta was not a live-in nurse. She had a room on Sherbrooke Street. But she showed up on time every morning and she obviously doted on little Joel.

On the evening of Saturday, June 14, Cyril and his wife went to a concert. They left Joel with Greta, who had agreed to stay the night. At 8:30 Mrs. Reitman phoned home to check on things. Greta assured her all was well.

At 1:30 Sunday morning the parents arrived home to find the house in darkness and the doors locked. Neither had taken a key. Thinking the nurse had fallen asleep, Cyril rang the doorbell. When no one answered after several rings, the parents became concerned.

Cyril broke a window to gain entry to the house. Greta and Jo Jo were gone. A note had been left on a table. With horror the parents read:

"Now the time is coming to take your boy way. We want 10,000$ ten thousand in cash 200 50$. If you don't give the money to us we will kill your son right now. Your father did sometink to us many years ago. Now we have sometink to do to you."

The letter instructed them to leave the money in the women's washroom of a Montreal bus depot.

"We expect the money on Monday after 11 a.m. o'clock. Don't call the police or the radio. The first time we hear sometink we will kill you boy and we don't care for the money. Perhaps a woman will pick up the money. If the police catch the woman your son is to be killed.

"P.S. We expecht nobody in house and find woman here. We have to take her too. She will be killed to. Maybe we will kill her after we have the money. She is too smart. Perhaps she can pick up the money. Do not mark the money."

There was no signature on the handwritten note. Cyril immediately called the police. Officers were at the door before he had even completed the call. A neighbour had seen him breaking into his own house and took him for a burglar.

The note was puzzling. Why did the kidnappers say they had expected to find no one in the house? Did they actually think the parents would go out and leave the child alone? Also, $10,000 seemed a rather small amount. Kidnappers usually demanded a king's ransom from families as wealthy as the Reitmans.

Cyril Reitman wasn't concerned about such quibbles. He quickly arranged to have the money delivered to the bus depot. He and his wife — and old Sam — asked the police to keep the story out of the newspapers and off the radio so as not to endanger their son.

The police complied. But on Monday they watched the women's washroom of the bus station where the ransom money had been deposited. Nobody picked it up.

While the Reitmans were agonizing in Montreal — Sam no doubt tortured by memories of the Lindbergh case twenty-five years earlier — Jo Jo and his nurse were on a bus heading for Ottawa. When they reached the capital, Greta checked them into the Lord Elgin Hotel. She signed "Greta Braun" in the register.

Greta made no attempt to hide the boy. Sunday morning she took him into the hotel's coffee shop for breakfast. Then she called for a taxi. Cab driver Edward Royer picked them up, and Greta asked him to take them on a short tour of Ottawa. They drove around the city for less than an hour. When Royer dropped them back at the hotel, Greta asked for his business card so she could call him if she needed a cab again. Jo Jo had enjoyed the day. He liked going for car rides.

The following morning Greta phoned the cab company and asked specifically for Royer. When Greta got into the cab with Jo Jo, she asked Royer if he knew of anyone who could babysit while she went shopping. Royer said his wife would probably be willing to look after the boy for a few hours. He had a four-year-old son Joel could play with.

After leaving Jo Jo at his home on St. Patrick Street, Royer took Greta back downtown and dropped her at a department store. She told him to be back for her at 3:00 p.m.. Royer kept the appointment, but Greta didn't show up. Royer waited until 4:00 p.m., then notified the police. They told him to keep the child at his house while they contacted Children's Aid. Because the Montreal police were still keeping quiet about the kidnapping, the Ottawa police had no idea who the boy at the cab driver's house was.

That night, in a strange house, with strange — though kind — people, Jo Jo wouldn't eat and wouldn't go to bed. He wouldn't allow Mrs. Royer to undress him so she could put clean clothes on him. He kept asking for his parents. He finally fell asleep at 2:00 a.m.

In Montreal the Reitmans were frantic. By Tuesday morning, when no one had attempted to pick up the ransom money, they decided to appeal to the public. Mrs. Reitman went on radio. She gave descriptions of her son and Greta and pleaded for anyone who had seen them to contact the police immediately. The Ottawa police heard of the broadcast and suddenly had a pretty good idea whose little boy was at the Royer house.

Officers picked Joel up and took him to the home of Lawrence Slover, a relative of the Reitmans who lived in Ottawa. Meanwhile Cyril and his wife were in a car racing to Ottawa accompanied by a police escort. No one had any idea where Greta was.

There were tears of joy in the Slover house when Cyril and his wife rushed in and found Jo Jo happily munching a piece of chicken. The Royers were there, and Cyril embraced both of them.

"Thank you. If there ever is anything we can do for you ... Thank you," he gushed. He promised Edward and Mrs. Royer they would be rewarded. "Money doesn't mean a thing in a case like this," he said. "As long as the child is safe, that's the main thing."

Cyril phoned Montreal to tell his father the good news. But a phone call wasn't good enough for Sam Reitman. He wanted to see the boy himself. Cyril, his wife, and son got into their car for a fast, police-escorted drive back to Montreal.

Police were now searching for the blonde-haired, "foreign" woman Royer had described to them. He said she called herself Greta Braun. The police had little doubt she was Greta Goede.

Greta likely realized she wouldn't have a chance of picking up the ransom money without getting caught. Instead of returning to Montreal, she took a bus to Toronto and went back to a room she'd had on Quebec Avenue when she lived in the city previously. It wasn't long before two Toronto police detectives were at her door.

Paul Panico, the owner of the restaurant Greta had abruptly quit before going west, had heard Mrs. Reitman's radio broadcast and knew the police were looking for Greta. To his utter surprise, he saw her walking along the street. Panico phoned the police and suggested they try her old boarding house on Quebec Avenue.

Greta Goede was charged with abduction and kidnapping. The first charge carried a maximum sentence of ten years. The latter charge could mean life imprisonment. There was a further charge of extortion when police found that the handwriting of the Reitman's ransom note matched that of the threatening letters the Cobhams had received.

However, when Greta appeared in court in Montreal on July 8, she was tried only for abduction. Judge Lucien Gendron said it was in Greta's favour that she had left the child with responsible people rather than just deserting him. Nonetheless, the nurse had caused great anguish to people who had placed their trust in her. He sentenced her to seven years in prison and recommended that at the end of her sentence she be deported back to Germany. Greta said she was surprised that Canada did not have the death sentence for kidnappers.

Greta was in tears when she was taken from the courtroom. She hid her face with a kerchief and would not respond to reporters' questions. A police detective summed it up when he told the press, "She appears to be a very lonely woman."

BIBLIOGRAPHY

Books

Audett, James Henry and Gene Lowall. *Rap Sheet*. London: Cassel & Co. Ltd., 1955.

Bell, Charles W. *Who Said Murder?* Toronto: Macmillan Co. of Canada, 1935.

Butts, Edward. *The Desperate Ones: Forgotten Canadian Outlaws*. Toronto: Dundurn Press, 2006.

Butts, Edward and Harold Horwood. *Bandits & Privateers: Canada in the Age of Gunpowder*. Toronto: Doubleday Canada, 1987.

Carrigan, Owen D. *Crime and Punishment In Canada: A History*. Toronto: McClelland & Stewart, 1991.

Curtis, Dennis, Andrew Graham, Lou Kelly, and Barrie Wright. *Kingston Penitentiary: The First Hundred and Fifty Years, 1835–1985*. Ottawa: The Correctional Service of Canada, 1985.

Dictionary of Canadian Biography. Toronto: University of Toronto Press, 1966.

Encyclopedia of Newfoundland. St. John's: Newfoundland Book Publishers, 1981–1994.

Girandin, G. Russell and William J. Helmer. *Dillinger: The Untold Story*. Indianapolis: Indiana University Press, 1994.

Gray, James H. *The Boy From Winnipeg*. Toronto: Macmillan of Canada, 1970.

Helmer, William J. and Rick Mattix. *The Complete Public Enemy Almanac*. Nashville: Cumberland House, 2007.

Hornby, Jim. *In The Shadow of the Gallows: Criminal Law and Capital Punishment in Prince Edward Island 1769–1941*. Charlottetown: Institute of Island Studies, 1998.

Hustak, Alan. *They Were Hanged*. Toronto: James Lorimer & Co., 1987.

King, Jefferey S. *The Rise and Fall of the Dillinger Gang*. Nashville: Cumberland House, 2005.

Macdonald, Bill. *The True Intrepid*. Surrey: Timberholme Books, 1998.

McSherry, Peter. *The Big Red Fox: The Incredible Story of Norman "Red" Ryan, Canada's Most Notorious Criminal*. Toronto: Dundurn Press, 1999.

Murray, John Wilson. *Memoirs of a Great Canadian Detective.* Toronto: Collins, 1977 (first published in 1906).

Poulsen, Ellen. *Don't Call Us Molls: Women of the John Dillinger Gang.* Little Neck, NY: Clinton Cook Publishing Corp., 2002.

Robin, Martin. *The Saga of Red Ryan and Other Tales of Violence From Canada's Past.* Saskatoon: Western Producer Prairie Books, 1982.

Rowe, Frederick W. *A History of Newfoundland and Labrador.* Toronto: McGraw-Hill Ryerson, 1980.

Withrow, Oswald. C.J. *Shackling the Transgressor.* Toronto: Thomas Nelson & Sons, 1933.

Other Sources

Bates, Robert E. "The Truth About Blackie Audett." *On the Spot Journal* (Winter 2006).

Bowler, Phillip."The *Fly* Catches the *Black Snake.*" Unpublished ms, Vermont State Archives.

Burchill, John. "Bloody Jack." Winnipeg Police Service, http://www.winnipeg.ca/police/history/story8.stm

Capital Punishment in Canada, Canada Death Penalty Index, http://members.shaw.ca/canada_legal_history/

Files on the extradition of Sam Jackson alias Behan, No. 1639, Department of Justice, Library and Archives Canada, 1927.

Ormond, D.M. "Report of the Superintendent of Penitentiaries Re. Kingston Penitentiary Disturbance," 1932.

Outgoing Correspondence of the Colonial Secretary's Office, The Trial of the Power Gang, GN 2/1/A, Vol. 2, pg. 171–186, The Rooms Provincial Archives, St. John's, Newfoundland.

Tierney, Bartholomew. "A Statement of the Case of Bartholomew Tierney," privately published, Montreal, 1823.

Zeilig, Martin, "The Story of 'Bloody Jack' Krafchenko," Manitoba Historical Society, No. 35, (Spring/Summer 1998).

Periodical Sources:

The author found some source material in various issues from the archives of the following newspapers:*Calgary Herald, Chicago Daily Tribune, Fort Wayne News Sentinel, Globe and Mail, Halifax Herald, Indianapolis Star, Manitoba Free Press, Sault Ste. Marie Evening News, Toronto Star, Vancouver Province,* and *Winnipeg Free Press.*